The Lofty Rhyme

Other books by Balachandra Rajan

'Paradise Lost' and the Seventeenth Century Reader (1947)

'Paradise Lost': a Tercentenary Tribute (edited, 1969)

T. S. Eliot: a Study of His Writings by Several Hands (edited, 1947)

Modern American Poetry (edited, 1950)

W. B. Yeats: a Critical Introduction (1965)

The Dark Dancer. A novel (1958)

Too Long in the West. A novel (1961)

The Lofty Rhyme

A study of Milton's major poetry

Balachandra Rajan

UNIVERSITY OF MIAMI PRESS

Coral Gables Florida

Printed in Great Britain

Contents

Foreword   vii

1. *The Constant Core*   1

2. *The Nativity Ode:* in order serviceable   11

3. *Comus:* the inglorious likeness   23

4. *Lycidas:* the shattering of the leaves   45

5. *Paradise Lost:* the web of responsibility   56

6. *Paradise Lost:* the hill of history   79

7. *Paradise Lost:* the providence of style   100

8. *Paradise Regained:* Jerusalem and Athens   113

9. *Samson Agonistes:* the unsearchable dispose   128

Notes   147

Foreword

A student of Milton is required to be aware of the past. My own awareness includes the reminder that my first book on Milton was published twenty-one years ago. The figure is not quoted to suggest that I have come of age in the business of Milton criticism but simply to indicate that there has been time for reflection and for those changes of response and emphasis which are part of the movement of any mind.

The present book began with the recognition that there are intriguingly different patterns of continuity in the poetry of Milton, Yeats and Eliot. The nature of these patterns is outlined in the first chapter of this book. The Eliot pattern was explored in an essay contributed to Allen Tate's collection, *T. S. Eliot: The Man and His Work*. The Yeats pattern was substantiated in my 1965 book on Yeats. This book on Milton is therefore part of an undertaking larger than itself. But every book must stand on its own and this book in seeking to do so is not so rash as to attempt to stand on a single proposition. The aim is a more accurate understanding of the poems in their wholeness and I have not hesitated to use any approach that leads decisively into the poetry.

The book was begun during a visiting year at the University of Wisconsin's Institute for Research in the Humanities. I am grateful both for the leisure and the intellectual company which the serene ambience of the Institute afforded. The Staffs of the Beinnecke Library, The New York Public Library and the Rare Book Room at the library of the University of Illinois have afforded me every assistance without asking me what I thought I was doing. Professor Merritt Y. Hughes's kindnesses go beyond the writing of this book but he has the satisfaction for what it is worth, of knowing that this book could not have been written without him.

Parts of this book have appeared in *The East West Review, The*

Foreword

Huntington Library Quarterly, Milton Studies, The Modern Language Review, The Sewanee Review, Studies in Philology, The University of Toronto Quarterly, in *The Upright Heart and Pure,* edited by Amadeus Fiore and in *Paradise Lost: a Tercentenary Tribute.* My grateful acknowledgements are due to the editors and to the University of Toronto Press. Parts of this book have also been read before the Milton Society of America, The Modern Language Association, The Renaissance Society (North Central Chapter) and the Association of Canadian University Teachers of English.

I should like finally to thank Mrs. Lori Cole who has typed out this book with cheerful and unfailing diligence and deciphered a handwriting more baffling than Linear B.

London, Ontario
1969

1 *The Constant Core*

To read 'Tradition and the Individual Talent' today is to become aware of its distinguished obsolescence. The essay takes its place among those monuments, the ideal order of which it once sought to alter by the injection of the radically new. Literary judgement moves onward though not necessarily forward; and the expanding worlds of the collective and the anonymous, the growth of mass communications and the increasing difficulty of communicating the authentic, have given to words like 'personality' and 'identity', a rallying power they once did not possess. The struggle to achieve definition without exterior compromise is now a condition of the creative conscience. In such circumstances, it becomes almost necessary to remind ourselves that the famous words which follow were the clarion call of criticism forty years ago.

Poetry is not a turning loose of emotion, but an escape from emotion; it is not the expression of personality but an escape from personality. But of course only those who have personality and emotions know what it means to want to escape from these things.[1]

One test of a critic is his power to repent. As the times changed, Mr. Eliot changed cautiously with them. Fifteen years later he had carried his flight from personality sufficiently far to look detachedly over his shoulder at whatever was pursuing him.

The whole of Shakespeare's work is *one* poem; and it is the poetry of it in this sense, not the poetry of isolated lines and passages or the poetry of the single figures he created, that matters most. A man might, hypothetically, compose any number of fine passages or even of whole poems which would each give satisfaction, and yet not be a great poet, unless we felt them to be united by one significant consistent and developing personality.[2]

The juxtaposition is not offered as a lesson in historical irony. To change one's mind, as has been suggested, is an indication that one's mind is alive though with some critics there is unfortunately, no other evidence of life. With Mr. Eliot the change is important not only because it is not unreasonable but because of the weight it assumes in his later critical doctrine. In the same year as the essay on John Ford from which the passage above is quoted, Mr. Eliot had expressed a similar view on Herbert: 'Throughout there is brain work, and a very high level of intensity: his poetry is definitely an *oeuvre* to be studied entire.'[3] In 1939, in considering Yeats's growth as a poet, Eliot found the merit of the later poetry to lie in the fuller expression of personality within it.[4] In 1944, the test of wholeness was applied to Milton:

The important difference is whether a knowledge of the whole, or at least of a very large part of a poet's work, makes one enjoy more, because it makes one understand better, any one of his poems. That implies a significant unity in his whole work. One can't put this increased understanding altogether into words. I cannot say just why I think I understand *Comus* better for having read *Paradise Lost*, or *Paradise Lost* better for having read *Samson Agonistes*, but I am convinced that this is so.[5]

Finally, in his last critical essay, Mr. Eliot reiterates in a more specific context of judgement, the earlier view he had expressed on Herbert:

To understand Shakespeare we must acquaint ourselves with all of his plays; to understand Herbert we must acquaint ourselves with all of *The Temple*. Herbert is, of course, a much slighter poet than Shakespeare; nevertheless he may justly be called a major poet.[6]

Mr. Eliot has described his criticism as a by-product of his poetic workshop. The self-deprecation in the phrase has tended to obscure the element of truth in it, which is that Mr. Eliot's criticism has always been enmeshed in a given literary situation and has found its strength because it has usually been charged with the forces needed to make that situation creative. Since part of the milieu which the criticism illuminates and moves forward is formed by Mr. Eliot's own poetry it is reasonable that motifs predominant in the criticism should find their substantiation in the creative work. Those who regard *Tradition and the Individual Talent* as the best of commentaries on *The Waste Land, Dante* as the best commentary on *Ash-Wednesday* and *The Music of Poetry* as the best commentary on *Four Quartets* will not think it rash to sense in the passages quoted a clue to the understanding of Mr. Eliot's poetry as a whole. The implicit criterion is one of continuity, sometimes expressed in but not necessarily identified with, the presence of a literary 'personality'. The important thing is that the continuity should possess the power of development, that it should be capable of creating and sustaining a significant process or a meaningful world.

Continuity is a concept which one tends to resist, partly because modern criticism has educated us so successfully in the self-sufficiency of the individual poem. It becomes desirable to tell ourselves that one critical hypothesis does not exclude the other and that because a work of art stands by itself it does not necessarily have to stand alone. Literature stripped of all contexts is unusual, if only because the language which enters literature is wrought from a context of both history and experience. Given the nearly unavoidable presence of a context, that of the *oeuvre* can be as instructive and at least as fully designed as the context of *genre* or of *milieu*.

The problem with each poet is to find the right metaphor of wholeness, one that will grasp but not deform the full range of the poetry, holding it firmly in its implicit shape. Such a metaphor must naturally be applied with caution and in seeking it, it is prudent to remember, though the warning may seem naive, that poets write poems which are sometimes sheerly themselves and which decline to belong to anything larger. These eddies do not prove the absence of a mainstream; they merely add to it the richness of occasional dissent. Yet even the word 'mainstream' can be misleading since the basic metaphor (or the figure as Rosemond Tuve might have called it) can be one of pattern as well as of movement or process.

With Yeats, for example, more than one metaphor may be necessary, but one of the metaphors would be quasi-biological. The poetry is written out of a series of lived positions fitted into the trajectory of an individual life; and the whole truth is given by a series of lives fitted into the wheel of possibilities. Truth can only be experienced and not known; it cannot be talked about but only presented and embodied. To live the truth is to live only part of it because to live is to make choices, to accept exclusions, to be both the child and the victim of natural necessities. Man achieves his particular fragment and maximizes the size and validity of the fragment, by moving through the possibilities that are permitted and by ensuring that each possibility is both completely and intensely lived.[7]

With Eliot, the curve of accomplishment is not based on the natural trajectory of life; its outline is rather that of an achieved and consolidated advance into knowledge. Each poem represents a step forward, or upward, building on the position won in the previous poem. The stairway is thus the vertebral metaphor; but the garden into which the stairway leads, the 'time of the tension between birth and dying' is such that the perilous balance of understanding requires the quest to be entered again and its conclusions renewed. The movement of *Four Quartets* is essentially cyclic

We shall not cease from exploration
And the end of all our exploring
Will be to arrive where we started
And to know the place for the first time.[8]

The shape of Mr. Eliot's poetry is thus composed by two forces: the spiral of process and the circle of design. Each necessitates the other and both stipulate the search for reality as a condition of man's being. It is not a search which can end in decisive findings: humankind cannot bear very much reality and the enchainment of past and future protects mankind from heaven as well as damnation. The sea of doubt is man's natural element and the hints and guesses at the truth which illuminate that sea are designed not so much to end doubt as to save it from the whirlpool of despair. Eliot's poetry as an *oeuvre* is thus given an unique and as it were, double honesty, by its sense of a pattern won out of experience and by the manner in which the nature of the pattern entails a further commitment to experience through which the pattern is once again validated.[9]

With Milton, the structure of achievement is best defined by going back to that famous autobiographical interlude in *The Reason of Church Government*[10] – an oasis of contemplation in a desert of 'hoarse disputes' which reveals both tenacity of commitment and a firm sense of poetic destiny. In the 'spacious circuit' of its musings Milton's mind proposed several alternatives to itself. There was the patriotic epic, either 'diffuse' according to the model of Homer, Virgil and Tasso or 'brief', according to the model of the book of

Job, seeking to 'lay the pattern of a Christian *Heroe*' in some 'K or Knight before the conquest'.[11] There were those 'Dramatick constitutions, wherein *Sophocles* and *Euripides* raigne' and of which the Apocalypse of St. John provided a 'majestick Image'.[12] Finally there were those 'magnifick Odes and Hymns' of which Pindar and Callimachus provided classical examples but in which 'those frequent songs throughout the law and prophets' were found 'over all the kinds of Lyrick poesy, to be incomparable'.[13] Milton dealt with the rival attractions of these forms in a fashion which is best described as Miltonic: he enlarged his achievement so as to encompass all of them. The totality of his work includes a hymn (which also describes itself as an Ode), a classical epic, a brief epic, an Athenian tragedy, and for good measure, a pastoral and a masque. The patriotic obligation is discharged in the defence of England which cost him his eyes.[14] The perfect Christian hero proves, not illogically, to be Christ, a conclusion implicit in an early comparison of Christ to Hercules,[15] echoed at the climax of *Paradise Regained*. This is a range and variety of accomplishment unapproached by any writer in the classical or Renaissance past; and even Milton's inclusion of that execrable fragment, *The Passion* not simply in 1645, but in 1673 when his later achievement might have rendered it superfluous, can perhaps be traced to a stubborn competitiveness, a determination not to be 'overgone' by Giles Fletcher.[16]

Variety treads a thin line on the edge of virtuosity and indulgence in overgoing can result in athletic rather than poetic performance. Milton's best work is never even remotely approached by these dangers because of the deep constancy which emerges from and shapes it. In forty years of writing during which radical shifts in understanding seemed to alter the fate of man and the fabric of the universe, years in which a millennium was promised and a revolution betrayed, the creative force of the poetry thrusts again and again towards a single centre. It is a centre cumulatively defined both by the changing perspectives of experience and by the varying literary forms that move into and explore the constant core. From *Comus* onwards the shaping concern is clear: it is that of man's responsibility (if one may use a first approximation with crude but necessary confidence) and four times in five forms that responsibility is focused in the specific theme of temptation. Even *Lycidas*, interpreted liberally, offers the temptation to sport with Amaryllis and to retreat from reality into the pastoral illusion.

This feature of Milton's work is obvious and indeed so obvious that it has not been explored. An early article by Hanford and a relatively late chapter by Watkins are exceptions to the general taking for granted of what is evident.[17] But Hanford's approach is bio-critical, seeking to establish through the temptation motif the 'conflict between the Puritan and merely human sides of Milton's nature'. Watkins, perceptive in his comparisons and contrasts, is not really concerned to establish a logic of the *oeuvre* in which the connections he develops can be displayed. Le Comte studies Milton's reiterations with care[18] but to pillage his sub-title, it is not merely verbal and psychological pattern which is involved but also and more decisively a pattern of understanding. Even a cursory examination will reveal how fully this pattern is shaped, how thoroughly Milton covers the sweep of the possible. We have temptation both simple and multiple, temptation succumbed to and temptation rejected. Our agents are perfect man, man falling to imperfection and fallen man inheriting imperfection. We see error resisted, error defined and overcome in debate, the process of sinning and that of regeneration from a sin that is past. Our settings are the dark wood of confusion, the bleak, wild desert that surrounds the inner wisdom, the garden on which eternity and infinity press, the locked-in theatre of the blind, groping mind, moving into engagement with the nature and mystery of things. Merely to enumerate the variations is to evoke their richness, to point out how naturally they fall into a larger understanding and to suggest how in each instance, the form chosen answers the concern and shapes the exploration. To take examples, the natural magnitude of the epic allows an infinite area of involvement to be 'zeroed-in' on an area of decision, minutely small but by that same token infinitely potent; the dimensions of responsibility are thus inescapably maximized. In *Samson Agonistes* the smaller compass of tragedy is used to contrive a minimum instead of a maximum theatre; blindness (used here with intricate symbolic power) encloses a prison more confined than Gaza's mill; and one proceeds from an inner nucleus of decision to the powerful paradox of that final act which redeems a nation while redeeming and destroying a man.[19] The line of movement may be different but there is an important sense in which both poems reach to the same truth, whatever may be the direction of their reaching. What the form does in each case is to make alive the specific thrust of exploration.

No poem can uncover the whole truth; but each uncovers as much of it as its decorum and action allows.

When man acts he acts beyond himself. Adam feels the 'Link of Nature' draw him to Eve at the very moment when he is cancelling and tearing to pieces the great bond of the cosmic contract. Samson's failure must be measured by more than Israel. Christ looks down the perspective of three civilizations to define the terms of that kingdom which his self-control brings into being. No man is an island, though every man's soul must forever be a battle-field. This is one central lesson of responsibility and Milton more than any poet in the language, drives it home with organized, inexorable power. The cumulative momentum of statement after statement achieves a weight of conviction that must be felt and known in the whole.

Though man acts beyond himself, the decision to act is his own. No one can share this dreadful freedom with him. Milton's insistence on the loneliness of temptation is firm, with that instinctive clarity of the artist, in which moral awareness grows with aesthetic recognition. The two brothers in *Comus* abandon their sister with an ineptness that has irritated others beside Dr. Johnson. One of them could have stayed with the lady; but both must be diverted from the action, not only to theorize about platonic philosophy, but so that the lady can face her enemy by herself. The stars are closed up in the lantern of the night, 'black usurping mists' signify the reign of chaos and the forest itself is a 'close dungeon of innumerous bowes'.[20] Only the steady light of virtue illuminates the duel of Christian warfare. In *Paradise Lost* the separation is arranged with far greater skill. A difficult bridge is crossed as the disagreement between Adam and Eve humanizes those who are about to fall into humanity; but the consequence is that Eve too faces her temptation alone. Then the serpent slinks away, afraid of confronting the first Adam, though in a later poem he compulsively crosses swords with the second and perfect man. The discrepancy helps to remind us that Adam also must be closeted with his tempter, that no distractions are to be permitted from the unrelenting pressure of the individual act of choice. In *Paradise Regained*, the 'world's wilderness'[21] surrounds and isolates the combatants; the desert is a place of destitution and clarity, with the self defined progressively in the higher commitments that constitute the new man. In *Samson Agonistes* the device of the third actor is discarded so that the hero can grapple alone with the temptations that strike individually into the world of his blindness. The chorus steals softly upon him and then stands apart from the action. There are no allies in this battle where the blaze of noon encircles the dungeon of the self seeking the light.

In the combat evil is not without its apparent advantages. The Lady's 'corporal rinde' is 'immanacl'd'. The blind fury cuts the thread of a commitment which the 'uncessant care' of the poet has laboriously spun. Christ is 'exposed' to Satan, and Adam and Eve are placed in what Beelzebub gloatingly describes as 'the utmost border of his Kingdom, left / To their defence who hold it'. Samson grinds bread and is made to perform at circuses. The Lady's mind may be free but with him the outer confinement encases the inner prison.[22]

'All other things have a nature bounded within certain Laws. Thou only [Adam] art loos from all, and according to thy own Counsel in the hand of which I have put Thee, mayst chuse and prescribe what Nature thou wilt to thyself.' The author of this doctrine that existence precedes essence is not Jean Paul Sartre but Thomas Traherne and Traherne in his turn is virtually transcribing a passage from Pico's oration on the dignity of man.[23] As Kristeller notes, the distinctive feature of the oration is that it distinguishes man from the inferior creation by virtue of the power of choice rather than by virtue of the gift of reason.[24] When Milton tells us in *Areopagitica* that 'reason is but choosing' and echoes this thought in a crucial scene of *Paradise Lost*,[25] he is showing his characteristic awareness of two ways of thought and bringing them together in such a manner that they bear with double force on his central theme. Nevertheless he would not have agreed entirely with the full application of these ideas to us, since fallen man, at any rate, cannot totally make himself. His annihilation is already inscribed on the map of his being and the question is only whether his will to survive has sufficient strength to reach up to that mercy which alone is able to undo his fatal contract. This radical act, perhaps coextensive with the long crisis of life, is one from which man cannot flee and which he is not permitted to delegate. Good and evil fight as armies in the outer consequences which it generates, just as the first and second Adam confront each other in the inner world of the mind where it begins. Whether the destructive force will prevail and gather momentum or whether the counter-force of grace will turn back into being the obstinate, downward spring which is man's nature, is a matter for each man to shape from his own struggle. Every man can write the outcome as he wills though no man can will himself not to write it. Out of these acts of making and unmaking, infinitely accumulated, the nature of society and of history must flow. The direction history takes may be either progressive or degenerative and the shaping of it involves both the strength to act and the power to desist from action. As Adam and Eve left Paradise 'The World was all before them where to choose / Their place of rest'. There is a sense in which freedom gives us this opportunity (with its attendant dangers) but it also requires us to turn away as well as to move forward, to learn to look down a hill and to renounce many empires.

These then are the specifications of our liberty; the unremitting pressure of decision, the lonely choice, the infinite consequences and the assault directed inexorably at the point of possible weakness. It is not simply that Milton knows these facts. They are his creative assumptions. Though his poetry affirms them it would be more accurate to say that it uncovers them in finding and developing its identity. To this process of definition and discovery an unusual range of resources is applied with impassioned skill. The received forms, the inherited traditions, the unique power of synthesizing the classical with the Christian, gather into a whole that is aesthetic but more than aesthetic. As the perspectives shift around the constant centre one is conscious of a larger definition coming into life than any poem is capable of creating singly.

Perhaps these preliminaries might have been better left unsaid. A poet's design ought to emerge from his writing; to suggest it from the beginning is also to suggest that the process of definition will be staged and that only those facts which fit the pre-ordained pattern will be permitted to assemble themselves. Still worse, it suggests that the writer starts from a blueprint, that he is in fact no more than a mechanic with metaphors. This is scarcely fair to Milton who is an organic as well as an architectonic writer and who as much as any writer in English, has the power of aesthetic perseverance, the single-minded and almost obsessed sense of literary shaping. If certain preliminary approaches have been outlined, it is because of the very magnitude of Milton's achievement. Modern criticism, with its felicities of the microscope, is not always well-equipped to deal with Milton's sweeping structures or to evolve a critical procedure which is adequate for his inherently large units of realization. It is perhaps even less applicable to the macro-strucures which are the concern of this book. To see the whole with lucidity, one is obliged to bring to it a certain sense of its shape. All that can be said in extenuation is that the preliminaries indicated here were won from an educated reading of the poetry and are meant to dissolve again in the experience of the work.

To suggest a pattern of constancy in Milton's accomplishment is by no means to imply that change is not possible within the pattern. As the poetry moves through the appointed positions on the circumference its sense of the centre alters, not only because the mind behind the poems has changed, or grown, or hardened (there are critical schools for each of these alternatives) but because the very process of passing through a position alters alignments in the experiencing mind. One cannot write *Paradise Lost* over the course of a decade without becoming a different person, both because of the decade and because of the poem. Part of this possible deviation can be discounted since a poet only writes the poem for which he is ready; he achieves a certain position on an aesthetic circumference only when that position answers his creative necessities. It is also true that in that deep act of learning which the creation of a poem can become, a poet may be fulfilling rather than deforming a pattern. Some inconsistencies will remain since a poet like other men is flesh and blood and blindness and because any pattern that is won out of life will reflect that life and be warped by some of its pressures.

With Milton, the overall pattern is therefore best described in terms of that seventeenth century symbol of perfection, the circle. Five different literary forms reach from the circumference into a common centre of recognition. Each form conducts its own exploration of this centre according to its inheritance and resources. Each, so to speak, creates its own individual strategy of insight. The resultant literature is, in a sense, generic but the collective design adds richness to the specific vistas opened by each form; and a powerful sense of inevitability is created as all roads end in the controlling truth. That this should be so is an aesthetic consequence of that spacious and inclusive vision of order which Milton was perhaps the last man to feel in its entirety; wherever one begins and however one proceeds, one must in the end, uncover the same pattern.

2 *The Nativity Ode*

In order serviceable

Since *The Nativity Ode* was written when Milton was twenty-one it is natural to observe that it marks his poetical as well as his legal coming of age.[1] Milton's own dating of the poem would seem to encourage such a remark[2] and his placing of it at the beginning of both the 1645 and 1673 collections suggests clearly that he wished us to regard it as opening the door to his achievement.[3] The poem is certainly Miltonic enough, both in its use and in its ignoring of precedent; the technical skill displayed in it (despite one notorious stanza where it overreaches itself) marks a decisive step forward; and it is evident that we are dealing with a writer who has heard and recognized the quality of his own voice. The coming of age may also be real in the deeper sense that the *Ode* measures Milton's firm commitment to a graver subject conceived in Christian terms. In the *Sixth Elegy* where the *Ode* is spoken of in some detail, Milton visualizes the abandonment of light elegiac poetry for the lofty rhyme written by abstemious poets. Perhaps the call to vegetarianism is not entirely serious; perhaps also, it has the cautious seriousness of a man mocking himself lest his performances mock him.

At any rate *The Nativity Ode* needs no ironic discounting. It is also not the work of an ascetic or of that man, who in Comus's words

Should in a pet of temperance feed on Pulse
Drink the clear stream, and nothing wear but Freize.[4]   720 – 21

Felicity, in Traherne's sense, is a keynote of the *Ode*. It celebrates a happy event with a kind of crystalline joy. Even the stanza that Milton creates[5] embodies this joyousness. The to and fro movement swings through two trimeters, coming to a temporary rest in the semi-close of a pentameter. Then the movement is repeated and the semi-close solidified through its rhyme-link with the previous pentameter. The rhyming pair which follows is not a trimeter or a pentameter couplet (as one might expect from the metrical scheme so far) but a tetrameter rhyming with an alexandrine. The slight asymmetry echoes the to and fro movement, swings it through a wider arc and brings it to a resonant, decisive close. The effect is reminiscent of a carillon of church-bells and its aptness for the occasion hardly needs to be stressed.[6]

For those who prefer poetry to descend in tidy channels from definable sources, Milton's poem is confusingly unlike its English inheritance. Attempts have been made to suggest that the line of transmission can be restored by seeking a European rather than a native parentage and Tasso's *Pel Presipio di nostre Signore*, Mantuan's *Parthenice Mariana* and Sannazaro's *De partu Virginis* have been cited as precedents.[7] It is small comfort however, to learn that Milton's poem is about the Incarnation rather than the Nativity or that he is indebted to Italian practice for such strategies as the mingling of the classical with the Christian. The affiliations traced are plausible enough; yet the truth is that Milton would have done certain things which the poem requires even if Tasso or Sannazaro had not done them. Johnson castigates *Lycidas* for its unseemly conflation of two idioms. He would not have been impressed by the suggestion that Milton's misdemeanours had an Italian origin. He might have been impressed if he had been shown how the conflation was demanded by the driving, imaginative logic of the poem. This is not to belittle the sensitivity with which a critic such as Rosemond Tuve explores the manner in which an awareness of antecedents is a shaping factor in our response to Milton's *Ode*; but the word Miltonic to connote anything must connote a stubborn residue of uniqueness by which the past is taken over and transformed; if the *Ode* is truly Milton's coming of age its music should ring with the sound of this uniqueness.[8]

Paradox has been called the natural language of the Incarnation as oxymoron is the language of mystical ecstasy.[9] Milton shows comparatively little interest in this language. Nothing in his poem looks forward to Crashaw's pyrotechnics, though Crashaw's rhetoric is sufficiently traditional virtually to echo Beaumont's *Psyche*.[10] The poem has its conflicts, resolved in decisive harmonies; but the conflicts do not centre round the Incarnation so as to manifest it as the ultimate concord.[11] The miracle and ardour of the word made flesh, the supreme act of love involved in the descent into humanity have little imaginative weight for Milton and in this respect his poem differs radically from its English predecessors.[12] His Christ is like Samson armed with celestial vigour though in different ways and to an infinitely higher degree. This is a Christ of creative power and unifying energy, who looks forward to the Christ of *Paradise Lost*, vanquishing Satan and creating the world out of chaos. The imagery which surrounds him is that of power and dignity. Heaven is parliamentary and the manger royalist. In between, the *logos* enters history as the irresistible champion of the light. This sense of the main weight of the poem seems justified not only by an overall reading but by such details as the apparently disproportionate attention given to the rout of the pagan gods, and the placing of the poem in the 1645 and 1673 volumes, with *Psalms* 114 and 136 succeeding it. Finally, we need only to compare the climactic line of stanza xxv (all the more significant because Milton has shied away so markedly from Incarnational paradox) with the words 'unable to speak a word' of Lancelot Andrewes's Nativity sermon, to realize what is involved in such matters as coming of age.

We can cautiously call the *Nativity Ode* baroque since even Douglas Bush is prepared to use the adjective.[13] But if it is baroque, it is so in a manner decidedly Miltonic. The controlled exuberance of the poem finds echoes in unexpected places such as the eulogy of discipline in *The Reason of Church Government*.[14] More important, the time and space perspectives which have been characterized as baroque in Milton's later poems[15] are used in the *Nativity Ode* with a confidence which perhaps makes us less aware of the sheer immensity of the poem's theatre. The movement is from the creation to the last judgement, from heaven and hell to the 'courtly stable' and the 'rustic row' of shepherds on the lawn. It is not simply the dimensions of this universe that anticipate irresistibly the universe of *Paradise Lost*, it is also the technique of moving in from the outer limits to the enclosed moment of decision or of meaning. In *Paradise Lost* the movement functions so as to create an infinite pressure of responsibility; in the *Nativity Ode* it brings about an infinite extension of significance. The miracle of the Nativity takes place whenever and wherever the entire truth is made living and manifest; even the device of placing the poet in the poem is intended to suggest tactfully that the author lays his work before the author of all meaning so that the true meaning can be radiated into it. We, like the shepherds, cannot anticipate the onset of significance; but when the truth shines forth we are profoundly aware of the pattern.

In a sense (though not in every sense) the poem is about this moment of astonishment, of 'sudden illumination', of a revelation which is also an act of radical ordering.[16] The adroit mixture of tenses helps, in creating this effect, working with the poet's use of time and space to involve the timeless in the immediate and living. This device has also been called baroque but artistic relevance is a rarer gift than the capacity to emulate a style.[17] What matters in the use of these devices is their assimilation to the need and voice of the poem and the assistance which they afford us in defining the personal tradition which the poem sets in train.

Barker's account of the structure of the *Nativity Ode* has not been challenged and no quarrel with his tripartite division is proposed. Perhaps he is too categoric in maintaining that the poem's three equal movements are held in relation 'not by the repetition of a structural pattern but by the variation of a basic pattern of imagery'.[18] The shifts in the quality of the imagery are certainly emphatic enough to ensure that they do not pass unrecognized; but it would be reassuring to discover that there is something further in the shape of the poem which defines the points at which it turns and the manner of its turning. Such a mapping-out is indeed possible and its effect is to confirm and elaborate Barker's conclusions. The first movement sets the scene, hushes the theatre and indicates something of the theatre's spaciousness. It begins and ends in the minute but momentous area of significance: the babe in the manger, the shepherds on the lawn. The second movement is a flashback in time to the creation, once again beginning at the still point and ending with the babe in 'smiling infancy'.[19] The third movement is a leap forward to the last judgement, balancing the flashback and ending inevitably in the stable where meaning begins. Within the flashback, is a comparison linking the golden age to the creation; within the movement forward, is a simile relating the giving of the Mosaic law to the last judgement. These contra-movements widen the main thrusts of expansion, reinforcing the sense of symmetry in history and looking forward in the process, to the still larger symmetries of *Paradise Lost* and the Celestial Cycle. At the same time these audacious excursions are controlled by being rigorously brought back to a constant centre of meaning. The point at which the timeless enters history is the only point at which we, standing in time and rooted in our finitudes, can apprehend the process of which we are the agents.

The first two movements of the Hymn are of eight stanzas. The third is three stanzas longer. The asymmetry points to a more important asymmetry. It takes four stanzas of the second movement for the gathering music of the spheres to transport us to the music of creation. The carefully judged crescendo comes to its climax at the centre of the movement and is prolonged by the reference to the golden age and by the double reference to *Psalm 85* and Virgil's Messianic Eclogue, suggesting the return of the golden age if the music should last. The movement is one of lingering rapture. In the third movement, on the contrary the thrust forward is of ferocious brevity. One stanza brings us to the last judgement and the reference to the Mosaic law instead of being added on, is telescoped into this very stanza. Strict symmetry is thus violated in a manner which looks forward to the far more sophisticated tactics of violation in *Lycidas*. Here, as in Milton's pastoral, creative energy overflows its boundaries; and here too, as in *Lycidas*, the poet is aware of his irregularity and draws attention to it. 'Time is our tedious song should here have ending' is not simply a modest disclaimer of poetic talent. The third movement is long-tailed enough to consist of virtually nothing but the tail. Milton is putting the fact before us, reminding us of the symmetry he has transgressed and helping us to understand that the apparent lack of balance conceals a real balance. The deepest affirmation of the *Ode* is its sense of the power and glory of God, of the inevitable victory of the light when it elects to shine forth in its radiance.[20] It is not wrong that the structural asymmetry of the poem should direct our attention to its imaginative centre of gravity. Years later, in *The Reason of Church Government*, Milton was to speak of 'glorious and lofty hymns' which would celebrate 'the throne and equipage of Gods Almightinesse'.[21] The *Nativity Hymn* fits this specification tolerably and it will be noticed that Milton is at some pains to remind us of the 'equipage' even in the stable.

One more observation deserves to be made about the three part structure of the *Ode*. When we recognize the designed asymmetry of that structure we can better appreciate the extent to which it is reflected in the designed asymmetry of Milton's stanza. The stanza consists of two balanced units of three lines with a third that superficially seems to throw the whole out of balance and actually provides it with a greater stability. The stanza is in fact, the poem in miniature. To integrate to this degree, the major and minor units of realization is an accomplishment which indicates an unusual power of cohesion, a power which as we shall see, displays itself even more strikingly in the verse paragraph of *Paradise Lost*.[22] It is the kind of fitting together which suggests music, not only through the content of the imagery but through the poem's repetitive and yet varied intricacy, its simultaneous sense of both development and pattern. This is as it should be since the poem is a kind of musical offering, informed by an occasion when the music of meaning was born.

Since the *Nativity Ode* stands at the beginning of Milton's first volume of poems it seems reasonable to regard it as initiating the personal tradition of his work. The undertaking need not be called perilous but it should be carried out with critical circumspection. Whatever weight is given to the personal tradition it should not be such as to carry away the poem from itself or undermine its capacity to live on its own basis. Yet self-sufficiencies lead to other self-sufficiencies and no order in nature is so inviolably self-sustaining that it is incapable of fruitful connection to other orders. When this has been admitted we have still to remember that Milton was among the most refined of generic artists and that apart from the *oeuvre* and the poem, we have also to listen to the third voice of the inheritance. Such a remark is intended to compass Northrop Frye's view that the accumulated inheritance may have a mythic foundation. There are thus at least three forces at work which the artistic achievement releases and balances creatively. Some degree of virtuosity is evidently called for, but any poem is more than a performance, though how it is more can only be understood by attending to the skills of the performance.

It is apparent that the *Ode* leads into the *oeuvre* through its sense of power and providence of God, the amplitude of its theatre, its confident excursions through time and space and most important, through the contention of light and darkness which is to play so vital a part in Milton's writing. Having made these (it is to be hoped) unexceptionable remarks it seems more rewarding to turn to the living felicities of detail by which these large observations are given shape and put in their place as large observations deserve to be.

Milton used the alexandrine only to discard it but no writer has charmed this 'wounded snake' of a line into a greater variety of effects. To look back to its use in *On the Death of a Fair Infant* is to realize how rapidly technical skill can mature; and to look forward slightly to the alexandrines of *The Passion* is to realize how flaccid and even regressive, technical skill is, without creative energy. In the *Ode*, Milton is usually able to avoid those two menaces that beset the alexandrine, the resounding thump and the inert debacle. Jubilant sonority and clanguorous discord are taken with equal ease into the line's compass; but perhaps the most striking manipulation, since it seems so contrary to the ineluctable properties of the line is the pianissimo to which the fifth stanza quietens: 'While birds of calm sit brooding on the charmèd wave.'

Dante, in a more famous climax, uses the same open vowel to achieve a deeper peace. But Milton's less searching effect is proper to a poem which remains closer to enchantment than to awe, which is concerned with the power of the word rather than with its mystery and which sees that power in pastoral terms as the sun dissipating the pale shadows of error. When this has been said we can note the manner in which the link between 'calm' and 'charm' preserves the sense of bewitchment and how the potentially disturbing effect of 'wave' is arrested by its metrical placing and smoothed out by the spreading of the *a* sound into it. The scale of accomplishment can be larger and can unlock deeper reaches of the responding mind but much less than this degree of accomplishment would be indicative of notable technical skill, possessed imaginatively and applied with relevance. Hughes cites Ovid (*Met.* XI, 745–6) but the anticipation of *Paradise Lost* is no less rewarding.

... Thou from the first
Wast present and with mighty wings outspred
Dove-like satst brooding on the vast Abyss
And mad'st it pregnant: I, 19 – 22

 Darkness profound
Cover'd th' Abyss; but on the watrie calme
His brooding wings the Spirit of God outspred,
And vital vertue infus'd and vital warmth   VII, 233 – 36

When the higher mood touches Milton it often touches him with a deep perception of God's power. But the delicate hushing of the *Ode* has not been forgotten; it revives in the juxtaposition of 'mighty' and 'dove-like', the intense co-presence of power and fragility, the force of order and the calm of peace. The chaos of *Paradise Lost* is not so much charmed as subdued. It belongs to a subsequent universe with energies of assault far more radical and threatening than the joyous effervescence of the *Ode* can allow. Neither universe ultimately excludes the other; both have their place in any continuum that is reasonably representative of the totality of man's vision.

That the creation and incarnation chime together in the music of meaning is of course, a recognition much older than the *Ode*. It is a recognition that crystallizes not merely in the implicit comparison referred to, but more deliberately and expansively in stanza xii. Here again, it is the dissimilitudes as well as the resemblances which matter in suggesting how the *Ode* complements and opens into the more solemn harmonies of *Paradise Lost*. The 'welt'ring waves' of the *Hymn* differ significantly in their imaginative dimensions from that 'outrageous' sea 'dark, wasteful, wild' on which Christ and Satan embark for contrasted reasons; and the 'oozy channel' which the waves are bid to keep suggests with equal felicity the less troubled compass of the disorder which is disciplined into creation. In *Paradise Lost* we move into a maelstrom of non-being which measures by its very turbulence the power needed to command it into form.

> Silence, ye troubl'd waves, and thou Deep, peace,
> Said then th' Omnific Word, your discord end.   VII, 216 – 17

To explore these differences is not to suggest that the *Ode* is *Paradise Lost* in miniature or even in embryo. In moving along the network of the work, the graduation from pastoral to heroic becomes expressive of aesthetic growth, of the maturing of the poetic mind and of the stern passage from innocence to experience that results from the mind's steadily sustained engagement with reality. The whole achievement must have the sweep of life as well as the shape of a pattern. Yeats, more than any other poet, seems aware that while poems grow from each other and therefore have a developmental logic that seems to resound to the logic of living and aging, they are also parts of a whole, each occupying its place in the spectrum of the imaginatively possessed. We can understand this and also understand that whatever its contributions to an overall design or process, every poem has its own propriety, its power of containment and its chosen exclusions. This is what decorum means when it is organic as well as formal as it is in every poem that earns its title. The overall view must always be maintained in sharp consciousness of this individual decorum.

Even a superficial reading of the *Ode* suggests how it has its own personality, as well as its membership of the Miltonic family. It is exuberantly formal, moving with assurance on the edge of extravagance, remarkably varied within what could be a strait-jacketing stanza, never 'confined and cloyed with repetition of what is prescribed'. It has both blitheness and solidity resulting from its connection with Elizabethan song and the manner in which that connection is modified by the weight of the stanza and the scale of the imagery. Jubilant and yet serious, it is a poem written in the world of light. The darkness is an otherness to it, not the stuff of our minds, out of which our minds must struggle. Its visual evocativeness need not be called painterly[23] but has been compared to the masque and has something of the tableau in its carefully-ordered groupings.[24] When the poem speaks of the 'well-ballanc't world on hinges hung' it is not too fanciful to see it as speaking of itself, as well as of the act of creation which the Renaissance liked to see as the perfect poem.[25] Milton remembered the line and in remembering it remade it, so that it reflects with the accuracy that comes only from instinctive skill and impassioned understanding, the different poem within which it is remade.

And Earth self ballanc't on her Center hung.   *PL* VII, 242

The step from 'well-ballanc't' may seem a small step but it is one which momentously alters the field of vision.[26] The self-balanced earth is expressive of self-balanced man 'sufficient to have stood though free to fall'.[27] Dependence is not forgotten in independence, since the earth despite its self-supporting nature also hangs from heaven by a golden chain. The point is that the whole equilibrium pivots upon us, upon man's unrelaxing steadfastness in order. We can defend ourselves till we destroy ourselves but we cannot give back our perilous autonomy. The cost of freedom is responsibility and *Paradise Lost* is a poem aware of the cost. Michael's much later vision of the world 'under her own waight groaning'[28] develops the image with sombre precision, with the quotation from *Romans* fitted into the cosmic structure, making the imbalance of sin into a gigantic deformity, a lopsidedness that rolls its way through history. A retentive memory and an accomplished craftsman's skill are scarcely enough for this kind of achievement.

The lines in which the *Ode* most obviously looks forward to *Paradise Lost* are those setting out its catalogue of false gods. Ten deities are mentioned in the *Ode*, nine by name and one by allusion. In *Paradise Lost* the list expands to twelve (including a seventeenth-century idol) and in keeping with the more spacious dimensions of the epic, 146 lines are needed to complete its indictment as against the 32 of the *Ode*. No less than seven deities are common to both lists. The persistence of this cavalcade in Milton's mind over something like thirty years ought to shake the confidence with which sources are sometimes proclaimed. Milton could have read Selden and Sandys by 1629 but he could not have read Ross's *Pansebeia*.[29]

The long tradition beginning with Lactantius which identifies the false gods with the fallen angels is explicit in *Paradise Lost*.[30] To be aware of it enriches our understanding of the *Ode* but its lesser prominence in the lesser poem also invites us to recognize that the concerns of the *Ode* are not quite those of the epic. Milton at this stage is not really anxious to 'deplore the general relapses of Kingdoms and States from justice and Gods true worship'.[31] Darkness in the *Ode* is something which the light dissipates. The description of the false gods as shadows is significant and differs designedly from 'darkness visible'. The 'pale-ey'd Priest from the prophetic cell' is not presented as an object of opprobrium; her supersession by the power of light is rather an occasion for rejoicing. The word 'cell' moreover is chosen for other reasons beside its pictorial qualities. Darkness in the *Ode* is uniformly embodied in images of constraint and confinement,[32] contrasted with the word in its radiance and openness. We do not even encounter stratagems such as those found in the description of Thammuz in *Paradise Lost*, where the shift of tone functions like a relieving simile bringing us back all the more decisively to the insistent moral voice. Moloch performing his 'dismal dance about the furnace blue' is a picture on a frieze rather than a force of evil. The idol we encounter in *Paradise Lost* is both more sombre and closer to ourselves[33]

First, *Moloch*, horrid King besmear'd with blood
Of human sacrifice and parents tears.   *PL* I, 392 – 93

It is not simply that the prophetic voice speaks here, that the heroic catalogue is purposively used as an instrument of the sense of moral outrage. Behind the voice is a mind which has come to recognize that the light does not triumph merely by proclaiming itself or in the controlled certainty of encounters such as that between Comus and the Lady. We live in the kingdom of darkness, coloured by it, even if we are not wholly its citizens. The hope of freedom discloses itself only when we know who is the enemy.

The attention given in the *Ode* to the rout of the false gods is, as has been argued, indicative of the real thrust of its concerns, its deep sense of the power and glory of God. It follows that so activist a poem should be interested less in what the Incarnation means than in what it does or, more accurately, in arriving at what it means through what it does. The *Ode* indeed sees the Incarnation as the transforming event in history, linking it to the creation and the last judgement and in an even more spacious movement, linking the first to the final paradise. In this it is only traditional but the eschatological weight is unusual in a poem designed nominally to contemplate or celebrate an occasion. The *Ode* is not really concerned with the inward significance of the Incarnation. It is concerned with it as a decisive event in the structure of events without which the other events are incapable of forming a structure. It is an intervention transforming the nature of history and the destiny of man.[34] The peace it establishes is a 'perpetual' and 'universal Peace'. All wars end when the ultimate war is won. In keeping with the buoyancy of the poem the view of this transformation it offers is optimistic and indeed verges upon a philosophy of progress:

And then at last our bliss
Full and perfet is,
  But now begins; for from this happy day
Th' old Dragon under ground,
In straiter limits bound,
  Not half so far casts his usurped sway.   165 – 70

It is a far cry from here to the bleak prophecies of Michael in *Paradise Lost*. Yet it is the later view which is the more traditional. Lactantius who joins with the young Milton in associating the final paradise with the Golden Age (and who interprets Virgil's *Fourth Eclogue* accordingly)[35] also believes that the days before the last judgement will be marked by general degeneration and the apparent triumph of iniquity.[36] A long tradition, including men closer to Milton's time such as Luther and Bullinger saw the True Church as increasingly beleaguered and declared with exultant pessimism that things had to get worse in order to get better. The period of the binding of the dragon was over and the beast was now rampant; it would rage on until it was destroyed. The forecast gained force from views of the decline of nature which were voiced early and influentially by Cyprian.[37] On the other hand a less sombre view of events was gaining ground in Milton's day, based on the assumption of progress in the true Church and on the implicit identification of the true Church with the elect nation, England.[38] In his early prose Milton carries these convictions to dizzy heights of millennial fervour. Even the author of the *Ode* believes that nature after Christ is not subject to old age; he would have been on Hakewill's side in the great debate with Goodman; and far from regarding the dragon as loose he regards his binding at the time of the Incarnation as only the beginning of a process of withering away. From that miraculous moment the light waxes and the darkness wanes until the fullness of perfection and happiness is achieved. In keeping with the radiance of a poem which as Rosemond Tuve rightly observes 'is not about paradise lost but about paradise made sure',[39] the victory of the light is almost effortless. Even Typhon, in a climactic image of binding, is presented as largely enmeshed in his own monstrosity.[40] This sense of a gathering progress to felicity is remarkable even after Hakewill. The later Milton returned to a sterner teaching but in doing so, spoke for a tradition as well as for himself.

The quiet close of a Milton poem sets it in shape, bringing the higher mood into consonance with the everyday. So the *Nativity Ode*, after its movement through space and history, comes back to a local habitation both humble and resplendent. The imagery of light endures but the lesser lights are subordinate and attentive to the prince of light. The 'handmaid lamp' and 'courtly stable' the 'polished car' and the 'bright harnessed' angels all suggest the proper deference of degree. The universal and mild monarchy of heaven has more than a touch of Renaissance splendour about it. Finally, the order which the last lines invoke is not directed to any climax of contemplation. It is 'order serviceable' designed for an active purpose, the intervention in history which is itself the decisive renewal of the hope of order. In this context the bright-harnessed angels are the energy of light, mobilized and held ready for a creative purpose. This is not quite the end of the felicities of the stanza. For Milton too, a serviceable order has been created and the instruments are at hand for the greater work ahead.

3 *Comus*

The inglorious likeness

Comus is a work that seems to invite sophisticated attention and many erudite gestures have been discerned in what Charles Williams once termed a 'philosophical ballet'.[1] Objections to this tendency have not been lacking. Marjorie Nicolson tells us that after many years of teaching and the overflow of much scholarship *Comus* remains to her 'what it was in my youth–the loveliest of English masks written by a poet-philosopher, whose philosophy was still very youthful and smacked of the schools'.[2] Robert Adams in a more substantial counterattack has trenchantly cautioned us against 'over-reading' *Comus*.[3] This is a warning that raises interesting issues. It would be comforting to know that there is attached to or ascertainable from each poem, a clear declaration of its density that would enable us to know when it is being over or under-read. Some extremes are obviously to be avoided–a limerick does not demand the same attention as an epic and the objection that *Comus* is too 'heavy' for a masque is not nonsensical even if it is not valid. The fringe areas of the unacceptable are however, comparatively small and in between there can be more than one view of that blessed source of confusion that is reverentially called the words on the page. Wanton ingenuity is to be spurned but perhaps the most we can do to define the wanton is to say that those interpretations are to be preferred in which the resources of the form and the details of deployment contribute to a whole, or at least do not detract from it and in which local life is most often interpreted so as to open into a larger totality. Artistic coherence seems to be our safest criterion and the deeper, wider and more inclusive the coherence, the more justified is the reading of which it is the result. A reading that leads to maximum coherence should not be objected to as 'too clever' unless something in the poem prohibits such cleverness.

The suggestion that only the poem itself can advise us how to read it will always be received with trepidation. It would be much more reassuring to argue that the poem should be read as the author directs, that is, when he is considerate enough to give us directions. Unfortunately the author, once he has put the poem into print, does not own it any more than the reader. He may have known most of what he was doing when he wrote the poem but there are some things he will have done unknowingly although he wanted to do them. He may have discovered what he wanted to do or modified it in the act of writing; and he may even have discovered what he did not want and none the less could not refrain from doing. The last possibility is familiar to readers of Milton criticism and all these sometimes threatening possibilities require to be entertained.

When this has been said it is safe to point out that Milton left at least two indications of how we might read *Comus*. The well-known lines from *Il Penseroso*

Of Forests, and inchantments drear,
Where more is meant than meets the ear,[4]

are usually glossed as referring to Spenser and Ariosto[5] but look forward even more strongly to the dark wood of *Comus* and the spell that binds the lady. To make the anticipation even clearer there is the line 'List mortals if your ears be true' which occurs in the Epilogue of *Comus* and the importance of which is emphasized by its insertion in the Trinity manuscript.[6] Both passages suggest a way of reading *Comus* which is not quite the way recommended by Professor Adams. Perhaps what they tell us is illuminated by an appeal made in not dissimilar language, by a very different poet, W. B. Yeats:

Nor may I less be counted one
With Davis, Mangan, Ferguson,
Because, to him who ponders well
My rhymes more than their rhyming tell.[7]

The connection with Yeats is all the more interesting because in his last play, *The Death of Cuchulain*, the Old Man speaks of wanting 'an audience of fifty or a hundred' and observes, not without satisfaction, that since 'I am producing a play for people I like, it is not probable, in this vile age, that they will be more in number than those who listened to the first performance of Milton's *Comus*'.[8] This is not to suggest that *Comus* should be read in the manner of a Noh play but the sense of an inner as well as an outer performance and possibly of a tradition of allusiveness are common to both Milton and Yeats. Yeats's demand is that the reader should be possessed of 'the old epics and Mr. Yeats's plays, about them',[9] a demand which one critic calls 'preposterous'[10] though it seems moderate enough when we think of Joyce and Pound. Milton's requirements would have been different and less definable: an awareness of Spenser though not necessarily as a subject for exegesis, an awareness not necessarily of specific masques but of the atmosphere of masques, a poetic interest in 'divine philosophy' and most important of all some sense of the Circe myth which Rosemond Tuve describes as the hinge on which the masque turns.[11] If however, the fable of Circe is central in our understanding of *Comus* it is largely because of the connections that are made to it and the manner in which it is involved with the Elizabethan frame of order, the balance of discipline and energy, the inescapable demands of Christian warfare and the ways of making and unmaking himself which are offered to man in the dark wood of his freedom. In creating these interrelationships *Comus* asks for an attention that is vigilant, educated but not esoterically schooled, that is aware of a pattern and rejoices in seeing its relevance proved and extended. Perhaps this is the kind of attentiveness that Sir G. M. Trevelyan had in mind when he described the Ludlow Castle performance of *Comus* as a high-water mark of English culture.[12]

Milton called *Comus* 'A Masque presented at Ludlow Castle'. He persevered with this title even in 1673 after he had spoken of the 'world's vain masque' and described Belial as reigning in those 'palaces and courts' where masques are supposed to be performed.[13] Milton's title does have the advantage of not enrolling him in the devil's party; it also suggests to us that the Bridgewater audience may have been content to receive *Comus* as a masque, appreciating what was singular in it but not feeling as Simpson does that 'The noble poetry of *Comus* only accentuates the perishable quality of the Masque form which it transgresses or ignores'.[14] The incongruity of celebrating chastity in a form consecrated to Hymen might have struck Milton's auditors as more apparent than real.[15] *Comus* ends not in one marriage but in three and if the marriages are out of the ordinary that only indicates the kind of attention that is invited from us. Complaints that Comus is no masque[16] should be related to complaints that the *Nativity Ode* is not about the Nativity, that *Lycidas* is definitely no pastoral, that *Paradise Lost* is not an epic, and *Samson Agonistes* not a tragedy. Now that Professor Lewalski has informed us about the requirements of the brief epic, it is time for somebody to declare that *Paradise Regained* while sufficiently brief is insufficiently epic. The moral is surely that it is Milton's habit to strain at the form, to oblige it to surpass its own dimensions;[17] yet the impression given is not of violation but of a highly individual fulfilment, of something latent being raised into imaginative actuality.

'The masque form' is a phrase which we use unreflectingly and which deserves a mild degree of scrutiny. The masque is not a form in the sense in which epic, tragedy and pastoral are forms. It has no classical past. It does not inherit an accumulated tradition which has become in effect an accepted way of insight. It is an unstable and precarious genre 'shaped and practised by a few men of genius for a single generation, during the first half of the seventeenth century'.[18] Moreover the men writing masques were in general too busy writing them to talk about them. Modern studies of the masque tell us much about the relationship of spectacle to total effect; but they are unable to point to a body of critical theory which tells us with some degree of authority what a masque is and what it may or may not do. Given the lack of theory and the wide variety of practice,[19] innovation is not only permissible but is among the major attractions an incipient genre can offer to a talent both deeply traditional and powerfully original. In any event, the perfunctory nature of Milton's allegiance to what are considered masque conventions can be much exaggerated. Simpson does allow that *Comus* is in conception 'a genuine and unmistakable Masque'[20] and it only remains to be added that the execution answers the conception with a tighter logic than is sometimes admitted. Milton moreover uses with some effect the symbol of the dance, the triumph over misrule, the visual reminders of design which the masque offers, the confrontation on which it often centres, the opening of a central myth into vistas of meaning, and most important of all the uninvolved character of the masque, which holds experience at arm's length and makes disorder a gesture in a dance rather than a threat to man's being. In employing what may be called the propensities of the masque as distinct from its devices Milton's touch is seldom less than revealing.[21]

Tillyard's interpretation of *Comus* has rightly had to yield to Woodhouse's pioneering essay.[22] As a result, insufficient attention has been given to his view that the masque reflects man's central position on the Great Chain of Being, confronted with the way up into being or the way down into self-annihilation.[23] This is perhaps the best way in which to look at *Comus*, both because it is universally accessible and because it couples and sets in motion a series of potent antitheses. It is also urged upon us by the masque to such an extent that no attentive reading can fail to be aware of it. More rarefied interpretations are not excluded but they take their place within the frame, enriching but not amending the structure of recognition that has already been built and engaged. This, as we shall come to recognize, is Milton's normal procedure: the immediate and the fully-educated response may differ from each other but the first grows towards the second as the result of alert re-reading. They are thus in potential consonance rather than in tension or ironic dissonance. The procedure is also evocative of reality, at any rate as Milton and his contemporaries would have known it. What we need to understand of the nature of things is given to us by the book of God. Exploration develops and deepens that understanding drawing it back from the Satanic betrayals which haunt it; it is an act of substantiation as much as of discovery.

The way up and the way down are part of the symbolic cosmography of *Paradise Lost*. The Ludlow masque initiates a similar opposition in the opening words of the Attendant Spirit. Descending from the 'calm and serene air' of his habitation (the tranquillity of being is set against the turbulence of becoming) he has inflicted on himself the smoke and stir, the low thoughts, the sin-worn mould and the rank vapours of the earth to guide those who seek the way to eternity. The platonic repudiation of the flesh need not be unreservedly accepted in a masque which is later to speak of 'Youth and Joy'; the gestures however stress by their very conventionality the difference between ascending and descending, with the Attendant Spirit as the guardian of one route and Comus as the overseer of the other. Comus, the son of Bacchus and Circe, a parentage which Milton suggests has never before been disclosed,[24] is 'Much like his father, but his mother more' meaning that his real interests go somewhat beyond mere revelry. His technique is to offer the 'weary Traveller', who by now is the wayfaring Christian as well as a member of Ulysses's crew, 'His orient Liquor in a Crystal Glass'. The characteristic light imagery, renewed in 672–73, suggests that we are to contrast Comus's false light with the true light of virtue, just as his false dance is to be contrasted with the true dance of order.[25] The metamorphoses which follow show precisely how Comus 'Excels his mother at her mighty art;' what takes place is not a total transformation into animality, but a transformation limited to the 'human count'nance', a pointed desecration of the image of God in man.

> Soon as the Potion works, their human count'nance,
> Th' express resemblance of the Gods, is chang'd
> Into som brutish form of Woolf, or Bear,
> Or Ounce, or Tiger, Hog, or bearded Goat,
> All other parts remaining as they were.   68 – 72

It is in the nature of alienation from God that one should rejoice in the experience of alienation:[26]

> And they, so perfect is their misery,
> Not once perceive their foul disfigurement,
> But boast themselves more comely then before,
> And all their friends and native home forget,
> To roule with pleasure in a sensual stie.   73 – 77

To receive the full effect of the last lines we must recall the platonic idea of life as an exile of the soul from its country, an idea of which the best-known English expression is Vaughan's 'My soul there is a Countrie'.[27] The conflation of this idea with the story of Ulysses's wanderings goes back at least to Plotinus:

> . . . Surely Odysseus is a parable for us here when he commends flight from the sorceries of a Circe or a Calypso, being unwilling to linger on for all the pleasure offered to his eyes and all the delight of sense that filled his days. The Fatherland for us is there whence we have come. There is the Father. What is our course? What is to be the manner of our flight? . . . We must close our eyes and invoke a new manner of seeing, a wakefulness that is the birthright of us all, though few put it to use.[28]

Milton is not greatly interested after *Comus* in the idea of earthly life as the soul's exile. He uses it in the masque because of the dimension it adds to the fable of Circe and because both it and the fable are attuned to a conviction that always remains close to the nerves of his own seeing. It is with an emphasis approaching fervour that he associates the image of God in man with the gift of reason and with the uprightness and erectness which are the sign of that gift: Thus, the Attendant Spirit warns the Brothers of Comus

> Whose pleasing poison
> The visage quite transforms of him that drinks
> And the inglorious likeness of a beast
> Fixes instead, unmoulding reasons mintage
> Character'd in the face;   525 – 29[29]

In *Paradise Lost*, our first sight of Adam is as the living affirmation of the image of God:

Two of far nobler shape erect and tall,
God like erect, with native Honour clad
In naked Majestie seemd Lords of all,
And worthie seemd, for in their looks Divine
The image of thir glorious Maker shon,
Truth, wisdome, Sanctitude severe and pure,
Severe but in true filial freedom plac't;   IV, 288 – 94

The repetition of 'erect' and the strategic inversion which by elevating the thought throws 'erect' into a position of controlling dominance are examples of technique at the service of conviction. Milton has little to learn and much to teach about the syntactical inversion which is also an act of valuing. Perhaps the most moving example of his sureness occurs in the *proem* to Book III.

> Thus with the Year
> Seasons return, but not to me returns
> Day, or the sweet approach of Ev'n or Morn,
> Or sight of vernal bloom, or Summers Rose,
> Or flocks, or heards, or human face divine;   III, 40 – 44

The carefully modulated rise through the hierarchies of being prepares one for the recognition that the loss of man's society is the deepest of all natural losses. The sense of judgement that creates the situation for the delayed and climactic epithet is almost insupportably exact. To be cut off from men is to be cut off from the constant and visible affirmation of God's image. Deprivation cannot have more poignant dimensions.

It has been shown that the initial speech of the Attendant Spirit, straightforward though it may seem, has deep sources and echoes in tradition. This is not however the only point at which we are advised of the two ways open to man. The alternatives set out by the Attendant Spirit in terms of the flesh and the spirit are also set out by the Elder Brother in terms of chastity and lust:

So dear to Heav'n is Saintly chastity,
That when a soul is found sincerely so,
A thousand liveried Angels lacky her,
Driving far off each thing of sin and guilt,
And in clear dream, and solemn vision
Tell her of things that no gross ear can hear,
Till oft convers with heav'nly habitants
Begin to cast a beam on th' outward shape,
The unpolluted temple of the mind,
And turns it by degrees to the soul's essence
Till all be made immortal: 452 – 62

In ascent, the soul refines its vesture into harmony with its quintessence. In descent it is trapped by the vesture, degenerating with it, imprisoning itself by the force of its own alienation:

  but when lust
By unchaste looks, loose gestures, and foul talk,
But most by leud and lavish act of sin,
Lets in defilement to the inward parts,
The soul grows clotted by contagion,
Imbodies and imbrutes, till she quite loose
The divine property of her first being.   462 – 68

He that hath light within his own cleer breast
May sit i'th center and enjoy bright day,
But he that hides a dark soul, and foul thoughts
Benighted walks under the mid-day Sun;
Himself is his own dungeon.   380 – 84

The body as the dungeon of the soul is a favourite image of the platonic tradition, but the words look forward also to the chorus's glimpse of the real nature of Samson's imprisonment,[30] to the paradox of darkness at noon and to the contrast between inward vision and exterior darkness, or blindness. *Comus* is a work of innocence. It may adopt the dark wood as its setting but it is not written out of it, or born from the perilous flood. Yet it has its persistent affinities with the more implacable world of the later work.

The elder brother is indefatigable in exposition to his captive audience of one. By refusing to take his sister's predicament too seriously he reminds us that that predicament is symbolic as much as it is dramatic. When the Attendant Spirit informs the two brothers of the Lady's situation and the younger brother comments a little reproachfully on the pretty pass to which platonism has brought everyone, the elder brother declines to have second thoughts. Instead, he provides himself with a resounding vote of confidence. He then develops in terms of good versus evil, the basic alternatives which have already been twice expounded.

> Vertue may be assail'd, but never hurt,
> Surpriz'd by unjust force, but not enthrall'd,
> Yea even that which mischief meant most harm,
> Shall in the happy trial prove most glory.
> But evil on itself shall back recoyl,
> And mix no more with goodness, when at last,
> Gather'd like scum and setl'd to it self,
> It shall be in eternal restless change
> Self-fed and self-consum'd.   588 – 96

Sin and Death are on the horizon here[31] though there is of course, in that macabre episode, a far greater depth and momentum of involvement than is sought for or appropriate in *Comus*. The destructive intent that issues in the greater glory of the good also represents a tradition which Milton will put to increasing use. At the same time, the references to 'glory' and to the 'happy trial' suggest to us that yet another tradition is being annexed to the imaginative structure. The dark wood of deceit and confusion[32] is the ideal setting for Christian warfare, and the elder brother in speaking of virtue is speaking of righteousness beleaguered, assaulted by the forces of worldliness, set on and hemmed in, yet

morally invincible. Virtue in *Comus* does not sally forth to meet its
adversary and the difference from *Areopagitica* is not without
significance. But virtue is also not 'fugitive and cloistered'. It
accepts the journey through the world, the inevitable 'surprise' by
'unjust force'. To confront this force it makes use of a power given
from above but also given over to man's keeping. If Chastity is
described as both 'sun-clad' and 'saintly' and spoken of in language
both militant and mystical it is because both understandings are
vital to the whole truth.[33] The differing associations are also a
reminder that *Comus* is a poem, not an arrangement of schematiza-
tions, or a cryptogram to be broken open by platonic or other
codes.[34] This applies particularly to the two main axes–Nature-
Grace and Reason-Passion, interpreted platonically–around which
the poem is usually seen to revolve. Milton criticism tends to
regard these two dispositions as exclusive of each other. In fact their
amalgamation is likely to be a primary objective in any poet
determined to consummate the classical in the Christian. Similarly,
light and darkness, stillness and turbulence, chastity and carnality,
good and evil, true being and its parodies, assume their places
around the centre of crisis. Yet the language in which each contrast
is described involves and interpenetrates the language of the
others. There is a homogeneity about the forces on either side which
make clear the peril and opportunity which surround the gift of
freedom. At the heart of decision, it is the nature of any commitment to take over, totally, the conditions of man's being.

The confrontation between the Lady and Comus seems to be set
in a dark wood of critical disagreement. The most popular view is
that the Lady wins largely by refusing to lose and that Comus walks
off with the debating and poetic honours. Other suggestions are that
the Lady is right but not the elder brother,[35] that both the Lady
and Comus are wrong and the Epilogue right,[36] that nobody and
nothing is right except the whole poem[37] and that even the whole
poem seems to have gone wrong somewhere.[38] No decisive solution
can be offered among or even to one side of these alternatives but an
attempt will be made to clear away deadwood. For the moment it
is sufficient to observe that while an agent in a Milton poem may
convey something less than the whole truth, the whole truth develops
so as to complete and not to repudiate the partial truths through
which it is disclosed. There are also occasions such as the celestial
dialogue in the third book of *Paradise Lost* when we must take it that

the whole truth is being spoken. In less exalted situations with less omniscient interventions, it remains true that the agents of good are fundamentally reliable just as those who speak for evil are fundamentally misleading. This is too simple a logic for some but any alternative logic (or lack of it) would result in bewilderment rather than poetic complexity.

Comus's language has been admired by F. R. Leavis[39] and where Leavis approves of Milton, further scrutiny seems rash. Nevertheless it is proposed to look harder at Comus's words. This is Milton's first temptation scene and there is a consistency in his language-tactics which attests to a firm imaginative possession of his problem. The word used is possession and not immersion for reasons which will become apparent. Comus begins with the kind of swelling prologue which should be familiar to every reader of Renaissance literature:

Wherefore did Nature powre her bounties forth
With such a full and unwithdrawing hand,
Covering the earth with odours, fruits and flocks,
Thronging the Seas with spawn innumerable. 709 – 12

This is the kind of language habitually employed to preach the proposition that the firmament displays the glory of its maker. Time after time, Renaissance moralists, teachers, thinkers and encyclopaedists had used the argument that the variety and plenitude of the creation attested to the power, glory and goodness of God. Milton's audience would have expected the surge of Comus's language to rise to its classic affirmation; the impact of the line that follows would have been all the more telling:

But all to please and sate the curious taste? 713

The enormous triviality of this conclusion would have been all the more decisive because of the sense of order in abundance which it violates. The balloon would have been deflated; at the same time the audience would have been made alert against a renewed assault of hyperbole. They would not have been disappointed. Comus's argument has been linked to Renaissance naturalism,[40] but no Renaissance naturalist went so far as to argue that nature would suffocate in its generative excesses unless it was relieved by the unrestrained hedonism of man. Such auto-intoxication gives substance to Douglas Bush's comment that Comus's rhetoric is indicative of his own moral disorder.[41] As his speech proceeds, his strange proposition that the wild exuberance of nature can only be pruned by an exuberance of impulse among its curious tasters, opens to a paradox of betraying dimensions. Those who preach temperance are 'nature's bastards', the children of the excess which they avoid; and those who preach wantonness are the true sons of nature's discipline. Nothing need be said about this preposterous proposition except that it should be recognized as preposterous. As Comus proceeds, his rhetoric becomes more and more strangled in its waste fertility. It winds up to a climax which has caused annotators trouble perhaps because its logic is slightly tipsy. The argument would seem to be that as the generative powers of the earth work their way inward, the uncollected diamonds at the centre would multiply, illuminating the underworld with their lustre, so that the inhabitants of hell would become accustomed to light and come to 'gaze upon the sun with shameless brows'. Since the Lady will identify herself a few lines later with the 'sun-clad power' of chastity[42] it is plain enough where Comus is placed by his argument. The Bridgewater text ends Comus's speech at this point[43] with Comus presumably gazing upon the Lady as he ends so that the dramatic effect underlines the logic of images.

The latter part of Comus's speech is not in the Bridgewater text but is in all other versions.[44] It represents only a nominal change of direction. An attack upon temperance is in order when what is being offered is a 'cordial julep'. But Milton elsewhere describes the julep as 'a thick intoxicating potion which a certain sorceresse the abuser of loves name caries about'.[45] It is natural that Comus should proceed from deriding temperance to dismissing chastity, revealing himself as a true son of Circe. In the process he also changes his argumentative stance and the Renaissance naturalist becomes the cavalier libertine. The language also becomes distinctly less clotted, moving closer to the style of the school which Milton was sniping at. To say this is not to deny the universality of the theme[46] or to forget that Marvell said similar things to his coy mistress. But it is plain whom Milton is referring to and would have been plainer at Ludlow Castle. When this has been said it should be added that Comus's smoother persuasion as a son of Belial also has its momentum, coarsening from 'Beauty is Nature's coin must not be hoarded' to 'Beauty is Nature's brag and must be shown' and ending in a warning the other edge of which is sharpened against himself:

There was another meaning in these gifts,
Think what and be adviz'd,   753 – 54

This is Milton's characteristic employment of the devil's rhetoric and is essentially the same in *Paradise Lost* as in *Comus*. The voice deepens, the depth of misunderstanding is more powerful but to the vigilant reader, the speaker judges himself in the very language that he finds to express himself.

There is certainly another meaning in these gifts but it is not clear that the Lady at this point provides us with the meaning. Milton's vacillation with the text here indicates his own recognition that he was not quite doing what he wanted. The Trinity Manuscript has Comus's full speech with the Lady's response ending at what is now line 778. The Bridgewater manuscript abbreviates matters further ending Comus's speech at line 735. The texts of 1637, 1645 and 1673 have the full confrontation substantially as we know it.[47] The problem becomes more complex when we consider the relationship of these changes to the Epilogue. An abbreviated epilogue which does not mention Venus and Adonis or Cupid and Psyche is cancelled in the Trinity manuscript. The Bridgewater manuscript gives us a further abbreviation. The full epilogue then appears on the next page of the Trinity manuscript and in 1637, 1645 and 1673.[48] There can be more than one meaning in these gifts as well, but the following explanation is suggested. Milton abbreviated Comus's speech in the Bridgewater manuscript, partly because Comus's suggestions about the Lady's chastity would have been less than tactful in the actual performance and partly because he was not satisfied with the scene as he had worked it out in the Trinity manuscript. He abbreviated the Epilogue to provide a song for Lawes. He now had a straightforward disputation between Comus and the Lady, restricted to temperance and the right use of nature. This did not satisfy him either. Milton then decided that his best solution in the circumstances was to have the Lady *repudiate* Comus rather than debate with him and to provide the 'answer' to Comus in the Epilogue. He rewrote the Epilogue in the Trinity manuscript, gave Comus back his full speech and gave the Lady twenty additional lines which dismiss Comus with a suitably scornful tongue-lashing.

The interpretation offered above turns on the proposition that the Lady is rejecting Comus rather than arguing with him. Scholarship has offered many views of the confrontation between Comus and the Lady but this possibility has not been explored. It is suggested now, not out of a desire to put everything on the table but because the text justifies it. It is only necessary to listen again to those crucial twenty lines to hear unmistakably the vehement voice of rejection.

> Thou has nor Ear nor Soul to apprehend
> The sublime notion and high mystery. . .
> And thou are worthy that thou shouldst not know. . .
> Thou art not fit to hear thyself convinc't.   783–91

To some, the thought that the Lady should disdain argument with Comus will be distressing but it has to be remembered that she is scarcely in a position for detached debate. She has been ensnared by an enchanter pretending to be a helpful shepherd, imprisoned in a chair, threatened with transformation into a statue and offered a drink which she has no reason to believe is other than poisonous. When she prudently refuses she is treated to an invitation to abandon her virginity. She goes through the motions of a reply to the less offensive part of Comus's speech and as for the rest she tells him where he belongs. The dramatic probabilities are suspended from time to time in *Comus* but there is no reason why they should be totally forgotten. The incident is plausible on the page and would have been entirely natural in performance.

If we are disconcerted, it is because the confrontation (the word 'discussion' is deliberately not used) has a symbolic as well as a dramatic effect. When good confronts evil we expect the great debate, with complete freedom of speech on both sides, culminating if all goes well, in the doctrinal and imaginative victory of the right. If all does not go well the poet has at least been honest. Milton's contemporaries may not always have been of this persuasion. Satan for them is to be recognized and rejected, not, necessarily, to be argued with. To enter into debate with the devil is to give him your little finger which means in the end giving him your whole body. Eve's mistake may have been that she slipped into conversation with Satan and the privilege of defeating the devil in debate may be one reserved for the second and perfect man. It is true that *Areopagitica* prescribes a different response in the encounter with error but even in *Areopagitica* the example chosen is Guyon who did not pause for discussion when he destroyed the Bower of Bliss.[49]

The suggestion advanced above is not put forward with resounding confidence. As Milton's creative mind engaged itself with a problem that fascinated it for over thirty years it is not unlikely that his sense of the encounter changed. It can also be argued plausibly though unpalatably, that the Lady is an example for Eve and the second Adam an example for the first. Adam's failure lies partially in his surrender to passion, in his failure after Eve's fall, to apply reason to their joint predicament. Eve on the other hand, argues with the serpent when she ought to dismiss him.

Part of our difficulties in reading the central scene in *Comus* arise because, even after Milton's many revisions, there are more than the elements of a debate embedded here. These gestures of argument suggest to us that Milton did what he did as a strategy of last resort and that the choice he made reflects his inability at this point, to achieve an imaginative supersession of error by virtue.[50] The first part of the lady's speech is not particularly good poetry by seventeenth-century standards and sounds to modern ears like a course in home economics. The second part is eloquent[51] but partly because of its hauteur. If the lady spurns Comus it may be because Milton can do no better. The point is that the dismissal has both dramatic and symbolic sanction and that the answer is not withheld but only postponed.

Milton's masque manoeuvres around the concept of chastity so that we know what the word means only as the poem regards it. It is considerably more than temperance of the soul. Allied to Plato's *Sophrosyne* particularly as Ficino read that concept,[52] it is a consecration of the soul to the good that rejects the other than good and the disproportionate claims of lesser goods. Out of this utter loyalty to the 'divine property of her first being' the soul derives a certain moral shapeliness which is chastity's 'unblemished form'. Chastity involves some sternness to the self. When Milton made the famous substitution in 215 he knew well enough what critics were likely to say[53] and risked their comments largely to suggest to us that while charity may be desirable in man's dealings with other men it is not desirable in his dealings with himself. Eternal vigilance is the price of Christian liberty and faith and hope can only be grounded in self-discipline. To be chaste is to be clad in the 'compleat steel' of spiritual armour; to see all things by the steady, certain light of

virtue; to be unpolluted in the temple of the mind whatever fate
may be bestowed on the body in the ordeal of life. Love of the good
draws down from the good the strength to persevere in that love.
It does not exempt man from the 'happy trial' but it does ensure
that Providence will see to the trial's outcome. The soul's seeking
of its form, its dedication to what is noblest in itself, is the true index
of chastity. Plotinus's treatment of the virtues as purifications which
he thought he had derived from Plato[54] thus leads naturally to the
view that chastity is the basis of all virtues. It is a metaphorical
interpretation of chastity and virginity that we must seek and
Comus in its approaches to the concept makes this reasonably clear.
Both Spenser's Britomart and Milton's remarks in the *Apology*[55]
substantiate the impression that there is no conflict between
chastity and married love.[56]

The Elder Brother begins by asserting that chastity is invincible
and ends by maintaining that it cannot be defeated. The Lady
begins where the Elder Brother ends and ends even more con-
fidently than he begins. It can be said that the one retreats under
the pressure of fact and that the other advances under the com-
pulsion of anger. But the Lady's words are not bravado and Comus
feels them 'set off by some superior power'. Chastity is lackeyed by
a thousand liveried angels but virtue is also feeble and must be
stooped to by heaven; the two recognitions have to be seen as
making the consistency of one poem. The power of the good may not
be fully put forth even on behalf of its unswerving champions, as we
learn from the sixth book of *Paradise Lost*; but it remains in being
and those who contend against it are sometimes aware of its infinite
extent. In *Comus* the Attendant Spirit is its delegated presence. He
cannot spare the Lady her ordeal but he has the means to limit it,
and when the two brothers bungle their rescue with the felicitous
incompetence without which the masque would not be possible he
has a second line of remedy to suggest. Preoccupation with the
function of the Sabrina episode and with the role of haemony in the
workings of grace[57] have obscured what should be evident: while
Sabrina may be an agent of grace she is also a water-spirit, a force
of nature. This other side of her significance is important because
Comus has posed as the champion of nature and has condemned
the Lady's doctrine of discipline as a frustration of nature's creative
energy. The Lady in turn has invoked nature as her ally, contend-
ing in her 'sacred vehemence', that even the dumb earth would be

moved to sympathy with her. Sabrina's liberation of the Lady shows on which side the truth lies and also shows that grace and nature ultimately act in unison. The part played by the reverse spell should also not be overlooked. Sandys's commentary on Ovid is as quotable as ever:

> For as Circe's rod, waved over their heads from the right side to the left; presents those false and sinister perswasions of pleasure, which so much deformes them: so the reversion thereof, by discipline, and a view of their owne deformity, restores them to their former beauties.[58]

What the Attendant Spirit describes as those 'backward mutters of dissevering power' are the restoration of the way up and the undoing of the way down, the consecration to true being instead of to animality. When this is done, things find their right nature by finding their real contexts, flesh and spirit stand in their proper and liberating relationships and the web of existence is freed from the weight of deformity.

Comus and the Attendant Spirit vie with each other in praising the Lady's singing, but Comus judges himself with unintended accuracy in invoking the Lady as a 'foreign wonder'. He and the Lady belong to different orders of commitment though the worlds which they inhabit may come into collision. Since he is not fit to hear himself convinced, the Lady's philosophy is not degraded by being put before him. The audience is presumably more eligible for enlightenment than Comus and has some right to expect the masque as a whole to be brought into doctrinal and imaginative balance.[59] From the pattern of the poem so far it is apparent that such a balance would have to show that the world of the senses is included and not annulled by consecration to the world of the spirit and that discipline forms the basis for the liberation of creative energy rather than the means for its confinement.

This is standard Miltonic thinking, proclaimed in the *De Doctrina* with the peremptory clarity so typical of that tract.

> For spirit being the more excellent substance, virtually and essentially contains within itself the inferior one, as the spiritual and rational faculty contains the corporeal, that is, the sentient and vegetative faculty.[60]

For those who prefer poetry to dogma there is the eulogy of discipline in *The Reason of Church Government*. There, in language that recalls *Comus*, discipline is described as not merely 'the removall of disorder', but if any visible shape can be given to divine things the very visible shape and image of vertue'. It is through discipline that the harmony of the voice of virtue becomes 'audible to mortall eares'. Even when there is no possibility of disorder, discipline is still present as a spontaneous movement of creative energy. The 'eternall effluences of sanctity and love in the glorified Saints' (the phrase is typical in its overflowing fervour) are not 'confin'd and cloy'd with repetition of that which is prescribed'. Such happiness will rather 'orbe itself into a thousand vagancies of glory and delight' and 'with a kind of eccentricall equation be as it were an invariable Planet of joy and felicity'.[61] The exuberance of the prose, its combination of the eccentric and constant, kindles the conviction into life, embodying for us the strengthening by each other of creative order and creative joy. Milton's strategies in *Comus* reflect what he found himself capable of doing. Perhaps the masque would have been more successful if the lady had forgotten her righteous indignation long enough to say something like this to her opponent. At any rate, this is what the Epilogue does say in language less direct and therefore more settled. As the knot of relationships is finally tied, the threads are brought together with a care and an allusiveness that justifies the injunction: 'List mortals if your ears be true.'

The ground is carefully prepared for the crucial lines of the Epilogue. The river imagery looks forward to Venus born of the sea. The Graces and the Hours were present at the wedding feast of Cupid and Psyche. The dance which triumphs 'O'er sensuall folly and intemperance' suggests the right coalescence of discipline and energy. The reference to the gardens of Hesperus sets in motion the imagery of Paradise;[62] and the contrast with the younger Brother's use of the same image reminds us that Paradise is made secure by inner righteousness rather than by the 'dragon watch' and its external safeguards.

Milton's reference to the Garden of Adonis cannot but recall and comment on Spenser's description. In *The Faerie Queen* the garden is the 'Seminarie / Of all things, that are born to live and die, / According to their kindes.'[63] It stands at the apex of the natural order with all things fetching their first being from it.[64] We can regard it as in and out of change. The scythe of Time troubles it, making it slightly less than a place of 'immortall blis' but it is also a place of 'continuall spring, and harvest'[65] and Adonis the 'Father of all formes' though subject to mortalitie is also 'eterne in mutabilitie' and 'by succession made perpetuall'.[66] The plentitude of the garden, with a variety and vigour beyond that of nature,[67] consorts with a strict observance of degree.[68] So far this might be Milton's garden but there is a marked difference between the way in which Spenser's Venus and Adonis possess each other

. . . she herself, when ever that she will,
Possesseth him, and of his sweetnesse takes her fill

There now he liveth in eternall blis,
   Joying his goddesse, and of her enjoyed.   *FQ* III, VI, 46, 48

and the picture given us by Milton

Beds of *Hyacinth*, and Roses,
Where young *Adonis* oft reposes,
Waxing well of his deep wound.
In slumber soft, and on the ground
Sadly sits th' *Assyrian* Queen: *Comus* 997–1001

The difference becomes even more clearly intentional when we turn to Cupid and Psyche. Spenser's two lovers are of the same world as Venus and Adonis, partaking with them of the same happiness.[69] In Milton they are both set apart and set above and the verse itself tautens and brightens as it rises to describe them.

But far above in spangled sheen
Celestial *Cupid*, her fam'd Son, advanc't,
Holds his dear *Psyche* sweet intranc't
After her wandring labours long,
Till free consent the gods among
Make her his eternal Bride,
And from her fair unspotted sides
Two blissful twins are to be born,
Youth and Joy; so *Jove* hath sworn.   1002–1010

As William Madsen remarks: 'Cupid is Venus's son, but he is far above her; Psyche's side is unspotted while Adonis is wounded. Venus sits sadly, while the offspring of Cupid and Psyche will be Youth and Joy.'[70] It might be added that Psyche's unspotted side recalls the 'unblemish't form' of Chastity and that the 'bliss' given to Venus and Adonis in Spenser's paradise is carefully denied to them in Milton's garden so that it can be found again in those 'happy twins' of 'divine generation', born of that love whose 'first and chiefest office' according to Milton 'begins and ends in the soule'.[71] To quote the crucial interlude in the *Apology* is to remind ourselves that the identity of the twins has altered. They are not 'knowledge and vertue' and while they may seem closer to 'pleasure', conventionally the daughter of Cupid and Psyche,[72] we must remember that in commentary on the myth, pleasure had come to have platonic connotations.[73] In associating the lower love with frustration and the higher with fulfilment Milton's thought may seem to have much in common with a writer such as Plotinus:

> Further proof that our good is in the realm above is in the love
> innate in our souls; hence the coupling in picture and story of Eros
> with Psyche. The soul, different from the divinity but sprung from it,
> must needs love. When it is in the realm above, its love is heavenly;
> here below, only commonplace. The heavenly Aphrodite dwells in the
> realm above; here below, the vulgar, harlot Aphrodite.
>
> Every soul is an Aphrodite as is suggested in the myth of
> Aphrodite's birth at the same time as that of Eros.[74]

The divergences, however, are as instructive as the affinities. Milton's Venus is no 'vulgar harlot' and his picture of the garden seeks qualified acceptance not rejection. It is a place of repose and healing but we cannot find in it the full meaning of happiness. To discover the reality above it is to liberate the lower reality into its full significance and the argument of images which suggest this also suggests to us that Plotinus would have looked askance at Milton's Youth and Joy. If these blissful twins are in the poem in this way it is surely to complete the answer to Comus. Comus has claimed that his is the right use of nature, but the poem has shown that nature is on the side of the Lady. He has taxed the Lady with letting youth slip by; now youth and joy are shown as the outcome of the restraint that he scorned.[75] Milton is giving poetic reality to his claim in the *De Doctrina* that 'the more excellent substance, virtually and essentially contains within itself the inferior one'. His is not a 'flight of the lone to the alone'[76] but rather a consecration to truths above this world which returns to this world to possess it in its plenitude, while always holding that plenitude in strict proportion in the order of things. Not to observe that proportion is to fall as Comus does, from the divine image to the inglorious likeness.[77]

In the twenty-seventh canto of the *Purgatorio* the angel of chastity greets Dante with the words 'Beati mundo corde', in front of the fire of purification that protects the sacred wood. After Dante has passed through the fire, Virgil can guide him no further. There is a point at which secular understanding must end and in *Comus* also a point at which the Attendant Spirit must declare at least by implication, the boundary of his good offices. He comes from the starry threshold of Jove's Court but he teaches a way of commitment which will carry those dedicated to it above the sphery chime of the created universe. Above the visible heavens there lies the heaven of heavens. Augustine's description of that heaven helps to put before us the climactic stage of the poem's upward movement.

I have heard your voice loud and clear telling me that that creation of yours (the heaven of heavens) is not coeternal with you: you alone are its happiness and in unfailing chastity it drinks you in and never and nowhere does it exhibit its natural mutability. . . . I can find no better name of this *heaven of heavens which is the Lord's* than your house–a house full of the contemplation of delight in you, from which there is no falling away to the contemplation of anything else, a pure mind, single in perfect concord, settled in the peace of holy spirits, the citizens of your *city in the heavenly places*–far above the heaven which we see.[78]

The world of *Comus* is carefully circumscribed and the manner in which the concluding and opening lines connect to each other both close the circle and point to what is beyond. Within its chosen limits the language of the poem is philosophic rather than religious. The Lady for instance, speaks of God as the 'supreme good'[79] and those who think it self-evident that *Comus* is a poem about divine grace ought to be better aware that the word *grace* is mentioned only four times in the masque and used only once with theological connotations. There is no reason of course, why a poem's centre of gravity should not be outside it, reached not by what it says but by its cumulative thrust of implication. Religious significances press in upon the world of *Comus* particularly in its central confrontation; but they do not transgress its decorum since the purpose of that decorum is to suggest how an action shaped in terms of a classical fable invokes and opens out into a Christian meaning. So the Attendant Spirit must bow himself offstage in an Ariel-like cadence leaving in the mind's eye the poem's final tableau of aspiration and balance: the upward effort of the individual soul, the downward reaching response of the divine and the meeting point of self-reliance and dependence where freedom is discovered in the total commitment to virtue.[80] This is the highest of the three unions through which the Epilogue has climbed heavenwards, but the treatment of Cupid and Psyche has already told us the lower reality is not annulled in the acceptance of the higher. Rather it is restored and stabilized and given its due function in the shapeliness of things.

4 *Lycidas*

The shattering of the leaves

Ever since Dr. Johnson forced us to recognize that *Lycidas* was about something more than Edward King, the depths of the poem have been variously sounded. *Lycidas* has been interpreted biographically, historically, musically and archetypally; as the climax of a tradition, as the casting aside of tradition by the individual talent and as a precarious mannerist balancing of the two forces; as a poem from which personality is virtually smoothed out and as one into which personality all but explodes.[1] Fortunately, the critic is left at the end not with the picture of confusion which this description suggests, but rather with a tangible though elusive sense of richness. No approach to *Lycidas* can be dismissed as wholly irrelevant; and yet none seizes the quintessence of a poem which continues to walk disconcertingly intact across the sounding seas of commentary.[2] If this map of partial successes teaches us anything it is that *Lycidas* is a poem built out of conflict. Criticism falls short of the whole, when it regards one term or other of the conflict as paramount; it is more likely to succeed when it recognizes how the struggle which is the poem's substance is created and pressed forward at a series of interlinked levels and then made to subside as the poem works out its peace.

Educated innocence is not easy to achieve but one should make the effort to see *Lycidas* under the morn's opening eye-lids and, if one may vary another poet's metaphor, to take the poem as its suddenness resists one. Perhaps the impact of that suddenness is best suggested by going back to what may have been Milton's encounter with it. When Milton sat down in 1637 to write the poem we know as *Lycidas* in the Trinity manuscript he may not have been writing the poem for the first time but rather transcribing and revising a previous draft.[3] Be that as it may, the poem as he wrote it, fell naturally and without disturbance into the reticent tones of the pastoral lament.

yet once more O ye laurells and once more
ye myrtl's browne wth Ivie never sere
I come to pluck yor berries harsh and crude
before the mellowing yeare.[4]

At this point Milton struck out the fourth line and replaced it by the line we know–'and wth forc't fingers rude'–a line which subtly imports a new note of violence into the poem. He then went back to exemplary pastoral diction–'and crop yor young'–and then striking the half-line dramatically out, yielded the poem to the power of its suddenness.[5]

hatter yor leaves before ye mellowing yeare
bitter constraint, and sad occasion deare
compells me to disurbe yor season due
for Lycidas is dead, dead ere his prime,
young Lycidas and hath not left his peere

Language is the poet's most basic resource and it is here, in the body and movement of the language, that we find the contentions of *Lycidas* at work. The explosive force of 'shatter', its harsh chime with 'bitter' into an assonance of anguish, are balanced against the gradualness, the organic decorum of 'mellowing'. Controlled by this interplay, the striking force quietens into 'disturb', to strengthen again in the repeated 'dead', with the caesura subtly spacing the drum-beat of grief. When we come to 'young', the word is stressed not only by its metrical position but by the lyric context in which it is made to reverberate. It is not simply a matter of untimely death; the whole theme has been stated with a tormented power that opens the lonely road to the blind fury. Looking back to the fourth line we now see that the 'forc't fingers rude' are more than the disclaimer of a young poet, writing before his time and under the pressure of circumstances. What is being 'forced' is ultimately the decorum of the poem, a decorum which as we shall come to recognize, is not simply formal but also elemental, powerfully symbolic of the sense of design in reality. *Lycidas is* the shattering of the leaves, not simply in the passage from innocence to experience, but in the angry challenge of the poem to the tradition which it inherits and finally, to its own security and indeed survival.

Inferences from the evolution of a poem can be treacherous and most of us have been obliged to learn that more than one conclusion can be drawn from manuscript changes. In the passage just discussed for instance, it can be argued that Milton's first two changes merely correct two errors of anticipation resulting from the transcribing of a previous draft and that the dramatic change to 'bitter' strengthens a design already in Milton's mind rather than one which springs to life on the page. Neither hypothesis can be disproved but fortunately acceptance of the less favourable hypothesis would not greatly affect the substance of this chapter; it would merely reduce what has been said so far to the status of an enlightening, prefatory myth. All that is suggested is that the view of *Lycidas* being developed here is consistent with the changes made by Milton and perhaps provides a perspective in which to see them.

As is well-known, the passages which are worked over most heavily in the Trinity manuscript are the 'Orpheus' passage, which is revised in the main text, rewritten in the margin and rewritten again in the 'trial-sheet', and the flower passage, which is struck out in the main text and rewritten in the trial-sheet. The first passage is *expanded* from four to seven lines; that menacing line 'downe the swift Hebrus to the Lesbian shore' is added to the marginal revision; its effect is intensified by the addition of 'when by the rout that made the hideous roare' in the trial-sheet; and the avalanche of horror is given further momentum as Orpheus's 'divine head' becomes his 'goarie visage'. In the flower passage, the number of lines is *reduced* by two; a certain amount of mythological exposition is discarded; and the passage takes on the quality of a procession with each flower given a distinct and vividly focused presence. The movement in one case is towards ferocious elementality; in the other it is towards conventionality in the best sense, the pastoral mood wrought to the height of its beauty. If Milton knew his business and everything in *Lycidas* suggests that he knew it considerably better than we do, revision in opposite directions can only mean that he wished deliberately to intensify rather than to diminish the oppositions that dominate the poem; he realized clearly that it was out of the struggle of contraries that the creative pattern had to be forged and won.

Professor Nicolson in her eloquent remarks on Lycidas, has threatened to haunt those who speak of digressions in the poem.[6] The word is certainly one which has unfortunate connotations and most of us would agree that it is not in the interests of accuracy to employ it. Nevertheless there is an interplay in the poem which Professor Nicolson herself treats as the intertwining of laurel and myrtle[7] but which is perhaps better described for our purposes as the attack mounted by the higher mood against the pastoral form. Convention and elementality are the basic forces of contention in the poem and the struggle between them is not one for supremacy, but rather for a vision which can include both, which can accept the shock of reality, without sacrificing the sense of design. Professor Barker who, with disconcerting ease, has taught us how to read *Lycidas*, in an essay which is actually about another poem[8], has suggested a three-part structure for Milton's monody which is by now, universally accepted; it only remains to be added that each part begins with a statement that the pastoral convention has been or is about to be violated. Two of these admissions have been noted;[9] the intention of the third ('Begin, and somewhat loudly sweep the string') has been obscured because it is a reminiscence of Virgil's Fourth Eclogue; but once the strategy of Milton's poem has been grasped, the kind of notice being served will be plain. After attention has been drawn to the previous or impending violation of decorum, a conventional passage follows: the remembrance of idyllic days spent in the fields, the procession of mourners and the procession of flowers. The assault of experience on the convention then develops and chaos beats against the wall of the poem's order, until an equilibrium is restored. There are of course, variations upon this pattern, as might be expected with an artist of Milton's subtlety and power of musical ordering. The long first section contains not one but two waves of assault, with the reworked 'Orpheus' passage functioning as the first wave. In the second section the brevity of the pastoral interlude gives force to the apocalyptic resolution. In the third section the pastoral mood is restored to a kind of intense fragility in which every detail is worked over with an almost caressing finesse. Then as the sounding seas muster for what threatens to be their most dangerous assault, the poem, instead of yielding once again to chaos, passes through it and is piloted to its peace. These variations help to remind us that we face in *Lycidas* a poet of supreme accomplishment writing a poem that is totally and tautly controlled. But we also face a poet who has moved beyond those academic groves that once formed the dark wood of *Comus*, who has decided to confront the anger of his poetry and to discover the truth on the lips of the blind fury. There is a difference between the 'honour'd flood' of the Mincius and that 'perilous flood' over which Lycidas comes to preside; the achievement of Milton's pastoral is that it is conscious of both of these forces, that it is able to outlive their perilous encounter and to absorb their struggle in a profounder sense of reality.

Some gathering of the threads is called for by now and perhaps one can suggest that there is involved in *Lycidas*, an assault upon the poem's own assumptions, which the poem in the act of making itself, recognizes and progressively strengthens. This attack is exemplified, both in the kind of microcosmic enactment of language that was studied at the beginning of this, chapter and in the larger tactical manoeuvre of the pastoral spectacle, thrice set up to be undermined. The total attack, both formal and linguistic, can be thought of as the stylistic correlative to the deeper assault of experience upon the sense of order; and the restoration of equilibrium in convention and language corresponds to, validates and intensifies the deeper restoration of a sense of design in reality. It is because of this inclusive and highly sophisticated strategy that the poem to quote Douglas Bush 'is at once an agonized personal cry and a formal exercise, a search for order and a made object, an affirmation of faith in Providence and an exploitation of pastoral and archetypal myth.'[10] One more paradox can be added to the description of this unprecedented poem in which everything has a precedent. It is both a powerfully allusive essay in a convention and a highly controlled denial of that convention.

Because *Lycidas* is so completely both a pattern and a process and because the pattern has so often been misunderstood, it has been necessary to run ahead of the poem and to suggest some of the definitions it achieves. It is time to resume the poem's own voyage of discovery and to note how the fringe of darkness grows out of pastoral peace, how from the very beginning the canker is in the rose and how the incipient suggestion is stirred at the outset that the sadness of things is also the fitness of things. The frost attacks all flowers including those of poetry but in what should be the open mind of the reader, seasonal death points also to seasonal rebirth. Not too much should be made of these implications; they are set up largely to ensure that the main current of assertion dominates but does not overwhelm the poem. These consolations of the pastoral decorum, the coupling of life and death to the rhythm of nature, are designed so that the violence which follows can sweep them aside; but they also remain alive for the eventual restoration. So, the traditional 'Where were ye Nymphs' blazes into the recognition that protection is useless, that the poet's fate is to be doomed like Orpheus. Large rechoes are stirred by the powerful image. Since Orpheus was a symbol of the force of civilization, his death connotes a reversion to barbarity and the dimensions of his defeat are given depth because in the sombre power of the verse, the fury that overwhelms him is now wholly uprooted from any rational order; the mourning of the woods and caves has broadened into the lament of universal nature and indeed in an earlier version of the passage both heaven and hell had joined in the chorus of grief. At the same time the context works, as always, in more than one direction: Orpheus as a type of Christ, keeps our minds open to that upward movement which the poem is eventually to achieve.[11] For the time being however, the nihilist momentum is dominant and it is against this threatening background that the first temptation to irresponsibility evolves. It is a temptation particularly striking for the immediacy it achieves within the pastoral tone. The buoyant consonants lend their sprightliness to sporting with Amaryllis and the line on Neaera's hair—surely one of the most voluptuous in all literature—is almost tactile in its quality of ardent entanglement. A few lines later, as the sudden blaze of fame is throttled down to the thin-spun whisper of frustration, we are made aware again of Milton's confident power to achieve what is currently called enactment. But something more than enactment is involved. If the verse is fully responsive to the immediate eddy it also sweeps on in the larger tide. As the higher temptation of fame succeeds the lower (in that ironical call of the clear spirit), we relinquish the world of casual living only to realize that dedication creates its own dangers. To live for the moment is to lose only the moment. But the commitment to a vocation, however warped by the pressures of earthly glory (the language is carefully judged to cover what it dismisses), opens, by its very seriousness, the door into a world of anti-meaning. The word 'slit' placed with almost malignant accuracy in the halting march of the monosyllabic line, is potent in evoking a calculating power of destruction, all the more challenging because it is driven by blindness.[12]

With the question posed, the answer has to follow. Professor Daiches has rightly stressed the tentative character of Phoebus's reply, though it is an exaggeration to describe it as a 'deliberately false climax'.[13] Professor Daniells agrees with Professor Daiches and uses the occasion to assure us that the 'refusal to promulgate a resounding resolution' is characteristic of mannerist restlessness.[14] This may be true but if the poem is successfully making itself, the weight of reassurance that is here offered must be precisely what the evolving logic demands; the justification is perhaps better sought in an inner necessity rather than in a current style. In any event, the resolution of the two-handed engine should be resounding enough for any taste and the poem, whether or not it is mannerist, does not at this point, cease to be itself. In fact neither resolution is sufficient and the difference in their quality is significant for precisely this reason. Both are temporary truces in the onslaught of questioning and both must give way to a different and superior order of recognition before the poem can attain its peace.

In the procession of mourners which initiates the second section *Lycidas's* death is once again made to stand apart from nature. All winds are imprisoned and the very phrase 'sleek *Panope*' reflects the mirror-like gloss of the sea's surface. The calamity is no part of the order of life; it emanates from a world of arbitrary destructiveness and the Fury's true function is to slit the thread of design. Thus, the natural logic of doubt is encouraged to flourish and one irrationality opens into another. If the fate of the innocent is to be struck down in the 'perfidious Bark' that carries them through life, then by the same injustice, the destiny of the wicked is to prosper. We are in fact making the first exploration of that world which Michael describes in *Paradise Lost* as 'To good malignant, to bad men benigne'. The second irresponsibility is now presented to us, neatly balancing the first, the personal questioning of one's vocation versus the public abandonment of one's calling. Complaint against ecclesiastics is not uncommon in late pastoral poetry and is indeed a fairly typical expression of that mode's social content. One might add that Virgil's Ninth Eclogue in which one of the speakers is Lycidas, includes a passing reference to social injustice. The muster of precedents should, however, serve to inform us that there are no precedents for the crescendo of indignation which the poem develops. In using what Professor Allen calls 'the inherited right of the pastoralist to be both satirist and allegorist' Milton is achieving effects which are far more than satirical.[15] Once again if an explanation is to be sought, it must take account of the poem's internal necessities, of the rage for order which has become a condition of its questioning. It is the mounting violence of that rage, pressed forward inexorably by the poem's dynamics that seems to reach up to and almost to call down the responsive thunder of the two-handed engine.

The return to the pastoral mood is now particularly fervent, as if the two previous breakdowns have made more anxious the search for security. Yet the caressing care with which the illusion is built up does not prevent it from being revealed as an illusion. The false surmise is not only that there is no laureate hearse; it is also the assumption that absorption in a ritual however ardent, can serve to protect one against the assault of reality. This is the third irresponsibility: the dalliance not with Amaryllis, or with the spoils of a desecrated office, but with that frail and precious sense of order out of which the poem has no choice but to advance. The forces of chaos muster for their assault and Milton in three daring revisions, makes clear not only his uncompromising sense of direction but the imaginative risks he knows he can negotiate. The 'floods and sounding seas' become the 'shores and sounding Seas' as if to destroy any residual sense of security and to suggest inexorably that, for those who ask ultimate questions, neither land nor ocean can provide a place of refuge. 'Sad thoughts' become 'frail thoughts', to stress the precariousness of the defence against chaos; and the 'humming tide' becomes the 'whelming tide', giving additional strength to the attacking forces.[16] Even nature which mourned Lycidas and lamented Orpheus, now seems committed to the 'monstrous world' of the enemy. As the pastoral mood faces its peril for the third time it appears to be confronted by annihilation; and precisely because of the poem's unitive power, a formal defeat must be also a failure of life. What is at stake in the inner world of the poem is nothing less than that sense of order and design in reality without which no man can survive in this perilous flood.

What happens next is of course known to every reader of *Lycidas* but bears repeating because it is so plain. In seven lines the poem is manoeuvred with startling authority from the desperation into which it has been deliberately plunged into an almost exultant recovery. 'Weep no more, woful Shepherds weep no more' is a line alive with both serenity and joyousness; the conviction that rings in it is not merely declared but achieved. This transformation is accomplished by an image which according to Eliot is for sheer magnificence of sound unsurpassed in the English language.[17] Little penetration is needed to see, however, that sumptuous noises alone cannot bring about what is accomplished here. It is also not sufficient to suggest that everything is contained in Mercator's atlas or that the angel looking towards Spain, is being advised to turn its attention to England's internal enemies. The image is clearly the turning point of *Lycidas*[18] and some attempt to elucidate how it works is necessary both to understand the poem better and to test those critical approaches that claim to possess it.

Lycidas, as one comes to realize progressively, is full of significant symmetries arranged as affirmations of its three part structure. The three forms of irresponsibility have already been noted and it is well-known that the outburst of questioning in each part is stilled on each occasion by a form of divine reassurance. The relationship between these reassurances is not undisputed. Professor Abrams considers that they disclose 'a gradual shift from the natural, pastoral and pagan viewpoint to the viewpoint of Christian revelation' while Professor Nicolson considers that the answers from above are uniformly Christian.[19] Perhaps it is best to say that each part discloses a different face of God or more precisely, a different form of man's recognition of God's nature. The God who calms the first wave of doubt is the god of justice and emphasis is laid on his impartiality, his 'perfect witnes', and on the 'all-judging' power that weighs all things fully and impartially in its balance. The god of the second part is the apocalyptic god of retribution whose single blow is sufficient to crush the armies of the godless. To make understanding doubly clear Milton defines the specific quality of each reassurance, immediately after the reassurance has been offered. Significantly, these definitions occur in those two crucial passages that admit the violation of the pastoral decorum. We return to normality from the 'higher mood' of justice; we return again to it from the 'dread voice' of retribution.

The third recognition of God is the one recognition that can truly answer man's agony. It is the consciousness not of justice but of the power beyond justice, not the might of him who wields the two-handed engine but instead the 'dear might of him that walk'd the waves'. To quote the language of another poem, it is the 'rigid satisfaction, death for death' which has dominated the first two 'resolutions' in *Lycidas*. The third resolution transcends the law and so reminds us that there are energies in this poem which even the law cannot silence. If peace is to be won it can be won only through the higher satisfaction of redemptive love. The angel mediates the movement into this recognition. Against the menace of the 'sounding seas' it stands steadfastly protective, guarding and yet guarded, vigilant and unassailable, looking out not only on a geographical panorama but also on the wide landscape of man's questioning and searching. The 'great vision' here is evocative of the blaze of understanding while the 'guarded mount' with its evocations of paradise, suggest distantly it is true, but strongly enough to give resonance to the verse, the redemption of man's nature and the protective finality with which God's grace surrounds that redemption. Finally, the angel looking homeward is not asked to wield the weapons of retribution but is implored instead to 'melt with ruth'. Just as power has modulated into protective strength, protective strength now modulates into mercy. Though legendary, archetypal and even political associations surround this great image, it lives also in a specific world of embattlement, drawing the self-wounding strength of the poem's conflict, into the conviction of design and peace. As the dolphins waft Lycidas to Byzantium,[20] they surely guide us also to the recognition that salvation lies not with the god of hosts, nor with the exact dispenser of Olympian justice, but in 'the blest Kingdoms meek of joy and love'[21] which establish both our dignity and dependence. The god of compassion will not be seen again with such tenderness in the sterner movements of Milton's later poetry; and though in an earlier poem, heaven had stooped towards a feeble but upward-climbing virtue, that, as befitted a masque, was a choreographic gesture, exquisitely felicitous, rather than a cry out of the heart of experience. The moment of comprehension in *Lycidas* is unique; it is not merely called but implored into being by the poem.

The unrhymed lines of *Lycidas* are no longer evidence that the poem is not quite anonymous.[22] Nevertheless, it is significant that the resolution contains no unrhymed lines.[23] The regularity is expressive of other mergings that are taking place: of the pastoral with the Christian, of the rhythm of nature with the death of man, of the poem itself with the forces of doubt which have invaded it and all but brought it to its destruction. It is also one more reminder of the fully-shaped economy with which the poem moves on its various levels of disturbance and achievement so that all that happens in it, however microscopic, acquires its full meaning in more than one dimension. In the end, even the shore and sounding seas are joined in a pattern of purpose, not a chaos of nihilism. Lycidas the genius of the one is also, through the hard-won achievement of the poem, an example to all those who fare forward upon the destructive element of life. All is in order now. If there is a time for grief there is a time to put grief behind one and to see the world made green again in the power of God's blessing. As the westering wheel of the poem sinks to its rest in the brisk finality of its last *ottava rima* a position has been established, a recognition achieved and the point has now been reached when even the poem must be put into its framework. The subtle shift from first to third person is a beautifully judged manoeuvre, distancing the poem, depersonalizing it and leaving it decidedly behind. The performance is over and a new day will begin.

If this examination of *Lycidas* is not wildly erroneous, we are facing a poem more intricately articulated than even the most elaborate dissections of it suggest. Every point on its surface inherits a long tradition to which it is competitively and creatively responsive. This is as it should be; since the singing match is a root convention of the pastoral, a late pastoral should have in abundant measure, the *élan* and the *brio* of performance. But *Lycidas* is always and inescapably more than a technical accomplishment of extreme sophistication. It is a voyage towards recognition, a poem that resolutely faces itself, that opens all windows upon the storm of reality and takes all assaults into its ultimate order. What gives the questioning its singular strength and the final resolution its inclusive validity, is the complete integration of experience, structure and language; few poems can have embodied and made alive their substance so fully, both in the large strategy and the minor manoeuvres of style. It is because of this total authenticity that the poem is able to accommodate and eventually to unify a range of dissension that would otherwise tear it apart. Rosemond Tuve is right in regarding *Lycidas* as 'the most poignant and controlled statement in English poetry of the acceptance of that in the human condition which seems to man unacceptable'.[24] But if the unacceptable is brought within the framework of order it is only by taking risks which are uniquely comprehensive. It is this perilous openness that gives Lycidas its character, that enables it to remain inclusively honest in its fidelity to experience, yet imbued throughout with a passionate sense of the *genre*.

5 *Paradise Lost*

The web of responsibility

When Raleigh contemplates the crisis of *Paradise Lost* he says decisively that 'there is not an incident, hardly a line of the poem, but leads backwards or forwards to those central lines of the Ninth Book'. The 'central lines' are those which recount Eve's plucking and eating of the apple. 'From this point', Raleigh continues, 'radiates a plot so immense in scope, that the history of the world from the first preaching of the Gospel to the Millennium occupies only some fifty lines of Milton's Epilogue.'[1] When Tillyard disagrees with Raleigh on the location of the crisis he directs our attention to Adam's and Eve's repentance. 'The whole elaborate edifice', he says, 'has been staged to give all possible weight to a quite uncomplicated and commonplace trickle of pure human sympathy, the first touch of regeneration, a small beginning but stronger than the pretensions of satanic ingenuity, like some faint flow of pale, clear oil issuing from a huge and grotesquely carved oil-press; all this complication of apparatus just for *that*.'[2] It is possible to have different views of where the crisis of *Paradise Lost* occurs.[3] It is also possible to believe that there is more than one crisis or to conclude, as Tillyard himself suggests,[4] that we should think not of a point but of an area of crisis. Most persuasive perhaps is the view of G. A. Wilkes that the search for a crisis results in misreading the poem.[5] For the time being we must refrain from committing ourselves to any of these fascinating and distracting alternatives. Rather, we must concentrate on what is suggested both by Raleigh's characteristic clarity and by that uncharacteristic flurry of excitement that invades Tillyard's normally bland prose. The two scholars disagree on what constitutes the crucial act of choice but they agree on the minuteness of the act and on the huge hinterland of motivation and consequence which converges on the act and radiates from it. Both accept the vast design[6] and the vulnerable

centre, the enormous pressures that are brought to bear on the enclosed moment in the walled-in garden.

As the times change the conditions of wisdom alter and what was
once indisputable as a pattern of truth becomes only accessible as a
metaphoric structure. It is not always easy to maintain that on the
22nd of April in 4004 B.C., an apple eaten in Mesopotamia where
apples do not normally grow, accounts for a decisive failure in ourselves. What we are dealing with is a fable of the human condition;
indeed three hundred years of the reading of *Paradise Lost* entitle us
to make use of the word 'myth'. This myth is sometimes described
as a myth of radical evil: in other words it invokes the recognition
that we are to some degree imprisoned in ourselves, that liberation
can only follow on moral transformation and that transformation
depends on our spontaneous dependence on a power beyond ourselves which restores to us the freedom of our proper place in reality.
The last books of *Paradise Lost* powerfully convey this recognition
both through the manner in which the trickle of sin broadens into
the torrent of history and through the manner in which the seed of
repentance grows into the harvest of redemption. But the last two
books are only a sixth of *Paradise Lost* and it has required some effort
by Milton scholars to show that they are organically part of the epic
and not simply the despairing postscript of a defeated reformer.
Radical evil has its place in the web of *Paradise Lost* but the web
itself is perhaps better explored by other guiding principles such as
infinite responsibility and the great movements of meaning and consequence that are made to centre round the gift of freedom.[7]

That *Paradise Lost* is the only poem to present the celestial cycle in
its entirety has been recognized[8] but due attention has not always
been given to Milton's shaping of the cycle. The typical chronology
maintained that the angels were created with the world and fell
during the creation. Milton's view that the angels fell before the
world was created was not without precedent but it was not the
view of his time.[9] We know from the *De Doctrina*[10] that he believed
in his account of events but *Paradise Lost* obliges us to look not so
much at what Milton believed as what he made of what he believed
in or invented. When both the true and the feigned seem to point to
the same aesthetic purpose we can be slightly more confident that
we are right in our sense of the purpose. To return to the celestial
cycle, Milton's more spacious planning enables him to set apart
human and heavenly history, to suggest more clearly how history

repeats itself, to link the fall of Satan with that of Adam and Eve, and to link the creation with the atonement. The rhythm of light out of darkness which is thereby established becomes not simply an assertion of the ways of providence but part of the poem's basic symmetry. The great confrontations of the epic have already been drawn and the shape they compose is seen as the pattern of time.

Milton's shaping of a work has always a deep creative consistency. All that he does is finely responsive to a controlling logic, putting around that logic the power and sweep of the poem. If he achieves certain results in his treatment of time, he achieves them again in his interpretation of space. In both dimensions the field of organization is the theoretical maximum and comprehensiveness becomes an aesthetic virtue because all things in that comprehensiveness are mobilized, interconnected and set meaningfully within an order of things the pivot of which is man's nature and his destiny.

Milton's universe is usually described as Ptolemaic; it is so only within what is hesitantly termed the hard outer shell of the created world.[11] The chaos which rages against the world is by no means the first matter of the *De Doctrina*[12] and while taking up hints and guesses from Lucretius, Spenser and elsewhere remains impressively Milton's own creation.[13] Ontologically, the world is a short 'walk' from chaos, to use a phrase by the 'Anarch old' which is both unexpectedly and arrestingly casual. It is hung from heaven by a golden chain which links classical precedents with Mediaeval and Renaissance ideas of harmony; but it is also joined to hell by a causeway which Milton's imagination built, even though its diabolic span encompasses scriptural and Virgilian texts. The decisions which confront man become all the more momentous when they are affirmed so insistently in the symbols of his universe.

God's eminence is 'dark with excessive bright'. Chaos is 'Darkness profound' and hell 'darkness visible'.[14] These discriminations are expressive of an alert poetic intelligence able not only to proclaim but to populate a universe, taking up the literary past when it can, but also ignoring it when it must. If chaos is Milton's creation, hell is its perversely disciplined enclave, an anti-world carved destructively out of the non-world. Milton's location of hell is like his chronology, his own imaginative decision, taken tellingly against the weight of precedent.[15] In placing it 'As far remov'd from God and light of Heav'n / As from the Center thrice to th' utmost

Pole',[16] he is expecting us to appreciate his talent in the solemn game of outdoing Virgil and Homer but also to recognize that there is more serious business on hand. Spatial distance from the light can also be moral distance, 'Glory obscur'd' is on the way to 'Darkness visible', and 'fardest from him is best' is meant to be heard as a cry not only of heroic defiance but of ultimate alienation.[17] The mind as its own place becomes 'myself am Hell'; the mind opened to God can become the paradise within. It is scarcely necessary to multiply examples; the principle is central and the reader should not be deprived of the pleasure of discovering and connecting its detailed manifestations.

As we read *Paradise Lost* we become more and more aware of the steady mobilization of what Blake and Yeats would call contraries: light and darkness, good and evil, reason and passion, creation and destruction, supernal grace and sinfulness. Each set of contraries evokes the others and is reflected into them, so that as we advance through the poem, we become conscious of a web of interconnectedness, steadily growing in its controlled complexity. The location of hell now takes its place in the poem, as everything does if we look for the place with patience. The purpose is to build into the cosmography of the poem our sense of the poem's massed polarities. The two armies under their creative and destructive Trinities confront each other across the created universe and like chaos beating upon the walls of that universe, the force of inescapable cosmic issues presses steadily upon the fragile peace of Paradise.

In a poem of the scope of *Paradise Lost*, oppositions of concept and imagery are not enough. A narrative poem must encompass and move through a series of dramatic oppositions. Few things in *Paradise Lost* are more striking than the manner in which Milton pushes satire almost to the edge of blasphemy in underlining his contrast between the divine and satanic Trinities. The two councils, infernal and celestial, play their part in this differentiation. Twenty years ago it might have been necessary to insist on the results made possible by this uniquely inclusive and dramatic structure. In the present state of scholarship such underlining is no longer required. But gains can seldom be made without paying a price; the price paid here is that a contemplative heaven must be renounced and that the divine must be disclosed in action rather than through its reflected radiance in things. Laments that Milton did not provide us with a Dantesque heaven are fairly frequent; these laments fail to recognize that poets like men of affairs, have only limited options and that to choose one option is to decide against others.[18] Moreover, the choice of an option is a choice decisive for the whole poem, assuming that the poem has some degree of integrity; what we discuss in seminars as the problem of Heaven cannot be treated as the problem of Heaven alone.

In the contrast between the two Trinities Milton makes it clear that he knows what he wants to do and that, like all artists who have felt within themselves the rights of their own poetry, he is prepared to run certain imaginative risks to do it. His design may not be the best of all possible designs, though those who feel this should ask themselves about the total and not merely the local alternatives. But Milton's sense of the design is consistent and decisive. In his presentation of Christ as much as in his treatment of the two Trinities, Milton shows his desire to give dramatic substance and animation to the oppositions of imagery and concept that extend and ramify through the poem. The web of responsibility proliferates and yet draws together; and the movement from mind to cosmos and from cosmos to mind, so characteristic of the fluency of the epic, bears with elaborated weight on the basic contentions within the nature of man.

It is unfortunate that in discussing what is unusual about Christ we should limit ourselves to a discussion of theology. Arianism or Subordinationism is not Milton's only way of being original. There are perhaps four occasions on which Milton's presentation of Christ departs from tradition. Three of these at least, have little to do with subordinationism; but all four of them have much to do with the poem. Though there is a well established practice of having Truth, Justice, Peace and Mercy consider man's fate before the throne of God, this constitutes no real precedent for a dialogue between two persons of the Trinity.[19] A true precedent is by no means easy to find. Again, Milton's treatment of the Battle in Heaven departs from typical interpretations of the Book of *Revelation* for as Milton himself points out, 'it is generally supposed that Michael is Christ'. In putting forward his view of events (which is also the view advanced in the *De Doctrina*), Milton is in the odd company of a mediaeval Catholic bishop; but the theologians of his own time seem almost wholly against him.[20] Once again, in interpreting the first chapter of *Genesis* the general opinion is that all three persons of the Trinity participated in the process of creation; the decisive role that Milton assigns to the Son is so unusual that the awkward reservation of VII 587–90 becomes necessary to preserve appearances.[21] Finally, in having Christ deliver the judgement on Adam, Eve and the Serpent, Milton is as far as we know, being unique.[22] Explanations can be offered for each of these individualities; but the one explanation which unifies them all is that Milton is determined to have Christ and Satan emerge as dramatic antagonists in the struggle of contraries which gives the poem its energy. It is an intention which emerges not simply in the shaping but also in the placing of Christ's victories. Thus in the two assemblies, Christ's redemptive mission follows immediately on Satan's destructive design. The Creation is carefully located in the poem to be succeeded almost at once by the undoing of the creation. Christ's victory in heaven is not as the leader of an army but single-handed, against the background of a military stalemate, the mounting violence of which threatens even the fabric of heaven with anarchy. Thus like every act of Christ, it too is an exercise of the power of creation, opening out into the creation which is to follow. In Christ's giving of the judgement it is subtly put to us that he is the ground as well as the instrument of order. He may be an actor in the scheme of things but he is also the force that encloses the action. It is no accident that the affirmation of the pattern comes at a time when Sin and Death are to be unloosed on the Universe. Thus at point after point in the struggle of contraries, we are kept aware both of the form of the struggle and of its agents.

A Renaissance critic's feelings can be understood if he complains of strangulation by the Great Chain of Being. If the figure is discussed here it is because it is necessary to show how every resource in *Paradise Lost* is made to point into the centre of decision. Sin is a violation of degree and while the violation may be upwards or downwards[23] the result of the sin can only be downwards, a tearing away of the sinful creature from the shaping principle of its own identity. Virtually Raphael's first act is to explain what Adam calls the Scale of Nature. In doing so he also puts before us the concept of 'bounds / Proportiond to each kind'. Satan's sin, shortly to be recounted, is a breaking of his bounds and the reader is surely meant to recall how 'one slight bound high over leap'd all bound' when the force of destruction made its entry into Paradise.[24] For that matter, Raphael's simile of the plant is meant to be remembered by the attentive when we come to the imagery of redemption in the last book.

Ulysses can speak passionately of degree in that great speech which none of us can promise not to quote. But Shakespeare's play is not about degree in quite the same way as Milton's poem. Degree is part of the cosmography of *Paradise Lost* and perhaps goes behind even that; the very act of creation is a setting of bounds and the drawing of the world's 'just Circumference'.[25] The golden chain evokes the Scale of Nature; and the chain and the causeway point to the way up and the way down in the architecture of both space and being. Reason and passion and flesh and spirit are two of the contraries which the chain traditionally couples. Because they meet in the mixed nature of man we are conscious of all the other contraries that Milton assembles, as involved in the struggle to preserve and refine that nature. To sum up, the chain is used structurally rather than evocatively. There is no other example in English literature of so fundamental and far-reaching a usage.

Aristotle in speaking tentatively of the unity of time, says that while tragedy endeavours as far as possible to confine itself to a single circuit of the sun the epic action is 'not restricted to any fixed limit of time'. Minturno suggests that the length should not exceed one year. The actions of the *Iliad* and the *Odyssey* have been reckoned as taking forty-five and forty-two days; that of *Paradise Lost* has been estimated to take precisely a month.[26] The statistics which are of no great consequence in anyone's response to any of these poems, are quoted to suggest that the main action of *Paradise Lost* is really extraordinarily concise, reflecting the dramatic origins of the poem. Indeed, shorn of its first three books, the epic would strikingly resemble *Adam Unparadized*. But the central action is widened in time by a flashback and a movement forward (both epic devices and both neatly arranged in two courses of angelic instruction), just as it is widened in space by the two assemblies (again an epic device) and by the scope of the opening movement from darkness to light. These thrusts of expansion are unprecedented in their extent and in combination with the confined setting of the crisis, they produce the impression for which Milton was always striving – the infinite structure encircling the infinitesimal nucleus. Perhaps it should be added that the beginning in *medias res* (another epic device) situates us on the circumference while directing our attention to the centre while the Satanic voyage (still another epic device, Miltonically inverted) transports us to the centre through what is by now a cosmos of meanings as well as a physical universe.[27]

Milton's use of the resources of the *genre* is necessarily selective and having asked himself 'whether the rules of Aristotle are herein to be kept or nature to be followed' he did what was right for the poem, to the distress of some neo-classical critics. The property of the epic on which he concentrates unerringly is what Aristotle called its 'capacity for extension'.[28] In so doing he takes to its theoretical limit Aristotle's view that 'so long as the plot is perspicuous throughout, the greater the length of the story, the more beautiful will it be on account of its magnitude',[29] with the difference that the concept of magnitude is applied to the total rather than to the primary action.

In creating the artifice of eternity Milton joins many things together and it is a personal as well as a public inheritance that we see coming to fruition in his poem. The *Nativity Ode* has the same panoramic movements through time and space that distinguish the epic and in both poems, the lines of force reach into and radiate from a centre carefully confined in time and space. The centre in the ode is one of meaning; in *Paradise Lost* it is a centre of decision in which meaning can either be preserved or undone. These differences put it to us that the *oeuvre* in achieving that fuller statement which is beyond the power of any single poem, must display both variety and wholeness. In *Comus* likewise, the theme of temptation is given its first enactment; light and darkness, vice and virtue, flesh and spirit, chastity and lust are brought together in a marshalling of contraries that anticipates *Paradise Lost*,[30] just as the catalogue of false gods in the *Ode* paves the way for the grimmer pageant of the epic. It is of course some distance from Comus to Satan or for that matter from Comus to Belial. The single episode grows into the long narrative of corruption. The 'curious taste' of misrule darkens into evil, engendering and devouring itself, a conception which the masque affirms but does not reach out to embody. The well-known comparison between Comus ravished by the lady's singing and Satan 'Stupidly good' as he contemplates Eve,[31] is exact in the differentiation which it also suggests. What is taking place is not simply development; it is in addition, the choosing of the right *genre* at the right time by the creative talent coming into possession of its own depths. We are asked to note the expert and supple observances of 'bounds proportion'd to each kind' and to discern how these observances contribute to a fuller statement of the unfolding theme. Thus in *Comus*, the place of decision is a place of confinement, looking forward beyond *Paradise Lost* to the almost claustrophobic confinements of *Samson Agonistes*. But the differences must be weighed with the similarities; the immediate setting for the crisis is a forest of deceit rather than a garden of order and the contrast is designed to suggest to us that whatever the environment, we cannot escape the ordeal. The Epilogue to *Comus* uses the garden to establish the peace of the poem, the settlement in symbol of its intellectual issues; *Paradise Lost* uses it as the focal point of the poem's war of energies. It is a war which cannot be avoided, whatever the position chosen or fortifications built. 'Within himself', says Adam to Eve, 'The danger lies, yet lies within his power.'[32] So the infinite theatre narrows to the enclosure of decision and the enclosure in turn contracts to the kernel of choice in the mind.

In this way Milton's own literary past like everything else that he inherits, is taken up into his poem providing him with his seminal oppositions, his characteristic strategies, his opening out of the meaning in time and space and with that central situation which he was repeatedly to explore and never to exhaust. The result is not monotony but a growing sense of the richness of a centre which can respond creatively to the different styles of insight regulated by the propensities of each *genre*. We also recognize, to return for a moment to Milton's heaven, that a contemplative presentation would have been foreign to his temperament. *The Nativity Ode* is a celebration of the power of the word; it rejoices not simply in goodness but in goodness at work in the redemption of history. In *Comus* for all its platonic apparatus, virtue is not simply reached up to by the aspiring mind but is held in battle against a plausible opponent. Milton's concern throughout is not with what the ultimate radiance is but with what it does and with how we are to respond to what it does. Given such a concern, the choice of a narrative form is all but inevitable; and while the form in its fullness contains introspective elements it seems unsafe to withdraw it wholly into these elements. *Paradise Lost* is a poem of the mind but it is also a poem of the mind's place in history and reality.

So far, our attention has been given to the web in its enmeshing and controlled intricacy and to those strong lines of convergence that direct the mind's eye along the web to its centre. It is time to inquire about the centre itself. At the point where all threads join we have neither a prisoner nor a manipulator, neither the spider nor the fly in marmalade. 'Sufficient to have stood, though free to fall' is the phrase most expressive of those mixed potentialities that flow from man's mixed nature.[33] It is expressive even in the see-saw of its balance upon the fulcrum of its own caesura. Significantly the phrase is used both of the angels and of man. On that height above all heights where past, present and future are seen together (and where the fall of man is described in all three tenses) it is natural that we should be made aware of the universalities of freedom rather than of its accidents.

In his speech from the throne God as might be expected, quotes the Bible frequently (a chronological purist might say that he provides a preview of it) and Sims cites no less than ninety-nine allusions in lines 80 to 342 of Book III.[34] This is not Milton's highest degree of allusiveness for in Book XII the reminiscences are even more thick-sown and as many as fifteen references to the scriptures are made in the opening thirteen lines of the poem.[35] Nevertheless the frequency of citation in Book III, combined with the imaginative context, put it strongly to us that we have reached the word itself, beyond which it is impossible to look. The scriptures may be an accommodation of truth to the understanding, but the very fact of accommodation indicates that we have arrived at a boundary. We may realize that the ultimate metaphor is a metaphor; but we cannot go behind what the metaphor reveals. Both the view of truth that was typical in Milton's time and the dramatic circumstances of God's statement make it evident that we are being confronted with the *données* of the poem, the conditions on which we are enabled to enter its universe. It is therefore all the more striking that lines 87–135 in which freedom is defined in relation to foreknowledge, contain only one biblical reference and that in lines 156–166 which set the stage for the whole process of redemption, the poetry speaks for itself without biblical support.[36] Milton is not alone in his view of the nature of man's freedom (or more correctly the freedom of intelligence) but the vehemence with which the view is urged and the cosmic elevation he accords it are unique. If the tactics are not quite successful it is because Milton in the last analysis, is unable to proclaim the absolute without justifying the absolute to the relative. 'The hidden ways of his providence we adore and search not', he says unexpectedly, in *The Doctrine and Discipline of Divorce*, but

Paradise Lost is distinguished more by searching than by adoration.[37]

God's affirmation of man's freedom is sometimes too strenuous to be convincing but when Raphael takes up the theme the vehemence moderates. We approach that quiet pride in responsibility which for Milton is part of the dignity of man.

> That thou art happie, owe to God;
> That thou continu'st such, owe to thy self,
> That is, to thy obedience; therein stand.
> This was that caution giv'n thee; be advis'd.
> God made thee perfet, not immutable;
> And good he made thee, but to persevere
> He left it in thy power, ordain'd thy will
> By nature free, not over-rul'd by Fate
> Inextricable, or strict, necessity; V, 520–28

Changelessness is the quality traditionally associated with perfection. If change is for the better, that which changes must be less than perfect. If it is for the worse, then that which changes has within it the seeds of corruption and is therefore imperfect. When Milton tells us that man is made perfect rather than immutable is he telling us that the peril of mutability is a price worth paying for the gift of freedom and that perfection must contain within itself the power to alter and indeed to destroy itself? It is a daring thought indeed and taken in conjunction with God's setting aside of the Bible in the third book the thought seems renewed evidence of Milton's determination to give the highest conceivable status to freedom. To relinquish such an interpretation is not easy but the probabilities are that Milton meant something less. The fact is that there are two kinds of perfection discussed in *Paradise Lost*. The perfection of the creator is changeless. That of the created on the other hand, must be involved in change if it is to proceed up the scale of nature within the bounds proportioned to its kind.[38] When we come to the perfection of intelligence the possibility must be faced of movement both upwards and downwards. Freedom of decision is part of the dignity of the higher creation and the price of that freedom is exposure to the risk of mutability. 'Reason also is choice' God tells us in the third Book, echoing a phrase from *Areopagitica* on virtue militant, as well as Pico's recognition of man's unique capacity to make or unmake himself.[39] We are also being told that since man like all created things, is involved in the time-process, the nature of man can only be completed in action. The highest form of action is responsible action and responsible action can only result from a freedom which includes the power to act otherwise. For this freedom, mutability, the great defections of history and the blood of the redemption are the cosmic prices which omniscience knows will be paid. The toll that is exacted is a testimony both stern and compassionate to the significance of the gift bestowed upon us.

If reason is choice it is also more than choice. 'What obeyes / Reason, is free' and not to obey reason is to be trapped in selfhood: 'Thy self not free but to thy self enthrall'd.'[40] But error can seem reasonable in *Paradise Lost* and reason can seem to be arbitrary. The dark wood of our condition is considerably more perplexing than the forest in *Comus* where enchanters who have shown themselves to be treacherous offer charmed draughts to ladies they have imprisoned. In *Paradise Lost* the devil's party consists of heroic democrats, gallant minorities resisting murderous force and serpents rising through the scale of nature upon the elegant coils of classical myth. The poem judges these pretences if it is read alertly; but there are times when Milton far from avoiding the confusion of appearances, seems intent on adding to it, perhaps as a test of the alertness of the reader. The prohibition against eating the fruit is in the Bible and cannot be escaped from; but the unexplained exaltation of the Son at the beginning of celestial history is neither in the Bible, nor in tradition,[41] nor in the *De Doctrina* and is therefore a difficulty which Milton chose to make for himself. To anyone sensitive to the larger symmetries of *Paradise Lost* it is apparent that one purpose of this 'invention' is to tie together the angelic and human falls and to link them within a circle that begins and ends with the exaltation of the Son. But though the pattern may be strengthened, we are also made sharply aware by the parallelism that the two falls proceed from divine decrees which are left unexplained. Substance is given to the argument that the universe that Milton is creating is a universe of *diktat* rather than reason.

The issue has been isolated as clearly as possible and Milton criticism is certainly adept enough to be capable of offering more than one explanation. It can be argued that Milton, the supreme structuralist, was prepared to pay the price for his pattern and that the price he paid shows the importance of the pattern. More popular would be the view that even Milton with his powers of artistic unification is not always fully in command of the varied resources that inhabit his poem. There are times when the totalitarian nature of his deity, or to put it more blandly, the force of cosmic will, breaks through the containment of Christian humanism which the poem is so earnestly seeking to erect.[42] The best explanation is perhaps the least persuasive when it is first offered. The infinite will always seem inscrutable in its crucial dealings with the finite. Expressed in decrees, the inscrutable will seem arbitrary. The correct response is not to recoil in rebellion at the apparent arbitrariness but to answer the will of God with the whole being of the mind. Even in the pre-lapsarian world there are things which cannot be understood until they are accepted. Acceptance indeed, creates the relationship out of which alone understanding can flow. Rejection is a turning away from God and the subtlest form of turning away is that which professes to foresake God for reason. Proclaiming the free intelligence as its standard, it is none the less profoundly unintelligent. This is the great paradox of temptation: the declaration of independence and selfhood which is in reality the testament of servitude and the spontaneous acceptance of dependence which is the discovery of the self in filial freedom.

Reason to the seventeenth century was an ethical and religious rather than an intellectual concept.[43] Right reason is the candle of the Lord. When God crowns his creation with the 'Master work' he brings into being a creature endowed with 'Sanctitie of Reason'

Magnanimous to correspond with Heav'n,
But grateful to acknowledge whence his good
Descends ...   VII, 511–13[44]

The moral connotations of reason are evident elsewhere. Love has its seat in reason. The 'mysterious Law' of wedded love is founded in reason 'Loyal, Just and Pure'. Reason whether discursive or intuitive, is Raphael tells us, the 'being' of the Soul, and reason, according to Michael, is virtue.[45] But because reason is part of the image of God in man, it is only right reason when it is founded in righteousness.

... in thir looks Divine
The Image of thir glorious Maker shon,
Truth, Wisdome, Sanctitude severe and pure,
Severe, but in true filial freedom plac't;
Whence true autoritie in men;   IV, 291–95[46]

'Reasons mintage' remains as in *Comus*, 'Character'd in the face',[47] but whereas reason in Milton's masque was set within chastity, reason in *Paradise Lost* is set within moral completeness. Filial freedom supersedes the freedom which flowed from the love of virtue. The more explicit terminology suggests no difference in kind; indeed the severity and purity with which truth, wisdom and sanctitude are invested may well be regarded as chastity reborn. What is taking place is the restatement of a familiar Miltonic concern: the relationship between discipline and liberty proclaimed on this occasion, as the indwelling presence of the image of God in man.

The divine image in the human countenance expresses the perfection of man. But man's perfection like every finite perfection, can only complete itself by reaching outside itself. The remarkable dialogue between God and Adam which Milton invents has more than one purpose; it suggests for example that Christ's function as mediator becomes necessary only after the fall; and since even the loyal Abdiel is not addressed so directly, the dignity of man is subtly emphasized. But the principal aim of the incident is to tell us of the circumstances of Eve's creation. Unfortunately, the argument of VIII 412–26 can scarcely be called a model of lucidity. Perhaps Yeats, whether or not he had read this particular passage, seizes the essence of it in telling us that 'we beget and bear because of the incompleteness of our love'.[48] God is perfect, deficient in nothing, containing within his unity every possible multiplicity. Man can only extend his finiteness by joining it in love to a complementary finiteness. The word 'extends' is important. Adam is not meant to complete himself *in* Eve and when he decides to do so he has fallen. Rather, he is meant to complete himself *with* Eve. The two enrich each other only as the dependence on God enriches them both. When the supporting relationship is abandoned, the auxiliary relationship which it sanctifies becomes engrossed in itself and wrenched away from reality. We remember then, that the birth of Eve recalls the birth of Sin, even in the springing into life from the left side.[49]

In his account of the fall, Milton faces peculiar difficulties. It is not easy to differentiate dramatically freedom to fall from a propensity for falling, or to paint a vulnerability which falls short of being a defect. The many poems and plays on the subject bypass the problem by not going behind the event. Milton is unique in his readiness to explore what has to be called the psychology of Adam and Eve. It is an exploration which is lengthened and given additional complexity by narrative flashbacks, by dreams which are also omens, by specific warnings not simply of the danger, but of the detailed shape of temptation, which those who receive them are persuaded to ignore, by probing dialogues between guide and learner in the cosmic hierarchy which set forth the principles of right action, and finally, by the style itself, by the allusions arching across the web, reaching backwards into the literary past and forward into the history of the poem. So sustained is this process that many of us react to it as a slowly accelerating slippage so that the eating of the fruit is merely the point at which the gathering weight begins to avalanche. The image is suggestive but not wholly reliable. The breakaway in the self can be pulled back and the forces which are involved in it are not so much forces of weakness as forces capable of good within their bounds. Reason and self-restraint can recognize and arrest the slippage. They have more than one opportunity to do so. When they fail to act, a point is reached when they can no longer act. The rash hand reaches out to rend the web and the self tears itself away from its position in reality.

No one denies that Adam and Eve are free to fall but some suggest that they are insufficient to have stood. Our courts of law refuse very rightly to accept from those made in Adam's image, the plea that they could not refrain from what they knew to be wrong; but the same plea is mysteriously more convincing when it is invoked for those made in the image of God. Some realism seems to be needed here. Eve's rehearsal of her sin in her dream is sufficiently detailed to put her on her guard; the ease with which she passes from 'damp horror'[50] at the possibility of eating the fruit to exhilaration in the eating of it, is more than fair warning. But her self-esteem, innocent in the Narcissus episode, becomes grounded in rather less than just and right, to quote Raphael's vain recommendation to Adam.[51] In the separation scene in the ninth book she is militantly self-confident, certain of her power to defeat her adversary and insistent on sallying forth to meet him.[52] Adam's sedate advice that two heads are better than one and that there is trouble enough even in Paradise without our looking for it, fall on an unreceptive mind. Even his laboriously diplomatic suggestion that the prospective assault on Eve's righteousness is an insult she should not be asked to endure, proves unavailing. Satan is far more

practised at winning his way into the lady's heart. Eve is sufficient
to have stood with Adam. She becomes insufficient when she deems
herself more than sufficient.

If Eve is left unprotected in any way, it is by Adam's desertion of
his hierarchical function. His learned lecture on psychology after
Eve's dream, evades the warning which he ought to deliver. In the
debate on collective security he capitulates abruptly, serving notice
of the more serious capitulation which is soon to come. His parting
advice to Eve is to let her reason beware lest 'She dictate false, and
misinforme the Will / To do what God expressly hath forbid.'[53] The
caution has its relevance but the blunter warning against Eve seeking to rise above her position in the scale of nature is not provided,
perhaps because Adam himself is more than inclined to deify Eve.
Adam's other statements that the will is truly free only in obedience
to reason and that the real danger to man comes from within become even more searching when they are directed against himself.

Adam's testing is more severe than that of Eve. He has to choose
between two loyalties and the depth of the lesser loyalty is measured
by his curious and touching suggestion that something of his essential self was subtracted in the making of Eve. He is perfect man with
one flaw designed into him; weakness 'Against the charm of
Beauties powerful glance.'[54] VIII, 540–46 makes it clear that
he is aware of Eve's real position on the ladder of being.
But the lines that follow make it even clearer that when he
approaches her loveliness, the minor brilliance overwhelms the
true light. The very language of the exaltation, the emphasis on
Eve's absoluteness and self sufficiency recall with saddening exact-
ness, Adam's recognition of God's nature in 414–16. The climactic
displacement is that in addressing an angel, Adam should speak of
an angelic guard surrounding the presence of Eve.

The angel not unnaturally, answers, 'with contracted brow'.[55]
Nothing essential he tells Adam has been taken from his nature; it is
merely that he is in danger of being unduly swayed by his emotions.
Those who find this judgement harsh are perhaps in a worse plight
than Adam, for Adam himself admits that he is fully capable of
discerning and choosing the good.

> I to thee disclose
> What inward thence I feel, not therefore foild,
> Who meet with various objects, from the sense

Variously representing; yet still free
Approve the best, and follow what I approve.   VIII, 607–11

Later in saying farewell to Eve, Adam returns to that crucial statement in VIII, 414–16, this time expressing correctly the mirroring of God's perfection in the finite perfection of man.

O Woman, best are all things as the will
Of God ordain'd them, his creating hand
Nothing imperfet or deficient left
Of all that he Created, much less Man,
Or aught that might his happie State secure,
Secure from outward force; within himself
The danger lies, yet lies within his power.   IX, 343–49

Adam is recorded as speaking these words 'fervently' which presumably means that his convictions lie behind them. Soon after he has spoken them, the edifice of perfection lies in ruins, overwhelmed by the danger within. The breakaway from the greater to the lesser love takes place with feverish celerity. It requires only eight lines for Adam to proceed from his shocked recognition of Eve's plight –'How art thou lost, how on a sudden lost'–to his desperate decision to share her fate.[56] 'Certain my resolution is to Die' is a declaration all the more telling because it is not until the eleventh book that Adam learns the meaning of death. The imagery has its own comment to make, for even before Adam begins to speak, the garland he has wreathed for Eve has withered. We realize that the poem too has its own ways of foreknowledge and its sense of freedom betrayed within that knowledge. Later when Adam begins to rationalize his decision, he uses in IX, 943–48 precisely the argument that Christ uses in the dialogue in heaven.[57] Adam hopes his sin will be excused. We know that it will be redeemed. The sacrificial gestures of romantic love are set firmly in the context of the true sacrifice.

Literature from the nineteenth century onwards has been largely the work of the devil's party but even readers whose affiliations are different may feel the bond of nature drawing them to Adam. The poetry allows us to make this identification. It also demands that we draw back from it and judge it. It is the double response which causes difficulty, encouraging critics to argue that the poetry is once again fatally unbalanced, with the intellectual plan at variance with the imaginative accomplishment. But the movement of judgement is unmistakable and is enforced by the poetry itself, rather than by the author's pointing finger. To go behind Adam's own metaphor, the forging of the link is the breaking of the chain and the sealing of the bond tears a greater bond to pieces.[58] It does not take long for wedded love to become lust and for Eve no longer 'blushing like the Morn' to look on Adam with eyes that dart 'contagious Fire' (recalling Satan's eyes that 'sparkling blaz'd').[59] The creative energy of nature 'boon' and wantoning as in her prime was earlier metamorphosed into the destructive energy of Eve 'hight'nd as with Wine jocond and boon'.[60] Even more pointed in its valuation is the manner in which Adam is made to surrender to Eve. The separate temptations which Milton employs are as has been shown earlier, part of his understanding of the nature of temptation, but Adam by giving Eve permission to leave, not only makes possible the encounter in solitude, but also reiterates his weakness and assumes responsibility for what is to follow.[61] After Eve has succumbed alone she plucks a bough from the tree and takes it with her. No commentator on *Genesis* seems to have thought of making her do this;[62] the result is that instead of Adam being brought to the tree, the tree is as it were brought to Adam. Nothing could exemplify more tellingly Adam's complete abdication from his functions of guidance and judgement. Adam then decides to share Eve's fate, Eve commends him lavishly and he passes into sin with her:

> from the bough
> She gave him of that fair enticing Fruit
> With liberal hand: IX, 995–97

Genesis III, 6 and 12 provide a foundation here, but the liberal hand plying the passive Adam and the bough which Eve has thoughtfully brought to the banquet put her somewhat masculine aggressiveness ('Forth reaching to the Fruit, she pluck't, she eat') in studied contrast to Adam's dazed and feminine acquiescence. The hierarchic roles have been reversed. 'The Feete must guide and direct the head' was Goodman's disgusted comment.[63] It might almost be said that Adam has regressed into infantility with Eve as his nursemaid.

More examples of this implicit commentary could be given, and the moral is not simply that we should read the poem with care.

Even when the conclusion is explicit as in IX, 997–99, the difference between the spontaneous and the directed response does not necessarily mean that the author's imagination has run away with him and that he is pursuing the poem vainly crying 'Stop, thief!' Rather, we are being invited to read the passage again. When we do so, our sense of the gap ought to alter. As our understandings grow up to the demand that is made upon them we learn more about the poem and possibly more about ourselves.[64]

At the centre of the web is the nucleus of freedom. But freedom must be set in a constellation of significance suggested partly by the web itself. It finds its nature in obedience to reason and in creative rootedness in the order of things. It extends itself in relationships which complete themselves in God. It is responsibility, obedience and guidance. It is the energy to act, curbed by the knowledge that sanctitude invests the power of choice. Its context is blood, imagination and intellect running together in devotion to the good. It brings to perfection the finite creature which it animates but the perfection consists of the power to walk a tightrope and when concentration relaxes the abyss opens. The mandate which Raphael is given conveys some of the feeling of this perilous privilege.

> . . . such discourse bring on
> As may advise him of his happie state,
> Happiness in his power left free to will
> Left to his own free Will, his Will though free,
> Yet mutable;   V, 233–37

There is a tentativeness here, a hovering in the verse, which seems expressive of the knowledge that freedom can make more than one thing of itself. The repetitions give additional weight to the concept; but they also seem to turn it around, exposing its various facets to the light. The under-cutting effect of 'though' and 'yet', carefully positioned at the climax of insistence, is confirmed, as the force of the thought comes to rest paradoxically on the word 'mutable'. It is the price that has to be paid not for perfection but for human perfection; and as the forces of the fable and of Milton's powerfully organized arrangement of it, mass themselves around the precarious centre, we cannot but be made intensely aware of the price.

Sin and Wisdom spring fully armed, from the mind. Hell is a place but within it lives a person whose fate is to discover that he himself is hell. Johnson spoke disparagingly of the confusion of spirit and matter in *Paradise Lost*[65] but perhaps the critic of today can see that one of the principal strengths of the poem is its fluency of movement between the interior and the outer world, so that each is an affirmation of the other and both lead to the consummation of the paradise within. The forces of the poem have moved inwards on the garden; now they erupt outwards from the violating nexus, stamping the deformity of misgovernment on the new nature of things. The interconnectedness which the poem has assiduously built up is now seen to mean that all falls apart when the centre fails to hold. The tenth book is concerned with the expansion of sin into space and the eleventh and twelfth books with its expansion into history. Yet as we are caught up in the momentum of this reversal, the crumbling of a great edifice exposed to the waywardness of freedom, we become aware that there is more to be said. Good comes out of evil and what providence achieves is not what the agent intends. Adam and Eve seek godhead and find debasement. Satan proclaims his new empire and chews the bitter ashes of his victory. The fallen angels debate upon a hill and find no end in the wandering mazes of philosophy. Adam is led through mazes to the admission of his own guilt. He ascends a different hill from which he sees both sin and salvation. The face of things may alter but the pulsation of things continues. Behind appearance and even behind experience, we are required to remain aware of the divine plan and its controlling ironies. Book Ten indeed is built on two dramatic contrasts between what is of present and what is of future significance. The eating of the fruit takes place against an inclusive and intricate statement of order, an order sufficiently comprehensive to draw into its scope energy, passion and movement. The repentance of Adam and Eve, their 'Sorrow unfeign'd, and humiliation meek'[66] takes place against a proliferating chaos, a declaration of war within and between things. Both acts are insignificant against their cosmic backgrounds and both tell us that insignificance is significant. Together they outline the condition of man.

'The War of Mankind with the Devil', Ussher informs us, 'is a lawful War, proclaimed of God, which is also perpetual and without any Truce.'[67] If fallen man fights this war, it is wholly by virtue of a power that is given him, a power which he can neither turn to nor repudiate. He is in truth a battlefield rather than a centre of choice. Good and evil contend for his soul; but if he is able to choose the good, it is only because the good has previously chosen him. In Luther's harsh and telling words:

Man's will is like a beast standing between two riders.
If God rides, it wills and goes where God wills . . .
If Satan rides, it wills and goes where Satan wills
Nor may it choose to which rider it will run, or which
it will seek; but the riders themselves fight to decide
who shall have and hold it.[68]

Milton agreed with Luther on the location of Hell[69] and on the abolition of the Law by the Gospel.[70] It is not clear to what extent he might once have agreed with him on the bondage of the Will. He was a Trinitarian at the time of the early ecclesiastical pamphlets and appears to have been a Calvinist when he wrote *Areopagitica* and *The Doctrine and Discipline of Divorce*.[71] When and for what reasons he changed to the positions held in the *De Doctrina* and *Paradise Lost* are matters which remain among the mysteries of a fairly well-documented life. To those concerned with the poetry however, it will be apparent that *Comus*, written much earlier, is scarcely a Calvinist poem. When the Attendant Spirit says 'Mortals that would follow me / Love vertue, she alone is free', he is not suggesting that only the chosen are capable of following him and that they having been chosen, are incapable of not following. In fact, the prolonged drama of temptation with which Milton was persistently (and some might say obstinately) concerned would not be very much of a drama if the man at the centre could only prefer what he was elected or condemned to prefer. Predestination may be grimly edifying but it has its deficiencies as a poetic spectacle.

These considerations as might be expected, apply with particular force to *Paradise Lost*. The entire cosmic mobilization has been massed around and made to converge upon an active, choosing centre. The war for the soul of man is decreed by Providence within the ground-rules of man's freedom. Eliminate that freedom and the entire apparatus so laboriously and compellingly built up is reduced to irrelevance by the eating of an apple. Man can destroy himself but poems cannot. If *Paradise Lost* is to survive as an entity, fallen man cannot be entirely stripped of freedom, of some share in the making of his destiny. 'The decree of Predestination', says Peter Du Moulin 'is that whereby God hath appointed what he will do with us and not what he would have us do'.[72] Similarly Elnathan

Parr argues that 'the will is no agent but a meere patient in the act of conversion to God'.[73] In *Paradise Lost* on the other hand, the turn to good is not possible without prevenient grace but prevenient grace by itself cannot ensure the turn.[74] Something in man remains to be uplifted, so that it can reach out to God and to reach out or to fall away remain possibilities within the unstable core of man's freedom. Whatever may be the dogma, the dramatic context shows us two people examining themselves, acknowledging their guilt and taking by virtue of something in themselves, the first tentative steps away from the abyss.

Arminianism was the great aberration of the early seventeenth century. By the time Thomas Edwards wrote *Gangraena* the rot had spread so far that he was prepared to admit that there were worse things than Arminianism though Arminianism itself had become considerably worse.[75] The principal threat by then was from the sectarian left rather than from the Papist right and Anabaptism was the reigning horror.[76] Nevertheless when Little Gidding was described as an Arminian nunnery, the anonymous author was joining two classic terms of Puritan invective in what was for him, a deft compounding of insult.[77] Milton's views on free-will are usually described as Arminian, an identification that has curiously gone unscrutinized, so that we look in vain for the work of scholarship on Milton and Arminius. It is a description which is fortunately less misleading than it might be. *Paradise Lost* is tactful about its theology. It is a poem designed to be read without anguish by those who do not share Milton's views. Consequently it is not always poetically wise to nail down the letter of its dogma. What can be said is that the spirit of the poem is far closer to Arminianism (as expressed in the Remonstrance of 1610 and in contemporary understanding of the movement)[78] than it is to the Calvinist position. This is as it ought to be and if Milton decided to bid good-night to Calvin[79] it was surely in the interests of the poem. Perhaps goodnight was said before the poem was written. Or perhaps it was said as a result of writing the poem. It is inconceivable that a man composing an epic over ten years, fitting piece after piece into the design that his imagination insistently presents, watching the whole become incarnate in the parts and the parts find their identity in the whole, should have learned nothing at the end except how to compose an epic. At any rate, if the structure of *Paradise Lost* is not to be washed away with Paradise, it must remain in being around a certain continuity between the situations of fallen and unfallen man.

That continuity is to be found in the persistent fact of freedom. Man after the fall is by his own act given over to darkness. But the grace of God, offered to all who turn to it, restores the balance of power, resurrects the reality of a choosing centre and permits the mind to hold itself away from its destruction.

> Once more I will renew
> His lapsed powers, though forfeit and enthrall'd
> By sin to foul exorbitant desires;
> Upheld by me, yet once more he shall stand
> On even ground against his mortal foe.   III, 175–79

The result is not meant to be certain victory. It is simply protection against certain defeat. Both the return to God and alienation from God lie equally within the scope of freedom. And salvation is not so much decreed as secured, won inch by inch by the cumulative exercise of the moral intelligence turning towards righteousness:

> And I will place within them as a guide
> My Umpire *Conscience*, whom if they will hear,
> Light after light well us'd they shall attain,
> And to the end persisting, safe arrive.   III, 193–96

The divine process never quite repeats itself and the order to come may not be entirely the order that was destroyed. But body can work up to spirit both in the individual and in the possible movement of history. Man stands where he stood and knows that the web defines him. Involvement, dependence and relationship are for him not limitations but the outline of his nature which right action must fill in and make perfect. Responsibility is the price of freedom; but it is also the means by which freedom finds itself.

6 *Paradise Lost*

The hill of history

Twenty-five years ago the high hill from which Adam looked down upon history commanded a territory which was largely unexplored. E. N. S. Thompson's defence of the last two books[1] had yet to be written and C. S. Lewis's dismissal of them as an 'untransmuted lump of futurity'[2] was the reigning judgement, challenged only by the imperceptive or by those who had no choice but to be original. Scholarship even more than nature, abhors a vacuum and there has been no lack of articles moving into those enticing, open spaces.[3] None of this scholarship has been less than interesting; and because the last books remain accessible only to the devout, none of it is interesting simply because it misleads us. The structural relevance of the last two books has been firmly defended; their place in the great pattern has been shown; and all is as it ought to be in the celestial cycle. Lewis's judgement is now a chastening warning that the race is not really to the swift but rather to the blear-eyed scholar with the true patience needed to struggle with sacred history. Yet despite these illuminations, certain areas of doubt remain. The argument from precedent is less compulsive than it seems when we remember that Milton's resolutely individual talent was fully capable of paying no attention to precedent. Structural coherence is not the same thing as structural inevitability and an extremely high order of coherence must be demonstrated if we are to deal with regrets that the mood of *Areopagitica* and *The Second Defence* is absent from the world of the last two books. To use Coleridge's proposition it has been shown how the last two books may well be as they are; it has still to be shown why they cannot be otherwise. The very variety of the explanations offered for the paradise within –more will be said of this diversity in its context–confess to the view that determined aesthetic manoeuvring might well have brought us to a less forbidding conclusion.

The view of the last two books put forward in these pages will not succeed in disposing of these doubts. If the doubts were to vanish there would be a lessening of the power to disturb us which is part of the poem's right to life. Time does not soften severity; rather it seeks to persuade us that there is aesthetic strength in the refusal to compromise. All that an interpretation of the last books can do is to suggest the shape of accomplishment in its sober, vigilant serious-ness and leave the reader to understand in what manner that shape is part of the demand which the whole truth makes upon him. From Adam's hill we ought to see more clearly the valleys into which the poem moves and the design which its momentum occupies. Another design may be possible and this is a way of saying that a given design is a design and not a destiny. But perhaps as the design is seen more clearly and the forces that go to its making are studied and weighed, it may be found that it was not easy to avoid and that it was the better part of poetry not to avoid it.

Paradise Lost is a poem of the infinite theatre, not in the sense that it is a drama grown monstrous, but in the sense that the massed resources of time and space are made to move inwards on the moment of crisis, intensifying that crisis and to some degree measuring it by its endless involvement in a web of meaning and consequence. The very cosmography of the poem and its massed oppositions of imagery and concept, strengthen the sense of man as the middleground and battleground. For this reason the pressures that shape history are made known in dramatic terms; what Satan appreciatively calls 'the fierce contention'[4] is renewed in the per-spectives that are seen from the hill:

> good with bad
> Expect to hear, supernal Grace contending
> With sinfulness of Men.   XI, 358–60

To read these lines is to realize that the terms of the contention have been subtly reformulated. The arena of combat is now the mind and history becomes the collective result of the individual struggle for moral transformation. XII, 79–101, a crucial and eloquent passage, makes this lesson more than clear and is in its turn a development from the clinical summing up of IX, 1121–31 Thus from the outset, the way has been opened to the affirmation of the paradise within. We see the inward movement carried further in the lesson which history is to inculcate:

thereby to learn
True patience and to temper joy with fear
And pious sorrow, equally enur'd
By moderation either state to beare,
Prosperous or adverse   XI, 360–64

In another context something could be made of the careful disposition of forces in the writing. Three caesuras in successive lines, varying in position only sufficiently to avoid a deadweight, create a point of balance on which the equilibrium of responses passively rests. But perhaps it is the very insistence of the 'tempering', the frigidity of the counsel which makes us hasten over it, so that we fail to notice that joy is the primary emotion called for by the last books. Few revelations have been considered more joyless than the vistas which are exposed from the hill; but we should know better by now than to tax Milton with a gigantic miscalculation of effect. Joy indeed becomes a relevant emotion when we decide to link it to supernal grace. It might be noted that Adam rejoices at the deliverance of Noah, that he is surcharged with joy on learning of the Incarnation and 'Replete with joy and wonder' when told of the last judgement and the final paradise.[5] Fear and sorrow are on the other hand the right emotions with which to contemplate the stubborn failure of the will to turn towards the salvation which is offered it. True patience is distinctly more than endurance. It rests upon knowledge and a sense of proportion and as Michael's presentation will reveal, it must take into account and to that extent rejoice in, the progressive commitment of the divine power to history.

The great contention is not the only glass in which the future can be viewed. When Adam's hill is compared to the hill on which Satan set Christ the aim is not simply to anticipate Ellwood or to indulge in Milton's typically tight-lipped irony (Christ refuses four kingdoms while Adam discovers what it means to claim one)[6] but also to suggest to us the traditional parallel between the six days of creation and the six ages of history. History is a redemptive process though it is also the chronicle of radical evil hardening itself to redemption. It is not just a matter of symmetry that at the end of the fifth day, the second Adam should stand on the second hill. The pattern was explained in the first five lines of the poem – before

Milton got to the predicate that launched the sentence into the movement of time.

The depth of the tradition behind the six ages has been ably detailed by Whiting, and MacCallum has argued persuasively for its presence in *Paradise Lost*.[7] That Milton knew the tradition and expected his readers to know it seems rather more than probable. But the six ages are not decisively marked in *Paradise Lost* and do not form the basis for any clear structure of interpretation or of emphasis. Indeed as the ages pass on, they are somewhat unceremoniously telescoped into each other. Milton is not the kind of writer to exclude any grist from his mill and the particular mill that is *Paradise Lost* was designed for the purpose of assimilating everything; but the right conclusion seems to be that the six ages are used evocatively, rather than as a rigorous scheme of analysis.

It is the contention which dominates history just as in its deeper form, it dominates the spaces behind history which the poem also occupies. *Paradise Lost* begins and ends with the exaltation of the Son and the references to the Platonic year at V, 582–83 and XII, 466–67 decisively mark the closing of the circle. Within the enclosure, Christ and Satan are the elemental antagonists, with Christ creating the world and then descending to ransom it, moving forward from a victory on an apparent battlefield to the higher victory of the higher fortitude. Smaller completenesses exist within the larger enclosure. History proper begins with Christ's judgement of Adam, Eve and the Serpent; it ends with Christ's carrying out of the Last Judgement. Milton with his sure eye for the apparent repetition which is actually a consummation, probably departed from convention to achieve this particular effect.[8] Similarly, the last line of Michael's account of history with its reference to 'fruits' of Joy and eternal 'Bliss' takes us back to the very first line of *Paradise Lost*, building arches across time and across the poem's spaces and reaffirming the paradox of good out of evil. Even the trumpet which summons the celestial assembly when Michael is given his mandate (Raphael is not given this special mark of prestige) rings with overtones of the Mosaic Law and of the Last Judgement. Such examples can be multiplied but what they lead to will already be clear. With the design urged on us, engraved on our attention, we are schooled to anticipate the eternal recurrence and the eternal perfecting. Post-lapsarian nature being what it is we must also expect the eternal obduracy. This pattern or more correctly this process which we contemplate is not inherently optimistic or pessimistic. Rather it is an indication of the poem's wholeness that the same struggle and the same pressures shape it in all its aspects. We may dislike the temper of the last books but to modify their structure may well be to tear them away from their moorings.

It is sometimes argued that it is the tone rather than the structure of the last two books which afflicts critics who have misgivings about them. The truth is that a firm sense of structure alters our response to tonalities. This does not dispose of the problem but it should make us more cautious about its disposition. Moreover a smattering of scholarship in the period will make it clear that the weight of woe in the last books is not excessive by contemporary standards and may even be less than is called for by the tradition. Taylor shows for example, that both the Judgement and the expulsion from Paradise are treated by Milton as examples of God's compassion rather than God's wrath.[9] Michael's mandate is to send Adam and Eve forth 'though sorrowing, yet in peace'.[10] The first requirement is scarcely to be avoided except by those who seem to think that Adam should leave Eden in a state of blurred elation, inebriated, as it were, by the *felix culpa*. In keeping with what is essentially a mission of consolation, Michael is described as 'milde', 'gentle', and of 'regard benigne.'[11] He, like Adam, is moved by the entrance of death into history.[12] Finally, Adam and Eve having found understanding and the peace of mind it makes possible, are led out of Paradise rather than ejected from it.[13]

A comparison of the epic with Milton's plans for a tragedy strengthens the view that the last two books are not meant to be intimidating or to be dominated by the flaming sword of God's wrath. In *Adam Unparadized* a 'mask of all the evills of this life & world' is made to pass before Adam. He is 'humbl'd, relents, dispaires'. Mercy then comforts him and promises him the Messiah. Faith, Hope and Charity are called in and Adam having been duly instructed, adds repenting to relenting and 'gives God the glory'.[14] In *Paradise Lost* Adam and Eve humble themselves instead of being humbled and the pageant of history is not a warning to the unrepentant but a means of enlightening those who have already repented. More important, what we are made to see is history and its significance, not a pageant of the world's woes with the Messiah at the end of it.[15] Good is presented to us as a shaping force, opposing evil as the power of evil evolves. Adam can see what the spark of his repentance has lit. The light burns more brightly even while the darkness intensifies.

History is not simply a combat but a combat with certain characteristics. Since the substance of man is corrupt, his natural movement is away from God. The inabstinence which is 'inductive mainly to the sin of *Eve*' and the licentiousness which proceeds from the 'effeminate slackness' of Adam do not fully describe the anatomy of sinfulness even though Milton in 1674 did increase by six, his lacerating roll call of diseases.[16] But the nature of the material is before us and even Adam's misguided view that all woes come from women[17] shows other inadequacies besides poor taste in puns. It shows among other things, that Adam himself needs to beware of backsliding. Because the property of evil is to recoil upon itself the turn towards good must necessarily take place against the resistance of the spring. That is why the basic cleavage of history is between the mass that falls away from God's true worship and the one just man who perseveres in the faith. Adam of course is familiar with the one just man from the example of Abdiel and in fact describes Enoch in precisely that phrase.[18] In doing so he demonstrates an encouraging capacity to apply in one tutorial the knowledge gained in another. Literary critics can also benefit from attempting to link the two courses of instruction.

In his succession of just men saved by faith Milton is following St. Paul's *Epistle to the Hebrews*.[19] The specific account of Enoch's translation into heaven may also owe something to the Geneva Bible.[20] Whatever the sources, the adaptation of sources answers clearly to the design, showing both in the example of Enoch and in that of Noah, the rhythm of the contention, the mass of evil, the small but immensely significant weight of good and the providence of God reaching down to the limited effort of man to restore himself. It is not so much a matter of punishing the wicked and rewarding the virtuous as of allowing man to work out his freedom, whether to find liberty or to exult in licence. If the deluge stands as an affirmation of the wrath which corruption merits, the rainbow stands as a declaration of God's covenant, witholding his anger from the scheme of things. The eleventh book ends with a promise ritualistically cadenced, that day and night, 'Seedtime and Harvest, Heat and hoary Frost', will hold their courses till 'fire purge all things new'. Both the solemnity of the assurance and the typological linking of the deluge to the final conflagration, invite us to recognize that there is an order in 'Heaven's great year', as much as in the lesser year of the four seasons.[21]

The twelfth book opens in the same style of inclusive ordering with which the eleventh book closes. The first five lines which Milton added in 1674, do not simply paper over a decision to divide what was previously one book. On the contrary, the interval between the world destroyed and the world restored is a moment of stability, a pause in the process where we remind ourselves of the pattern. Halting at noon is also not an accident. Dawn would be the natural time of transition between the world destroyed and the world restored but noon is the time of maximum understanding, as it is with Samson in the temple, and by ironic inversion, the time of maximum delusion, as it is with Eve and the Philistines. The insistence is clear that we should see more clearly and this indeed is what is asked of Adam in the last book.[22]

The shift in the last book from vision to narrative has intrigued more than one student of Milton.[23] That Adam's eyesight should fail as events move away from him is considered to be nothing more than a pretext. The highest hill of Paradise is not like that mount 'High Thron'd above all highth' from which God views 'His own works and their works at once'.[24] Nevertheless it is assumed to be high enough for Adam assisted by an archangel, to be able to penetrate history's haze of distance. A better basis must be found for the change in techniques and the dreadful prospect of seeing the whole course of Old Testament history in *tableaux* while reason enough, is not deemed a scholarly reason. It seems plausible that when Book X of 1667 was divided into two books a different mode of presentation should be allotted to each; but to those who seek a subtler propriety it can be argued that Adam's failure to see clearly with his outward sight indicates that he is beginning to see more clearly with the eye of the mind.[25]

Adam's education is a compendious and protracted affair and his formal instruction by archangels takes up nearly half of *Paradise Lost*. In the eleventh book his responses have been largely limited to outright misunderstanding or to ejaculations of dismay, addressed to the event as much as to Michael.[26] A different Adam confronts us in the twelfth book and his firm statement that God has given no man dominion over other men echoes Rutherford's *Lex Rex* as well as Milton's *Tenure*[27] and takes our minds back to Satan's misuse of the same proposition during his rebellion in heaven.[28] In other words Adam is learning to ask the questions that will find the important answers. We have attained the stage of student participation, that elusive ideal of the learning process.

Michael's answer has wide roots in classical thought, in commentaries upon *Genesis*, in the hallowed correspondences between macrocosm and microcosm and in the spacious circuit of Milton's own musings, from the clangorous opening of the *Tenure* and the troubled peroration of *The Second Defence*, to that high hill of the future on which Rome is to be refused.[29] Coming at this point in the movement of understanding and within a hundred lines of the prophesied destruction of the earthly paradise,[30] it makes it apparent that the final paradise can only be within. It also moves round the hill to the point where the mind must consider politics and in so doing takes its position against the view that social institutions can be modified to liberate rather than frustrate man's goodness, or that human nature, as the epiphenomenon of social institutions, can be transformed when those institutions are transformed. 'New styles of architecture, a change of heart'[31] is Auden's linking of cause and effect in a manner which spoke for progressive thought in the thirties. Milton's language is different and in turning against himself in that bitterness which is part of the taste of wisdom, he might have said that there can be no reforming of reformation till man, the instrument of reforming, is reformed. Society can be no stronger than its members and unregenerate man can only write larger and larger, the tyranny that looms within himself.

Man in his nature, covenants with darkness. God, in his goodness, offers to man's horizon the rainbow of the covenant with light. If there is Nimrod 'the first king', the beginning of whose kingdom was Babel[32] there is also Moses who set his people's lands in order. The fruit, the eating of which is death, leads to the seed, the planting of which is life. This flowering of the seed into its harvest is one of the basic images of the twelfth book, an image used with subdued but telling persistence. Its roots go back into the tenth book and Milton in having Christ deliver the judgement that foreshadows his own victory has completed yet another of those circuits of meaning within which so much of *Paradise Lost* is inscribed.[33] The judgement is made in 'mysterious terms' and Michael later refers to it as 'obscurely then foretold'.[34] Both phrases are invitations to a typological reading or more mundanely, both urge us to attend to the idea, to witness the blossoming of the force of goodness as part of the disclosure of the poem's logic. As we examine the occurrences of the 'thought' we cannot but be aware of the gradations which subtly move the thought into its fullness. Because Adam remembers the judgement and is able to interpret it partially, he and Eve are able to save themselves from suicide. When he repents, the promise glows more brightly; the turn to contrition strengthens the up-reaching of life.[35] When Christ offers to God the first fruits of the seed of repentance he describes them as worth more than all the fruit of every tree in an uncorrupted Paradise. The imagery recalls the 'Earth's great Altar' sending up silent praise to the Creator and later on the same day, in a threatening transformation, sending up 'the savour of Death from all things there that live.'[36] Christ's compassionate tendering of the first fruits of the faltering move-ment towards goodness establishes him not only in his theological role as mediator, but more movingly as the spokesman of humanity, foreshadowing that nature he is destined to assume. The small seed of repentance will grow into the tree of redemption. The micro-scopic decision flows into space and into history, however small the turn towards evil or good.

Michael's educational mission requires him to teach Adam how in the flowering of the seed, God's covenant with mankind is renewed.[37] The lazar-house miseries of the eleventh book and the nature of history prior to the deluge provide scant opportunities for such a demonstration. But as history repeats itself and the new world like the old one goes from bad to worse,[38] the single just man is not, as on previous occasions, taken out of history but is, as it were, entrenched more firmly in it, so that his descendants can become the chosen people. The idea of the elect nation was pro-claimed eloquently by Milton, at the zenith of his fervour in the forties.[39] It was an idea which became typologically impoverished when England failed signally to be the second Israel. But Milton still subscribes to the concept in the *De Doctrina*[40] and in *Paradise Lost* the elect nation and the bondages from which it is liberated are part of the onward and expanding movement to the ultimate deliverance in which all nations will be blessed. Michael who can be painstakingly pedagogical when first things are to be seen first repeats this crucial phrase on three occasions.[41]

When the flowering of the seed is intertwined with the renewal of the covenant we are better aware of the latter as the progressive commitment of the good to history. Escalation is the word that springs to the mind but people on moving staircases need only to stand and let the machinery work. This may be a suitable way of life in the Civil Service but it is by no means the best procedure for salvation. The word 'escalation' as used in other circumstances has become too tarnished to apply to Christian warfare. What we need to recognize behind the language we choose is that the widening deployment of evil is inherent in the nature of man and that the good must match the range and energy of that deployment. As the great contention moves to its climax the forces thrown into battle on either side will grow.

The widening intervention of the good is not part of a design peculiar to *Paradise Lost*. It is latent in the Bible and in the tradition Milton inherited but to say this is only to remind ourselves of Milton's singular capacity to shape what he received so as to bring out its own and Milton's meaning. We may note as characteristic in their strengthening of the pattern the careful contrasts which affirm the rhythm of the contention, the exactly poised statement with which the twelfth book begins and the strategically placed references to the embodying of Christ's judgement, which direct our consciousness both to the energy of the movement from the single just man to the chosen people and to history itself as the disclosure of that which is decreed in the seed of the divine will. From the individual to the nation and from the nation to humanity is the promise offered in the renewals of the covenant. That the sinfulness of man should turn away from the offer is the other and stubbornly dark side of the historic process which realism must acknowledge even in its sense of the light. What we need to recognize at this point is the mounting commitment of the good to the field of battle which is the human condition. Our awareness of this battleground is not simply a matter of the last two books; it is present in the cosmography of the poem, with the world placed between the forces of heaven and hell, in the contrast between the creative and the destructive Trinities and in the massed confrontations, elaborately linked and extended, which the epic urges irresistibly on us. The final shaping of the poem is anchored in the poem's logic. That is why we should respond to it not simply as doctrine but as the creative imagination cohesively at work.

If the vigour of Milton's underlining is not by now evident it should become evident in his remarkable treatment of the Incarna-

tion. Adam's response to the event in XII 375–85 shows a significant advance in his capacity for word-play but the pun also tells us
that Adam is using the lessons of history to read a certain meaning
into Christ's judgement. Indeed the very confidence with which the
Incarnation is recognized, notwithstanding the studied vagueness
of Michael's announcement, suggests that Adam has learnt much
in the last two or three hundred lines. The good pupil now goes
further and suggests that the purpose of the union of two natures in
the Incarnation is to bring God and man together in a grand
alliance for the defeat of evil. Michael disagrees with Adam, but not
on this suggestion. Indeed in XII, 388–90 he makes explicit and
confirms what Adam implies. While Milton's treatment of the
other aspects of the Incarnation has an appropriate weight of
tradition behind it, he appears to be without precedent at this
point; and as is usual when he speaks on his own, what he says is
called for by the logic of the poem. His audacious innovation both
expands the contention to its theoretical limits and states as
decisively as possible, the energy of redemption with which the
good enters history.

The commitment of supernal grace to the world of change is
progressive in more than one sense. It is not simply that the scope
of deliverance expands; the very nature of the covenant refines
itself in the process of renewal. The coming of the law is the decisive
stage in this upward movement, an act of ordering which affirms the
presence of God among his people and so looks forward to that more
radical ordering which the descent of Christ into humanity makes
possible. Michael in his somewhat hurried narration of Old
Testament history[42] pauses to take his time over the law and Adam
is ready with the helpful question, pointing out that the restraints of
law imply the persistence of sin and that if there are many laws
there must also be many sins. In other words, as a potential
Christian,[43] he is finding his way into the nature of Christian
liberty. Michael's answer is framed in a series of stately and perfectly sculptured progressions that have a relevance far beyond the
immediate relationship which they outline.

So law appears imperfet, and but giv'n
With purpose to resign them in full time
Up to a better Cov'nant, disciplin'd
From shadowie Types to Truth, from Flesh to Spirit,

89

From imposition of strict Laws, to free
Acceptance of large Grace, from servil fear,
To filial, works of Law to works of Faith   XII, 300–06

If the passage moves us it is not simply because it has the supreme
rightness of high poetry–the living out of thought in the only
possible language–but also because of the conclusiveness of shaping
which seems to gather and consummate the entire tradition to
which it is meant to respond. Much could be said about this process
of perfecting but the commentator must restrain himself. As the
movement is charted from Plato's cave to the light, from flesh to
spirit, from imposed restraints to ardent and disciplined freedom,
it is sufficient to recognize that each of these movements takes some
of its life from the others and that all of them have their roots in the
poem's history as well as in the history of doctrine. Raphael in
expounding the scale of nature to Adam, had pointed out how in
each created thing, body could work up to spirit 'in bounds / proportion'd to each kind'.[44] The 'better Cov'nant' is thus a restoration of the Covenant of creation. It is also the golden chain against
the causeway and the divine image which is 'reason's mintage'
against the 'inglorious likeness' which is Comus's substitute.[45] The
phrase 'just for unjust' reiterates God's statement in heaven, of the
power of mercy and defines in the careful disequilibrium of its
language, the only way in which the 'rigid satisfaction' of justice can
be transcended.[46] The nature of the movement from shadowy types
to truth has been prefigured in Raphael's earlier statement that
earth may be the shadow of heaven.[47] The difference between
servile and filial fear is suggested to us by our first glimpse of Adam
and Eve in Paradise

in thir looks Divine
The image of thir glorious Maker shon,
Truth, wisdome, Sanctitude severe and pure,
Severe, but in true filial freedom plac't;   IV, 291–94

and in Adam's understanding of the lessons of history:

Henceforth I learne, that to obey is best,
And love with fear the onely God, to walk
As in his presence, ever to observe
His providence and on him sole depend.   XII, 561–6

Fear in this context, is an indwelling sense of the holy. It is a consciousness of the order of things, imperative enough to make one shrink back from the possible violation of that order. If fear is not craven, obedience is not constrained. It is that 'free acceptance' grounded in righteousness and flowing from 'filial freedom', of which Christ's obedience is the perfect example.

The Law of God exact he shall fulfill
Both by obedience and by love, though love
Alone fulfill the Law; XII, 402–04

These linkages and completions should help to suggest how, as the poem comes to its climax, it does so out of itself, rather than by reaching out to a doctrinal summation. In its taking up and clarifying of its past, the poem's own history supports its sense of history. That the thing said should become the way of saying it is a proposition that is all but trite, but occasional weariness with it should not prevent us from honouring its accomplishment on this extraordinary scale.

The ascent from flesh to spirit and the supersession of law by an inner righteousness which issues in order instead of reluctantly yielding to it, are progressions which are invaluable in bringing us to recognize the character of Christ's final victory over Satan. To many readers, Adam on the hill looks forward to Christ on the hill only in the sense that his quietism stiffens and narrows into the total withdrawal on the ascetic mountain. Christ's victory is a repudiation of that 'tedious havoc' which the poet exults in and the doctrinaire castigates. Whether epics are meant to exhibit these processes of self-indulgence and self-chastening is debatable; and the alternative view of Milton blind, tired and defeated by history, retreating into the fastnesses of the interior kingdom, is scarcely more attractive as an aesthetic hypothesis. The merit, such as it is, of both explanations is that they attempt to come to terms with Raphael's militarism (possibly ironic) and Michael's emphatic turning away from the big battalions to the interior victory. Any explanation that claims to be more successful would need to do likewise and do better.

If an inconsistency is involved between the sixth book and the twelfth it is certainly not one which Milton seeks to blur. When Adam is told of the Incarnation and foresees the coming victory he naturally does so in the terms taught him by Raphael:

Needs must the Serpent now his capital bruise
Expect with mortal paine: say where and when
Thir fight, what stroke shall bruise the Victors heel.   XII, 383–85

Michael's response seems at first sight to be a chilling reproof of his
pupil:

Dream not of thir fight
As of a Duel, or the local wounds
Of head or heel: XII, 386–88

The best of teachers can disagree with each other and it is possible
that Michael thinks Raphael misleadingly corporeal, in 'lik'ning
spiritual to corporeal forms.'[48] But it can only be deliberately ironic
that the archangel chosen to preach the higher heroism is the one
who distinguished himself most in the lower laying-about-himself
with that two-handed sword which some see as the two-handed
engine.[49] The sword is mentioned again in XI, 239–41 when
Michael comes to earth 'as Man / Clad to meet Man', in a 'militarie
Vest of purple'. The language used to describe his descent from
heaven is the language used to describe the Sun's chariot as it
moves irresistibly to the defeat of his enemies. These remembrances
of things past are surely meant to suggest that the higher victory will
consummate rather than deny the lower conquest,[50] and that
corporeal analogues and local duels are no longer necessary to
suggest its magnitude. When we recognize this and look back on
Raphael's 'likenings' we remember that the rebel angels were not
so much belaboured into submission by the Son, as left 'Exhausted,
spiritless, afflicted, fall'n'[51] by the revelation of his nature. The
Son's chariot is a force of order[52] as much as a force of wrath. The
paralysis which grips the guilty who confront it is like that moment
of piercing enlightenment which comes to Satan as he falls 'smitten
with amazement',[53] having recklessly placed Christ on the pinnacle
of the temple. The seeds of the last battle are sown in the first conflict and Michael who learned the limitations of ordinary valour
and on the third day, saw the seed being planted,[54] is the best person
to proclaim its flowering. If war begins in the minds of men, the last
battle has to end here. Milton not unreasonably thought that an
ex-general would be an intriguing choice to preach UNESCO's
motto.

If the progress from flesh to spirit suggests the quality of Christ's final victory, it also leads us to the paradise within.[55] When the earthly paradise is carried away in the flood, its reduction to an island 'salt and bare' is meant to teach us that 'God attributes to place / No sanctitie, if none be thither brought'. The lesson looks back to an early line of the epic–'Before all Temples th' upright heart and pure'–and forward to a crucial argument in Christ's rejection of the temptation of Athens.[56] Typology also has its part to play and though Joshua leads his people into a promised land which Moses the law-giver may not attain, it is an 'earthly *Canaan*' contrasted with that 'eternal Paradise' to which we are led by the true Christ whom Joshua prefigures.[57] Finally, the idea is rooted in the basic dispositions of the epic. In a universe engineered to permit the maximum of movement from mind to cosmos and from cosmos to mind, with each world used to exemplify and interpret the other, it is but natural that mind should emerge as the superior and controlling principle. Satan sees this (though his perception is stamped by hell's deformity) in those great defiances that proclaim the fixed mind, not to be changed by place or time. In the massed and interlinked contrasts that dominate the world of *Paradise Lost* it is almost inevitable that 'myself am Hell' should be located in its true position as the diabolic perversion of the paradise within.

The Atonement, the victory over Satan and the Last Judgement, lead to the paradox of the fortunate fall, just as the flowering of the seed leads to the paradox of Eve the destroyer as Eve the preserver. Both paradoxes in turn are integrated into the disclosure of the providence of God, thwarting the anti-providence of Satan and shaping that destructive power to its own uses. By having Adam affirm the first paradox and Eve the second,[58] Milton makes them not so much doctrine as part of the legitimate human response to doctrine. Because of these tactics Adam is able to speak as man answering in gratitude to the source of all blessedness and affirming in joy his sense of the bounty of God. As the sentence spirals through the repetitions of the word 'good' our recognition of the divine goodness widens and augments itself; and the sense of growth and plenitude is strengthened as the second sentence spirals similarly through the repetitions of the word 'more'. The coupling of the atonement to the creation recalls firmly the rhythms of the celestial cycle and Adam's doubt whether to repent or to rejoice is audacious indeed in the presence of his stern mentor. That he is not rebuked shows that he has judged exactly what the occasion permits.

Michael has paused 'As at the World's great period', Heaven's year has completed its circle and the design has been revealed. Everything suggests that the end should be here and yet the Archangel proceeds to a narration of 'the State of the Church till his [Christ's] second Coming.'[59] Both the tone and the leaden sombreness of this Epilogue–the word is Louis Martz's and is meant to suggest how inessential Michael's remarks are–have deeply disturbed even Milton's most resolute defenders. Indeed almost every comment on Milton's pessimism and his 'abandonment'[60] of history will be found on examination to have its roots in this passage. To quote Martz again 'the fissure in the last two books cannot be healed; the weight of woe has gradually weakened the epilogue's connection with the poem's centre, and here the epilogue at last drops off'.[61] The comment is representative and is particularly telling since Martz is sensitively aware of those forces in the epic that demand the consummation of the paradise within.

Milton is not incapable of miscalculating his effects but the calculations that go wrong are considerably more sophisticated than we think. Michael's portentous pause may deceive us but it does not deceive Adam; that it fails to do so is proof of how far his education has advanced. There is something more to be said and as we move back into the current of history, we must remember that supernal grace has always been countered by sinfulness. The pattern may suddenly change but Adam has no right to assume that it will change. His duty is to remain aware of both forces in the rhythm of the contention. Michael's task is to teach his pupil true patience and the tempering of joy by fear and pious sorrow. He has given Adam an occasion for deep joy. Having responded to it, will Adam keep his response in proportion? Will he realize that in the coinage of the world there is always another side to felicity?

If these questions are slightly dramatized it is to persuade us to look more closely at the situation. Adam must move to the apprehension that history will repeat itself, with the solitary difference that the single just man will be collectivized as the community of saints that make up the true church. The pith of Michael's answer is that the chain of recurrence will not be broken. This is a melancholy reply but we must ask ourselves what other reply would respond adequately to the weight of the evidence. Even a poet cannot disregard the chastening lessons that are taught him in the world's wilderness. He has to explain to others as well as to himself how revolutions are betrayed and how new Presbyter becomes old priest writ large.

A writer is the product of his time but not its prisoner. Michael's answer is not simply Milton's or that of defiant Puritanism confronted with the failure of the good old cause. The beleaguered saints apart from their obvious relationship to the single just man, are part of the traditional interpretation of Church history and Milton in using the image, is calling upon a lineage that descends from Cyprian through Luther to himself. Ernest Tuveson has documented this tradition so fully that no further comment is required.[62] It is true that the *Nativity Ode* takes a more radiant view of the encounter between darkness and light. So for that matter does *At a Solemn Music*. The early ecclesiastical pamphlets are fervent with the conviction that the elect nation is knocking at the doors of Christ's kingdom;[63] and in the more settled prose of *Areopagitica* where sobriety tempers elation and good and evil are inextricably mixed in the field of the world, truth welcomes the encounter with error because the encounter leads to inevitable victory. These recollections perhaps distract us from the knowledge that the concept of the elect nation and its promise of the reforming of reformation, both ecclesiastical and social, formed a relatively brief chapter in the true church's view of its history. When the tide of opportunity was not taken at the flood and it became manifest that the English were not the chosen people, the optimistic view was set aside and the tale of woe was put back into the position that it had traditionally held.

Reading Milton we are conscious from the *Ode* onwards, of a deep sense of the power and providence of God, an eagerness for battle that rejoices in bringing on the great contention. It seems almost as if a personal tradition is being betrayed in Michael's prophecy. We need to remind ourselves that the other view also has its roots in Milton's sense of the human situation. The Lady has no choice but to journey through the dark wood. She will be left in loneliness and imprisoned in the enchanter's chair. Her body will be 'immanacl'd, while Heav'n sees good'.[64] Evil has its kingdom and we are obliged to live in it, while refusing to be its citizens. Whether in the confusion of the wood or the hard clarity of the desert, whether as the Lady or as the second Adam, the ordeal is upon us and to find our way through it is part of the terms of experience. What the individual undergoes in his life is what the true Church undergoes in its history. Finally, Milton's view of history, apart from its roots in traditions both public and personal and in the painful questions that his own time searchingly put to him, is not without affinities to the thinking of today. It is therefore decidedly not a view of history which history itself has put in a museum. The following remarks by Paul Tillich have of course, no connection with *Paradise Lost*, but they are a remarkably good summing-up of the interpretation of history embodied in the poem, strongly evoking both its structure and its colouring.

History is not fulfilled at its empirical end; but history is fulfilled in the great moments in which something new is created, in which the kingdom of God breaks into history, conquering destructive structures of existence. This means that we cannot hope for a final state of justice and peace within history; but we can hope for partial victories over the forces of evil in a particular moment of time.[65]

If we are dismayed by Michael's prophecy, Adam is not, Perhaps he is too seasoned in woe to feel dismay. But there is serenity in the poetry of his response, with the march of monosyllables slowing down the race of time till time stands fixed in the stasis of the language. The design stands sculptured with the abyss behind it to remind us of the limits of what we know. Adam contemplates it not only in peace but in 'peace of thought'. True knowledge has superseded forbidden knowledge, calming those raging winds that were let loose after the fruit was eaten.[66] As Michael and Adam descend from the 'top / Of Speculation' (the 'mirror' connotations of the word are not inappropriate) the music of the every-day gathers itself, not without sadness but also not without dignity. If it is the end of the poem, it is also the beginning of ourselves. Almost the last note to be heard is the affirmation of that freedom to choose around which the poem's significances have been so powerfully and consistently massed. If wrong choices have been made, wise ones are not excluded.

A poem is a whole and *Paradise Lost* is a whole the dimensions of which sometimes seem to approach the limits of the mind's eye. Its conclusion is founded in the growth of Milton's own thought, in the traditions he received and in answerability to the failures of his time. Most important of all, it is founded in the poem itself and in the unfolding of its own grave logic. Yet to say this and to show this is not to do enough. So far this study has operated under necessary restraints, since steady attention must be given to the poem's structure and movement before there can be any educated comment on how the structure is warped or the movement impeded. 'Warping' and 'impeding' moreover are words which mislead us in indicating where Milton falls short of success. It would be more correct to say that a design of significant and sustained intricacy is very nearly given its complete poetic life. What is withheld from us is the full range of recognition that is needed to give peace of thought to the reader as well as to Adam. Michael could say that the promise of grace means that man is forever at the crossroads, that the way up remains open however often we choose the way down, that history can redeem as well as repeat itself. Perhaps such understandings are precluded since Adam in the nature of his situation, must be made to face the future through the dark glass of his own guilt. But poems have resources for letting us know more than the agents can see. Milton does not make use of these resources and even in drawing on recognitions that are, so to speak, part of the Milton tradition, he significantly alters the quality of affirmation. Compare the Elder Brother's exultant faith in righteousness beleaguered

Vertue may be assail'd, but never hurt,
Surpriz'd by unjust force, but not enthrall'd   *Comus* 588–89

With Michael's sedate statement of the same truth

His Spirit within them, and the Law of Faith,
Working through love, upon thir hearts shall write,
To guide them in all truth, and also arme
With spiritual Armour, able to resist
Satans assaults, and quench his fierie darts,
What Man can do against them, not affraid,
Though to the death . . .   XII, 488–94

Again compare Michael's remarks on wolves in the church with the prophetic indignation that surrounds the same image in *Lycidas*.[67] The temperature is lower in *Paradise Lost* and we can argue that moderation is meant to prevail in the language as well as in the consolations preached to Adam. It is not apologetic to call the mood autumnal. But there are times when the tone approaches weariness.

Other contrasts can be cited to suggest what is withheld. 'Tyrannie must be,' says Michael sombrely 'Though to the Tyrant

thereby no excuse.' When we turn to *Samson Agonistes* we have come
to a different side of the hill

> Oh how comely it is and how reviving
> To the Spirits of just men long opprest!
> When God into the hands of thir deliverer
> Puts invincible might.   *SA*, 1268–71

The joy of battle and the exultation in the ordeal are muted in the
last books of *Paradise Lost*. The emphasis also shifts to the last battle
from the immediate encounter. Truth no longer closes up to truth
or irresistibly confronts error, as light dispelling darkness. The
eager confidence which runs through *Areopagitica* is as we know,
subdued by the recognition that the wheat will not be separated
from the tares till the Second Coming.[68] But the sifting goes on and
is another name for progress. In Michael's prophecy there is no
such optimism:

> Truth shall retire
> Bestuck with slandrous darts, and works of Faith
> Rarely be found: so shall the World goe on,
> To good malignant, to bad men benigne.   XII, 535–38

A poetic design dictates its proper exclusions but it should be
apparent by now that some of Milton's severities are in excess of
what the poem demands of him. But it is easy to exaggerate the
damage which results from such restrictions. Severity has its own
aesthetic virtues and a 'balanced' statement is not necessarily more
satisfying than a series of less inclusive positions chosen and given
substance by a man's imaginative life. Many years before *Paradise
Lost*, the young Milton, then a university student, stood on a different 'top of speculation' and surveyed the exciting empire of knowledge:

> He [the man of learning] will indeed seem to be one whose rule and
> dominion the stars obey, to whose command earth and sea hearken
> and whom winds and tempests serve; to whom, lastly, Mother Nature
> herself has surrendered, as if indeed some god had abdicated the
> throne of the world and entrusted its rights, laws and administration
> to him as governor.[69]

When Adam on his eminence affirms the teachings of obedience,
love with fear, dependence upon God, and an encompassing sense

of God's presence, Michael commends him on having reached a wisdom beyond that promised by the Faustian dream.

> This having learnt, thou hast attained the summe
> Of wisdome; hope no higher, though all the Starrs
> Thou knewst by name, and all th' ethereal Powers,
> All secrets of the deep, all Natures works,
> Or works of God in Heav'n, Aire, Earth, or Sea,
> And all the riches of this World enjoydst,
> And all the rule, one Empire; only add
> Deeds to thy knowledge answerable, add Faith
> Add vertue, Patience, Temperance, add love,
> By name to come call'd Charitie, the soul
> Of all the rest: XII, 575–85[70]

The words look back irresistibly to the sweep of the *Seventh Prolusiou*.[71] Some natural tears can be dropped because of the inconsistency between the two texts but we owe it to ourselves to wipe them soon. The point is not that the view from one hill is more acceptable than from the other or that a third hill might provide a fuller prospect. The point is that the writings of one man surrounded both hills and the valley between them.

7 *Paradise Lost*

The providence of style

'The style of *Paradise Lost*' is by now, an inevitable chapter in any book on Milton. The critic doomed to write it by the business of criticism would be less than wise if he sought to avoid his fate; but he should approach his subject with a double sense of betrayal, apprehensive not only of what he is required to do but of the manner in which he is called upon to do it. To talk of the style of *Paradise Lost* is to suggest that there is basically only one style whereas both critical precept and our experience of the writing itself put it to us that the poem comes to life in many ways.[1] There are strong unitive forces in the language of *Paradise Lost* which permits us to argue that the many blend into one and that this synthesis has a significance beyond the language;[2] but even given this unification, the attention of the critic must be directed to both the one and the many. More important, the word 'style' suggests that the language of *Paradise Lost* is no more than the garment of the thought or even a kind of plastering laid on the thought. We then discover as in some modern houses, that what we really have is plaster without a backing. The magnificent monument encloses dead ideas and the Chinese wall is a vast strategy for the protection of emptiness. Debate is always dominated by its initial terms and it is not until Arnold Stein's *Answerable Style* that we are advised that the manner of saying has something to do with the thing said. In its bareness, this may not seem a particularly profound proposition but as is well known, originality in Milton criticism is only attained by resolute attention to the obvious. Part of the effort of a critic today must be to find his way over the wall which the Milton controversy has built across our sense of Milton's poem.

The critics of *Paradise Lost* and its defenders are sometimes alarmingly alike in what they do. Both take what seems to be the natural way, which is to proceed from the literary specification to the literary performance. Dr. Leavis and C. S. Lewis agree on the performance but disagree on the specifications while a succession of critics of whom Christopher Ricks is the most impressive, accept Dr. Leavis's specifications but take issue with his estimate of the performance. The pattern thus constituted can be safely called the eternal triangle of the Milton controversy[3] since there is no prospect of its becoming a point or even a straight line. It will readily be seen that all parties to the dispute approach the language from external desiderata. The desiderata vary between the two main schools and even within the schools. It is possible to refine the requirements of what for convenience must be called the new criticism and even to allow sublimity a discreet place in the parade with ambiguity, tension and irony. It is also possible to go beyond C. S. Lewis's description of secondary epic, to bring Tasso into the picture[4] and to allow that the high style need not be destitute of new critical virtues. It can even be suggested that the language of *Paradise Lost* is singular in its satisfaction of two sets of criteria. The result will still be that we come to the 'Style' from the outside, from externalities however they may be chosen or combined. The attempt to derive the characteristics of Milton's language from a study of its typical formations (as in articles on Milton's 'suspension', his syntax and his similes) may seem to be better grounded in the facts but it too looks at the style as a thing in itself. It is the anatomy rather than the body, the frozen posture rather than the movement; but even if it were all it claims to be, it could only tell us what the style *is* and not what *it is for*.

Neo-Aristotelians will understand that the *is* can only be defined on the basis of the *is for*. To know the style we must know the poetic universe which the style both inhabits and affirms. In this as in many other ways, the language reflects the poem's sense of reality. Nothing in the world of *Paradise Lost* is known adequately by itself. All things are known only within a web of involvement and relationship; and these involvements and relationships tell us that in that greater world which the lesser world of the poem brings into concentrated life, we know ourselves only by knowing how the whole contains us. The presence of the whole poem stands behind each detail whether of structure or of language, completing it, locating it and giving it its meaning in the pattern of things.

When Milton described decorum as the 'grand masterpeece' he was probably paying his respects to external stipulations though one

critic has suggested that the word 'masterpeece' may be synony-
mous with 'gimmick'.[5] When Milton asked whether the rules of
Aristotle were to be kept or nature to be followed, he was suggesting
that every poem which respects itself has certain rights of its own.[6]
The organic, exfoliating decorum of which Coleridge is the chief
theoretical exponent may seem a strange principle to bring into
Milton's world. But Coleridge's insight is universal in its application; every poem must be faithful to the laws of its own life. In this
chapter it is proposed to reverse the traditional procedure, to
approach the 'style' of *Paradise Lost* from the inside and to suggest
that the poem's language-tactics are not only the best but almost
the only possible way in which it can become itself. It is probable
that the approaches from the inside and from the outside will come
together in their grasp of the poem. This feat if achieved, will prove
something more important than the accuracy with which literary
scholars dig tunnels.

Since truisms are reassuring it is best to begin with them. Because
the epic deals traditionally with demi-gods and heroes, it has a
more than normal distance to maintain against the 'pushing
world'.[7] The elevation of epic language becomes aesthetically
relevant in securing this disengagement. *Paradise Lost* improves on
other epics by dealing not simply with events that surpass the
ordinary, but with events that transcend and initiate the world we
know. The distance is therefore the maximum possible and the
style must be heightened accordingly. The force of removal must
also be far more persistent than in other poems which are not 'above
heroic'. Distancing however is not disconnection and though the
poem establishes its own world in a language which to a certain
degree is its own, it must demonstrate the organized relevance of
that world to the one in which we live. This, *Paradise Lost* succeeds
in doing through a structure in which all the poem's resources are
made to radiate into the condition of man and through a narrative
movement which leads us down from the cosmic and pre-human to
the human. The elevation of the style is thus neither inflationary nor
a force of dissociation. It is a magnification designed to intensify the
inherent pressures of the poem, so that the remoteness of the
language paradoxically becomes the main means of its relevance.
The epic similes depict this effect in miniature, with the carefully
controlled and pointed digressions reaching out to what the main
march of the language holds away. What this means is that in its

primary qualities and in its deflections, the language is living out the poem. And because the play of the language is so vitally linked with the tensions of the structure we feel the impact far more strongly and searchingly than if it were the product of one resource alone.

One of the objections urged against the style of *Paradise Lost* is that it is almost aggressively 'managed'. It is alleged to push and even to 'corner' the reader, depriving him of his right to respond freely to the evidence. There is an element of truth in this but only the element that is necessary if the poem is to be true to itself. The reader is not meant to avoid the sense of a present and unfolding design which survives and finally comprehends the assaults made against it by the anarchies of freedom. Milton's view of reality was along these lines and commitment to such a view is neither simple nor even single-minded. The imaginative realization of this view implies a language that to some degree conveys the feeling of management, if that is the right word to suggest a structure that is not so much imposed as won out of the character and resistance of its material. In its 'built' quality the style is meant to suggest to us what could be involved in the artifice of eternity.

'Conflict, more conflict!' is a cry which Yeats is said to have used when flourishing Sato's sword.[8] The designer of *Paradise Lost* would have agreed with Yeats. The mobilization of contraries extends through the epic, coupling its ontological, cosmic, moral and dramatic organizations, so that any specific confrontation is magnified and thrown back by the many mirrors of the poem's life. This is a feat of unification too sweeping and too intricate to be planned. It can only be created by the poetic mind possessed by a shaping principle. But the analytical critic can look at the achievement and draw its diagram from the outside, asking himself if the characteristic and repeated interplay of the poem can be reflected in the tactics of style. Having established the ultimate consistency, he can return to the poem to find his specification satisfied. Milton proceeds from the relatively simple proposition that the eye reads in one way and the mind in another. By the steady pulsation of his poetry he also ensures that with subtle variations, the ear reads in much the same way as the eye. The metrical and grammatical forces in the poem are thus brought into interplay and the unit of the verse recapitulates microcosmically the great contention that is Milton's subject. In keeping with his habits of creativeness, Milton having put his two forces into creative opposition, maximizes instead of minimizing the interplay.[9] He lengthens his paragraph, emphasizing its turns, varying the weight and location of his medial pauses, letting the prose rhythm counterpoint the insistent throb of the iambic line; and he strengthens the line itself, limiting his substitutions, restricting his feminine endings, and in general permitting only those variations which are necessary to make the norm more audible. For a demonstration of this intensified interplay we need to look no further than the beginning of the poem where twenty six lines are needed to bring the metrical and grammatical forces into coincidence. In the process we are taught to react in unison both to the structural affirmation and the sinuously responsive language. Out of the major conflicts of the poem the ordained purpose evolves. Out of the contentions wrought into the style we also gain the sense of onward movement through and even because of, the eddies, digressions, and apparent changes of course. The cumulative effect of these repeated enactments is decisive in a full reading of *Paradise Lost*. We come to recognize that however the language turns, the final turn will always be to order. The insistent shaping cannot but convey to us a searching conviction of the energy of form. Justifications of Milton's verse paragraph are not lacking. This justification is offered as evidence of how well a good poem knows itself.

A student once suggested that Syntax was the daughter of Sin. Critics of Milton may smile at this observation but several of them are not doing very much better. The syntax of *Paradise Lost* is still too often treated as the result of Milton's exasperation, following the discovery that English was not Latin. Less obstinate responses to the poetry have shown that Milton's inversions can usually be given a local justification and that the justifications are considerably more than appeals to sonority or rhetorical emphasis. Thus in 'Love without end and without measure, grace'[10] the word order first invites us to read 'without end' and 'without measure' as if both phrases were attached to love, then to read the first phrase as describing love and the second as describing grace and then again to read both phrases as defining the kind of love which is the content of grace. The reader is not called on to choose between these alternatives but rather to superimpose each upon the others; it is the simultaneous presence of all three which gives the line its subtlety and force. Other examples of such felicities could be given but perhaps Milton criticism is by now adult enough to do without a series of demonstrations which might limit the reader's right to his own alertness. In any event what is being suggested is a larger propriety rather than an immediate relevance. A fluid syntax is necessary if the movement of the paragraph is to play with any variety against the containment of the line; once again the effect is to give complexity and vigour to the interaction of forces. More strikingly, the delayed resolution which is the typical result of Milton's syntax, reproduces the drama of the poem in the drama of the language. We are watching not merely style or even answerable style but the manner of saying as the poem's way of life.

The life of a poem by Milton is varied and it should not be assumed that the contest between line and paragraph is capable of only one resolution. Many effects can be discriminated but perhaps it can be said that in the Satanic world, the interplay frequently works to compound confusion while in the celestial world, it is directed towards clarity. Two examples may hint at the range of subtlety offered. The first is taken from Satan's encounter at the gates of Hell:

The one seem'd Woman to the waste, and fair,
But ended foul in many a scaly fould
Voluminous and vast, a Serpent arm'd
With mortal sting: II, 650–53

Reading with the line as unit, we have the pseudo-finality of 'fair' (nicely betrayed by 'seem'd'), followed by the strong close of the second line on 'fould', a closure strengthened by the pun, which Milton's spelling underlines. This could be the end of the matter in the mind. But the bottom of deception is not so easily reached and the sentence coils back into 'voluminous and vast'. Donald Davie's curious remark that this phrase has nothing to recommend it but alliterative sonority[11] disregards an etymological pun that has been noted by more than one annotator and which follows scathingly upon the earlier word-play. The 'Serpent arm'd' is not the end of the business either, even though we are looking at the scene through the eyes of another armed serpent confronting its mirror image. It is only with 'mortal sting' that the movement comes for the moment, to its deadly point of rest. Thus there is more than one 'scaly fould' in the sentence and the mind is taught to recognize that as we penetrate falsity, we will find more falsity. From this labyrinth we turn to the celestial example.

Man shall not quite be lost, but sav'd who will,
Yet not of will in him, but grace in me
Freely voutsaf't;   III, 173–75

As the first line comes to its rest it seems that man's will can bring about his salvation. Then the second line acts as if to annul the first, with grace overwhelming the reality of will and with 'me' strengthened by its emphatic position and by the rhetorical contrast with 'him'. It is tempting to add to these underlinings the emphatic 'mee' printed by Darbishire and Wright, but honesty obliges one to admit that the spelling is not found either in 1667 or in 1674. Even without it the affirmation has been reversed and 'Freely voutsaf't' does not exactly restore the balance. Rather it obliges us to respond to the proposition as a whole and to recognize that the turns are necessary to present the thought in its integrity. The emphatic 'will' of the first line is no deception. It defines the effort that is necessary for salvation, that is needed to bring down the redeeming power of grace. Behind the joint effort there is meant to stand the knowledge that all things are of God. Self-reliance is not excluded; but it can only find its footing in humility. Using the deliberately sparse resources of syntax and contrast, the verse achieves a lucidity of affirmation beyond the reach of argument. The intense effort to come close to clarity makes us aware of what might be meant by the poetry of understanding.

Deception finds its fulfilment in self-deception. It is against this recognition that the ringing Satanic defiances must be judged and a scrutiny of one of them will not be out of place. As Satan accepts his new kingdom he does so in 'obdurat pride'; the energy of the pride is such that the reader is caught up in its momentum.

The mind is its own place, and in it self
Can make a Heav'n of Hell, a Hell of Heav'n,
What matter where, if I be still the same.   I, 254–56

The sound lives out the sense here, with the five times repeated *i* encircled and protected by the movement of the first line. The self creates its stronghold of inviolability and then as the line overflows, the outburst of pride reaches out to impose itself on its surroundings The third line in its 'high disdain' seems to embody both possibilities – the invulnerable self and the mind remaking its environment in its image. The onward force of the rhetoric is designed to sweep the reader through the passage, so that vigilance is required to maintain the sense of judgement. But a careful reading puts it to us that the balance of the second line, shaped to complete the symmetry of phrasing and thought, actually results in the destruction of Satan's position. A hell is very nearly made of heaven in the sixth book. Degradation is the mark of Satanic transformation. Transformation in the other direction – the mark of which is redemptive, not destructive – requires not stoic self-sufficiency, but the attainment of the paradise within. That paradise is to be found not in heroic defiance, but by the establishment of true identity in a profound act of relationship and dependence. Neither Satan's fixed mind nor Mammon's policy of economic development are capable of making a heaven out of hell. The third line now takes on a different and grimmer meaning. The environment can only be doomed if the centre which dominates it is sterile. The mind as its own place leads to 'myself am Hell' and Mammon's alternative is dealt with when Michael teaches Adam that outward freedom is lost when Christian liberty is surrendered. Deception in this example declares and defeats itself; the effect is suggestive not so much of clarity, as of rhetorical traps which the mind seeking clarity must learn to discern and evade.

The weight given to sound effects and metrical placing in the above discussion may seem excessive but experience teaches us that it is not uncalled for. Momentum does not mean the sweeping aside of subtlety or the failure of the language to run with or run creatively counter to the thought. When the Son asks:

And shall grace not find means that finds her way
The speediest of thy winged messengers
To visit all thy creatures and to all
Comes unprevented, unimplor'd, unsought.   III, 228–31

the tentative, halting movement of the first line is in studied contrast to the proposition in the second. The result is to put before us both the efficacy of grace and the resistance it encounters. We move through the resistance to the efficacy because that is the normal sequence in experience; and the inversion of the first line first suggests attainment of the objective, then makes us aware that there are two tasks, not one, and by obliging us to reconsider the whole process brings us to recognize how finding the way falls short of finding the means. The entry into the prison is only part and perhaps the easiest part of the rescue. The rhetorical repetitions of the fourth line are an accumulation of apathy (II, 185 and III, 373 show the same device put to different uses) and the effect is eloquent in its deadly inertia. The celestial style has been chosen for examination here and elsewhere because of its widely-advertised barrenness; the pressure of interpretation it accepts shows us how much can be found in Milton's 'failures'.

If overflow achieves one result in hell and another in heaven it is not to demonstrate anything so simple as versatility or even to keep the reader's mind on the poem. *Paradise Lost* creates a symbolic universe: internally symbolic in the sense that each element in the poem tells us something about the other elements and externally symbolic in the sense, that the intricate coherence of the poem tells us something about the far greater intricacy of a design that necessarily lies beyond the mind's grasp. Even the poem's encyclopaedic quality, the remarkable inclusiveness that is settled in order, is designed to suggest to us an order from which nothing is excluded. Therefore the language tactics of the poem always spring from the shaping forces of its life. If overflow and word-play achieve different results in heaven and in hell it is because the character of all things depends on their orientation. Heroism is not the same thing on both sides of the battle. It realizes itself only by virtue of the right commitment. When the commitment is misdirected the heroic attributes will be eaten away, however impressive they may appear in the world's eye. By insistently changing the shape of things the poem obliges us to see all things in their context; and as part of the same effort it insistently changes the shape of words. Glory is one thing in heaven and another in hell.[12] Mazes are one thing in hell and another in heaven, one thing in the 'Fould above fould' of the serpent misleading Eve (the language remembers the description of Sin) and another in Adam finding his way to his guilt.[13] Nature is 'boon' and wanton in its creative energy. Fallen Eve is both things in a different sense.[14] The words educate us to look beyond the words and to see behind them, the valuation of the whole poem.

The presence of the whole poem behind its details is also the presence of pattern behind process and of aesthetic form behind dramatic disclosure. There are many devices to persuade us of this presence. The great symmetries of the celestial cycle (strengthened by Milton's arrangement of that cycle), the cosmic architecture, the mobilization, and interconnection of contraries, the elaborately developed parallelisms and contrasts all put the structure and momentum of the work behind the life of the moment. There are also the backward and forward movements of narrative and prophecy and the 'simultaneous present' of all things, spread around the height of God's omniscience.[15] Nor must we forget the images that end Book IV and initiate Book XII, which whatever else they may be doing, also suspend process to make us aware of pattern. There is finally the syntactical manipulation of the very first lines, where the end is symbolically in the beginning and the pattern stands in suspended isolation before the movement of the sentence begins. Thus from time to time, we are taken out of time to become aware of the perspectives which control time; and always the structure with its insistent placing and judging of events, obliges us to give our attention to the larger span.

We must now ask ourselves how the poem's language-tactics succeed in realizing this quality of the poem. First, there are the paradoxes with which the divine language is charged. These are not the characteristic paradoxes of the *via negativa* but are rather directed downwards into action, shaping that action through the ironies of providence. The divine language therefore both discloses and adjusts itself to the basic force of the poem, the persistent turning of evil to the ends of good. Moreover, by its insistence that the end of the event is other than where the event seems to be tending, the divine style urges us to the larger view and to the knowledge that the text requires the context. Secondly, there are effects in the poem which move the poem ahead of its own flow. This may seem a contradiction but it is one put forward to suggest that Milton is as good a man as any in contriving his escape from the Gutenberg galaxy. If we now return to II, 650–53, (and we can do so with confidence since these are by no means the best lines Milton wrote) we will see that the armed serpent is not the only anticipation of things to come. There is also the 'mortal sting' which suggests the nature of that 'other shape' which has still to be encountered. Thus both the infernal father and his son are already involved in the seething life of the image and the macabre allegory is presented in compact form before the poem unfolds it for us. This is not the end of the process of anticipation. The Biblical context of 'mortal sting' is meant to recall Christ's triumph over death and the same phrase is used in III, 253 when the Son offers himself for the redemption of man. It has already been noted that the description of Sin looks forward to the description of the serpent tempting Eve. In short, to the attentive reader, the whole poem is present in four lines of local description. If, keeping resolutely to the activities of Sin and Death, we now move on to II, 1021–30, we will notice that the difficulty with which Satan moved through Chaos is contrasted with the manner in which that same chaos 'Tamely endur'd a Bridge of wondrous length'. The imagery of exploration and seafaring is extensively used in connection with Satan's journey.[16] One suggestion being made is that though the first voyage is dangerous, the trade routes follow and are tamely endured. But Satan's laborious journey is also meant to be contrasted with the ease with which Christ moves through chaos on his creative mission; the tame enduring, considered against this contrast, is a significant comment on the progress of evil. Finally, when we come to the actual building of the causeway by Sin and Death, we are regaled by a simile which compares this engineering feat with the bridge built by Xerxes over the Hellespont. We thus move from archetypal into human history. But the simile invites us to think of the fate of Xerxes and as we move back into the archetype, the apparently casual flourish ('if great things to small may be compar'd') recoils with suddenly augmented force, telling us that Nemesis will insist on its sense of proportion. We thus move from the second book, to the seventh, to the tenth, and to the final victory. Similarly in I, 253–55 'myself am Hell' is latent; the battle in heaven is anticipated; Hell's 'Universe of death' (II, 622) becomes an extension of its sterile nucleus; and the ground is laid for the crucial distinction which will lead to the affirmation of the paradise within. In each instance we run ahead of the flow of the poem sensing the presence of the links; and then in the main movement itself, we look forward and backward, understanding what the links really mean.

Three passages have been examined but the reader, once he is aware of the possibilities, will have no difficulty in finding many more examples for himself. Milton may have invented the anticipatory simile:[17] if he did so, it was because the technical pioneering was necessary for the life of his epic. The innovation takes its place among other movements in front of and across the poem's unfolding:

the weeping trees of Paradise, the premonitions with which Eden is haunted, Eve's dream, and the accumulating gravity of what Arnold Stein calls 'gestures' of temptation.[18] The restorative forces are prefigured also, from the great sweep of foreknowledge in the third book, to the sombre chronicle of the eleventh and twelfth books where typology joins prophecy in the disclosure of what is to come. It is by the insistent persuasion of these devices that Milton is able to make pattern consonant with process and his success in doing so is characteristic; he maximizes rather than minimizes the distance he is called upon to bridge. No poem has more propulsive power than *Paradise Lost* or conveys more of the feeling of events evolving from their own momentum. At the same time, no poem can lay claim to a more intricate or more inclusive design, a deeper establishment of energy in form. Here as in almost every other way, the poem is characteristic of the reality it commemorates.

The various movements of anticipation are part of the general tactics of *Paradise Lost*. But applied specifically to the fall of Adam and Eve, they suggest something of the feeling of foreknowledge. We know what is to come and cannot but know it. The poem cannot annul our awareness of history. But it also cannot offer inevitability as a substitute for suspense. By their inherent obliquity and tact, the premonitions of the imagery avoid this danger and at the same time the gestures of temptation which for all their gathering weight, can at any time be arrested or reversed, keep the situation dramatically open. We begin to sense some of the subtleties at work in an extraordinarily difficult and delicate undertaking; the translation from doctrine into the life of poetry of that which is foreknown, yet not decreed.[19]

The approach to the style from the inside has now proceeded far enough for us to see how every detail of Milton's language-tactics springs out of the basic needs of the poem, discovering it and establishing its identity. No other style could bear witness so powerfully to the nature of providence, the timeless pattern and the onward movement, the tension of contraries evolving into design, the order in which all things are justified and settled, yet which is also the basis of true energy and freedom. The style of *Paradise Lost* can be described in a formal sense, as the style of secondary epic but while the letter may be followed with fastidiousness it is also given a life which it has never quite possessed. Milton succeeds in meeting with what one can only call creative fidelity, the demands of both architectural and organic decorum. This double propriety is a singular accomplishment but perhaps it is the interior relevance which is both more difficult, and rewarding to explore. To discover it and to respond to it is also to understand how far we must travel in our reading of *Paradise Lost*.

8 *Paradise Regained*

Jerusalem and Athens:
the temptation of learning in *Paradise Regained*

1

When the devil offers Dr. Faustus the riches of infinite knowledge all of us (including Marlowe, according to recent critics) disapprove of the doctor's choice. When Christ in *Paradise Regained* rejects a similar offer from a more insidious antagonist he is greeted with anguished cries of *et tu Brute!* Donne can describe a 'hydroptique immoderate desire of learning' as the 'worst voluptuousness'[1]: but more moderate language in Milton's brief epic is generally found to be far less tolerable. These remarks are not made to subscribe to the familiar lament that critics are inconsistent but rather to suggest that there is a problem of how to respond involved here which is more than the problem of what Christ says or even of how he says it. For this reason the search for precedents is only of limited usefulness. To prefer Jerusalem to Athens is not solely a late Puritan or a patristic privilege. Sidney can be quoted to the same effect and so can Nicholas Ferrar.[2] Plotinus' concept of the virtues as purifications and his specific definition of magnanimity as the scorn of earthly things can also be made to point in the same direction.[3] On the other side, Luther and Calvin can be quoted on the benefits of literature.[4] This exchange of accepted positions can serve to remind us that the circulation of ideas is rather more complex than it appears to be in the first stage of scholarship. It also becomes apparent that it is not in this way that we can discover why Milton did what he did.

Douglas Bush's concern at watching Milton 'turn and rend some main roots of his being'[5] is eloquently put and widely shared. The other side of this observation is hardly ever mentioned. It is that the position which Christ articulates has itself a main root in Milton's being.[6] The much-quoted digression in *The Reason of Church Government*[7] suggests strongly the superiority of the Bible to secular accomplishment not simply as wisdom but as literature. Certain contrary

pulls or to continue with the previous metaphor, certain entangle-
ments in the main roots are necessary if the whole mind is to preserve its wholeness. As time passes and a man's sense of the truth as
he finds it alters, it is natural that one element or another in these
conflicts should predominate. *Paradise Regained* presumably
disturbs us because what is taking place in it seems to be more than
a mere change of emphasis; crucial attachments which we are
accustomed to call Miltonic are being not so much minimized as
driven out of existence. Critics aware of these obliterations have
suggested that Christ turns his back on history because history
chose to turn its back on Milton and that it is the failure of the
millenium to materialize which leads to the proclamation of the
paradise within. These justifications from life, or from literary life
are reassuring only up to a point. A man may be constrained to say
certain things but that does not mean that his saying them is
aesthetic. The force of rejection is a powerful component in any
mind that is God-oriented but there is no obligation to construct a
poem which is designed primarily as a demonstration of this force.
It is the consistency of the undertaking which deters us. Renuncia-
tions, including even this one, are acceptable as gestures or even
commitments but not as commitments of the whole man. They
disturb us when they are fitted into a process of refusal which drives
both the poem and the reader against the wall.

One of the results of a historical examination is that it shows us
how unnecessary the wall is. There is no temptation of learning in
the Bible and Elizabeth Pope in her pioneering study of the traditions behind *Paradise Regained*[8] has been unable to point to any
tradition which sanctions such a temptation. Poets of course, are
free to invent what the past fails to offer them; but unless a poet is
obstinately obtuse he does not box himself in a situation from which
he is unable to escape, at least to his own satisfaction. The question
which Satan asks may allow only one right answer. But why,
precisely, does the question have to be asked? This is perhaps the
most teasing of a number of Miltonic perplexities, including the
battle in heaven, Michael's postscript in the last book of *Paradise
Lost* and the confrontation between Comus and the Lady.

Despite its provocativeness, the temptation of Athens has
received relatively cursory treatment in studies of *Paradise Regained*.
The fullest scrutiny of it so far is by Barbara Lewalski[9] and even Mrs.
Lewalski in her zealous examination of the genre, can find only one

other brief epic on Christ's temptation.[10] A temptation similar to the temptation of Athens apparently occurs in Quarles' *Job Militant*.[11] This is an interesting but scarcely substantial precedent. For the rest, Mrs. Lewalski tells us that epics both brief and compendious, include episodes on the education of the hero.[12] This is a fragile basis for the confident assertion that the need for a temptation of Athens was, so to speak, found by Milton among his données.[13] An education involving the rejection of education is a striking reversal of not very compelling precedents. When the reversal is placed in its setting it may well strike us as characteristically Miltonic, but to make it less (or more) than an obsession with renunciation we need to locate it in a larger movement of irony.

Originality invites but seldom receives evaluation on its own terms and that is why, at this point in the poem, arguments from the genre, the times and the life will not suffice. There is a driving internal logic to the poem. We have to possess it, or at least to recognize it, before we can understand how the force of that logic annexes precedent or disregards it in the momentum of its unfolding.

Loyalty to its own dramatic decorum can be decisive in shaping the way in which a poem reveals itself. That Christ ought to be Christ rather than John Milton is a proposition which few would want to dispute but it is unfortunately not naive to ask how this proposition operates in the dispositions of *Paradise Regained* and in the specific tactics of what Louis Martz terms the 'meditative combat'.[14] One of the more important among Professor Pope's recoveries of tradition is her insistence that Christ suffered the temptations in his human aspect.[15] This fact like the dialogue in heaven in *Paradise Lost*, provides a dramatic 'cover' for Milton's theology; but it also means that Christ enters the combat with a crucial unawareness of himself. Both the achieving of identity and the rejection of those masks which offer a superficial at the expense of a radical function are caught in counter-movements, exactly opposed and balanced. Every retreat from Satan is an advance into self-realization and on a more spacious stage, every abstention from history helps to create even in its apparent withdrawal the only basis on which history can be transformed. It is for this reason that the emphasis in Milton's brief epic falls so heavily on the second and central temptation.[16] Readers familiar with Milton will recognize a typical strategy: the redistribution of formal weights so as to reveal the direction and energy of the main thrust.[17] The inner kingdom must be constituted with almost vehement purity if the world of creative action (as distinct from mere turbulence) is to come into being around it. The perfect man can only become himself through an unqualified fidelity to the commitments which create him.

To know these facts the reader of the poem does not have to be a seventeenth-century reader though he cannot but profit from the attempt to pass imaginatively through the seventeenth-century response. What is essential is that the reader should encircle the poem with some general knowledge of Christ's function and his destiny, watching the circle shrink as Christ's realization of himself advances. Then, in the climax on the pinnacle, it will be Christ's knowledge which surprises the reader's knowledge.

Accidents are rare in Milton's poetry and it is no accident that three temptations (or inquiries) in the abstract precede the specific offer of the kingdoms of the world. 'Riches' and 'Fortune' are suggested first, then 'glory' and finally 'zeal and duty'. The movement is from the material to the apparently 'moral', from personal fulfilment to public service. Christ's answers progressively declare his nature: the emphasis on sovereignty in the kingdom of the self needs to be followed if it is to be saved from egotism, by the conviction that glory is found only in serving the glory of God and finally by the realization that even fitness for action must wait on the ripeness of things. The sequence shows Satan's imprisonment in his own earlier manifesto–'Honour, dominion, glory and renown'[18]–and also suggests the nature of what may be called Christ's vertical allegiance in contrast to Satan's horizontal involvement in the world.

It is only after Christ has demonstrated what we may doubly call his uprightness that Satan transports him to that hilltop from which he views history and is exhorted to enter it. The first Adam also saw history from a hilltop and *Paradise Lost* XI, 381–84 carefully makes the link; but the link supports dramatic differences. The first Adam looks on a river of destruction which flows from his sin and which he is powerless to modify. The second, offered the means of decisive involvement, remains the detached and seemingly indifferent observer. Christ's answer has the clarity of Michael's in *Paradise Lost* XII, 82–101 and clarity of certain kinds must skirt the edge of cruelty. But Christ does also add with a confidence increasingly threatening to Satan, that what will be will be irresistibly in its due time. The poem as elsewhere has its tact at these points, its carefully limited boundaries which it asks the reader to cross, bringing his own knowledge into the poem so that he can measure Satan's blindness and Christ's advance into self-realization. What happens in the poem is never the poem's whole story. The stingingly harsh judgement on Rome for example

> What wise and valiant man would seek to free
> These thus degenerate, by themselves enslav'd
> Or could of inward slaves make outward free?   IV, 143–45

work in many ways on the reader's responsiveness. The words 'wise and valiant' are meant to recall our first glimpse of the first Adam in Paradise (IV, 297). The coupling between interior and exterior freedom embodies a conviction that Milton states in many places and in many ways but always with a persistent fervour of commitment. The controlled play of the sibilants is also remarkable, curling as it were, in the air of the speaker's scorn. But most important of all, the reader should be aware that Christ *is* that second Adam, that wise and valiant man who is destined to rescue mankind from slavery. The knowledge undercuts the otherwise patrician hauteur of the statement and helps us to realize that Christ in rejecting one kingship is establishing another. Limited interventions are no substitute for radical transformation. This is surely the purport of the images of kingship in IV, 146–51.[19] Too little and too late is not part of the strategy of the divine will. There is no reason why Satan should be advised of these facts but the reader errs in adopting Satan's blindness.

The division between the second and third books of *Paradise Regained* cuts perplexingly across the temptation of the kingdoms. One result is to bring Rome and Athens together, thus giving additional weight to the rejection of the classical world and compounding Milton's 'betrayal' of himself. Another consequence is to arouse a sense of uncertainty regarding the unfolding of the poem, since a new book can scarcely begin where a crucial temptation is traditionally supposed to end. Satan himself (IV, 85–90) suggests strongly that after Rome he has no more kingdoms to offer and when Rome is rejected he can do no more than offer again with additional conditions, something that has already been rejected. This is a nice touch of dramatic verisimilitude, bringing us firmly to the end of the temptation in *Luke* and also suggesting the exasperation of an outwitted opponent who has made his last throw. The second round is over and yet there are indications that it may only be beginning. Other readers besides those in the seventeenth century can draw the conclusion that the devil is most dangerous when he appears to be defeated.

If we look back on IV, 88–9 we will note that Satan says only that he has shown Christ all the kingdoms of the world. Of course there is a kingdom not of this world. Christ has been saying so throughout the poem, sometimes to the extent of appearing to say nothing else. What can be more artful than to offer him that which has hitherto made him invulnerable, to seduce him with those riches in the name of which he has refused all other riches? Seen in this light the temptation of Athens has little to do with Milton's 'disillusionment', with his zeal for precedent or his passion for innovation. It is a move issuing strictly out of the logic of combat. In the nature of things it cannot be the *coup de grâce* but reserved applause should not be out of order.

Satan's offer is necessarily tainted. Being a citizen of the world (the use of the phrase reminds us how to measure it) he has offered both Parthia and Rome as prizes of the lower glory. Now, in prefacing his most insidious temptation with the words 'Be famous' and in his betraying reference to 'empire' (a categorical imperative of the Satanic mind) he forgets Christ's calm dismissal of these lures in III, 44–47. More important, as a citizen of the world, he can only offer that wisdom which the world has accumulated in its history. He cannot know that there is a higher wisdom; but the reader should know it and Christ should not only know it but should remind us through the shaping of his answer that he is destined to incarnate that wisdom.

The preamble to Satan's temptation is hardly ever quoted. It is among the most crucial passages in *Paradise Regained* and it is essential that we grasp its implications firmly if we are to know what is happening in the poem.

> All knowledge is not couch't in *Moses* Law,
> The *Pentateuch* or what the Prophets wrote;
> The *Gentiles* also know, and write, and teach
> To admiration, led by Natures light; IV, 225–28

What is being offered is the completion of the world of understanding, with natural knowledge supplementing the wisdom of the law and of the prophets. Christ can agree with the first two lines of the statement; but he cannot agree with the consequence since he himself is to bring Old Testament wisdom to a far more decisive and transforming fulfilment. Satan offers all that he can within the limits of his knowing but Christ at this point in his 'becoming', not only knows but *is* something that Satan cannot understand. A deep irony turns here on the reader's recognition of what is going on. Christ must refuse Athens to declare his nature, not necessarily in his capacity as perfect man but rather in his capacity as the historic Christ who is to bring down into history a power of grace beyond the light of nature.[20] His reference to the inner light, received from the fountain of light is not, as critics tend to suggest, a walling-up of himself in the interior kingdom. Rather it is a statement of the additional dimension that is to be bestowed upon the kingdoms of the world. It is also an oblique affirmation to Satan that Christ is truly the Son of God, deriving all that he knows and is from that allegiance. Satan's difficulties with the concept of sonship are recurrent and characteristic but once again the reader is not called on to adopt his exclusions.

'Error by his own aims is best evinc't'[21] is the devil's invitation to engage in the wars of truth. Christ's answer can only be that error is trapped in its own being and is best shown to be error by virtue of a source outside itself. If the light of nature is to be redeemed by the light of grace, if the law is to culminate in the gospel, he who brings the higher wisdom into history can scarcely accept the lower as a substitute. It is indeed the higher understanding which gives structure and cohesion to that lesser knowledge, which is not really knowledge but vanity, until what is above it puts it into order. Christ who commands the power of creative ordering (as he did in the seventh book of *Paradise Lost*) can scarcely surrender that power to the very substance which it is supposed to transform.

Comus has his fling at Stoicism's 'budge doctors' and Stoic apathy is on the agenda of the philosophic angels in hell.[22] Christ attacks Stoicism with a distinctive earnestness which is only understandable when we think of him as himself rather than as an articulation of Milton's disappointments. Christ has defended the interior kingdom and is now being offered that kingdom precisely because of the consistency of his defence. Stoicism is the affirmation of that kingdom as an end rather than as an instrument for the service of God's glory. Noble in its indifference to the world, it is potentially Satanic in its self-centredness: this is the cutting edge of Christ's reference to 'pride' a reference that is not without dramatic pointedness when we remember to whom Christ is replying. Christ's dismissal of the schools has a finality for which 'frigid' is almost certainly the wrong adjective. We are facing the decisiveness of a man who has come to judge the world rather than to receive it, or rather to receive it and to redeem it as its judge. The strangely neglected lines which follow make abundantly clear where we ought to be in our own minds.

> Alas what can they teach, and not mislead;
> Ignorant of themselves, of God much more,
> And how the world began, and how man fell,
> Degraded by himself, on grace depending?   IV, 309–12

It is the accents of compassion rather than scorn which are dominant. Regardless of the injunction of the Delphic oracle, man cannot know himself until he finds within himself the primeval act by which he was undone. Philosophies which evade this fact have set themselves upon the road to delusion. The second line of the statement is carefully ambiguous. If we are ignorant of our limited selves we must be far more ignorant of God who is unlimited. But our ignorance of ourselves is also the result of our not knowing God and so the greater ignorance, in the movement of the thought, reflects back on the lesser and inexorably enlarges it. As for the beginning of the world, Satan has reason to remember that; it was the response of divine creativeness to the damage done by his own rebellion. The fall of man is also an event of which Satan is keenly and perhaps delectably aware. A common knowledge denied to Athens is thus being assumed between the combatants and it might almost seem at this stage in the response, as if Christ were reminding Satan as a privileged individual 'in the know', of the philosophic delusions of the Gentiles. Yet the very next phrase 'Degraded by himself', is a stab at Satan's vanity and 'on grace depending' carries us into a realm with which Christ's opponent is totally unfamiliar. The reader must remember the stern distinction of *Paradise Lost*, III, 129–32, a distinction which was well-known outside the epic. Even more important than the drawing of the boundaries of Satan's world is our sense of the point that Christ has reached in the affirmation and becoming of himself. For the first time, he knows himself as the instrument of grace, implicitly answering and softening the question which he had implacably posed in rejecting the temptation of Rome. He also makes clear what he must do with Athens. The light of nature though 'not in all quite lost'[23] has been drastically dimmed by man's fall. Christ's task is to restore that light and not to use it. Satan cannot know of Christ's redemptive mission (an ignorance which gives depth to the angry bewilderment of IV, 368–72) but the reader ought to know and is now put on notice of what he ought to know. Seen in this frame of understanding, Christ's remarks all fall into a firmly shaped perspective. His historic function is not to live in Athens but to make what is of value in Athens live in him.

The content of the *genre* and of interpretative tradition are thus not quite sufficient for the reader of *Paradise Regained*. There is a dramatic encirclement which irradiates the poem and which is drawn into the poem by the poem's shaping forces. As the duel of the mind evolves in its stripped clarity we are meant to measure each movement of the combatants with an intentness not inferior to that of the writing itself. Irony is the word which seems to be called for however much the term may have been debased by usage: both the irony of Christ's increasing self-embodiment, abutted against Satan's static yet sedulous resourcefulness and the irony of the reader's larger knowledge, measuring both the growing and the imprisoned identity. When Christ's words are interpreted according to the logic of combat and according to the destiny he is to take on and increasingly knows, they cease to be intrusions of the poet into the poem and become aesthetic facts rather than aesthetic disturbances. Not all problems of imaginative acceptance disappear, since the basic commitment set forth with typical severity, is well beyond our powers of adherence and also involves the disconcerting paradox of using literature for the denial of literature. But a properly constructed dramatic whole calls for contemplation of its forces rather than endorsement of its doctrine. Moreover, every rejection in the poem is meant to be subverted by the reader's realization that it is only through the quality of his refusals that Christ is able to construct that historic personality which is destined eventually to redeem what is rejected.[24]

The question of what can be legitimately read into a poem will always remain debatable and provocative. There are many poems which in the course of their tactics, invite the reader to write part of them himself; the act of reading thus becomes a specific foundation for growth in the reader's own mind. Any student of rhetoric also knows that the most effective persuasions are better left unsaid. This kind of poetic tact is not always easy to separate from incompetence but in *Paradise Regained* the evidence is all on the side of a tact that is finely controlled and purposive, drawing its boundaries with precise insinuation so that we always move across them into a surrounding and creative irony. There is yet another kind of 'extension' of a poem for which we must be prepared to allow. As the reading situation changes and traditions drop away, connections which were once 'live' cease to exist and crucial lights in the poem may no longer shine as the reader reads. Historical scholarship can switch on these lights; its temptation is perhaps to switch on too many of them and so to minimize the poem's powers of self-illumination even in the darkness of today. *Paradise Regained* is a poem difficult of access but when one has become familiar with the special kind of alertness that it calls for, it is remarkable to what an extent it is capable of sustaining and validating itself. Rich associations that once invested it can and should be drawn back into it; but a reading educated in vigilance and freed from unaesthetic distractions, can still perceive much that remains on the poem's own grounds.

2

The first Adam when first seen in the garden is described as formed for contemplation and valour.[25] It is a description which follows and thereby sums up an ardent affirmation of the image of God in man. Christ in refusing Rome, remembers both the balance and the sequence of qualities[26] and so calls on us to look at what lies beyond the refusal. The perfect hero may be presumed to be perfectly schooled in wisdom. Quite apart from the promises of Milton's own consistency, the rejection of learning invites a reference to the *Tractate on Education* where, as might be expected, we are presented first with a 'contemplative' definition: 'The end then of learning is to repair the ruins of our first parents by regaining to know God aright, and out of that knowledge to love him, to imitate him, to be like him, as we may the neerest by possessing our Souls of true vertue, which being united to the heavenly grace of faith makes up the highest perfection'.[27] It is a definition which looks backward to the Epilogue of *Comus* and forward to Christ on the hill. But it is only one aspect of the truth and the active definition is needed to complete it: 'I call therefore a compleate and generous Education that which fits a man to perform justly, skilfully and magnanimously all the offices both private and publike of peace and war'.[28] Once again, we are to bear in mind the sequence as well as the balance. Both have their share in that misalliance of valour and wisdom which Samson comes to perceive as the driving force of his downfall.[29]

The Christian hero who is the source of Christianity may seem to have forgotten the double definition amid the frigidities of the meditative combat. But the elaborate and extended second temptation, the emphasis on the shaping of the interior kingdom and even the rejection of a displaced allegiance to learning are part of an insistence that first things should clearly come first. It is no accident that the prolonged central temptation which serves to establish the primacy of mind is enclosed by two notably brief temptations to false action. The first is an incitement to premature action, before the interior kingship that governs right action has been established. When Christ by contemplation establishes his capacity for valour, the third temptation calls on him to act under the pressure of panic.

It is typical of Milton's way with paradox that Christ acts ultimately by refusing to act. What happens on the pinnacle is less the result of something done than of something revealed. Satan is not struck down by any thunderbolt. He falls 'smitten with amazement' and it is reasonable to suppose that the amazement covers more than the unexpected sight of Christ standing on the pinnacle. The affirmation of identity reaches its climax at this point and Satan's fall is the result of some catastrophic recognition. When error knows truth it also knows its own defeat as error. But this is the ultimate statement and there must be in front of it and evoking it, a more specific confrontation born of the facts of the poem. The oracular warning 'Tempt not the Lord thy God' is obviously crucial and has been variously interpreted.[30] In understanding it, it may be helpful to look at the immediate context. Satan has placed Christ on the highest pinnacle of what he himself, 'Swollen with rage', has described as 'thy Father's house'. In quoting *Psalm 91* which is a hymn of trust in God[31] and of confidence in the power of his protection, he challenges that power in its sanctuary. It is an act of precipitate *hybris* and if Satan is twice described as 'proud' in thirty lines it is to remind us that pride is the first of the devil's sins to be mentioned in *Paradise Lost* and to suggest that we are witnessing the re-enactment of that 'impious Warr in Heav'n and Battel proud',[32] in which the contention that shapes history began. When Christ replies to *Psalm 91* with *Deuteronomy* 6, 16 we are made aware how scrupulous the etiquette of duelling must be to require the exchange of texts in such precarious places. But we must also recall that the previous verse of *Deuteronomy* is a statement of God's wrath. At this point Satan realizes where his passion to know his adversary has led him. He has recreated the old battle. Now, on the pinnacle, he recognizes his old enemy. He has by his own recklessness surrounded himself with the conditions that inexorably lead to his defeat. Inevitably he repeats the rhythm of an old fall. Even the 'heavenly anthems' sung after the Son's triumph describe Satan as the 'infernal serpent' (the first phrase used to describe him in *Paradise Lost*) and speaks of the infernal legions as hiding terrified amid a herd of swine, recalling that 'Heard / of Goats or timerous flock' in the likeness of which the rebel angels were driven from heaven.[33]

To suggest this way of looking at the climax on the pinnacle is not to exclude or to minimize the other ways. Mrs. Lewalski has as usual, summarized most of the alternatives.[34] The Son stands in affirming his dependence, in trusting in God in the spirit of the text that is hurled at him.[35] In saying 'Tempt not the Lord thy God' he both declares the wrath of the Father and finds himself as the Father's perfect image, warning that there are limits to presumption and that his office now is to ensure that these limits are kept. But a deep and double act of recognition is also involved, with the Son reaching the pinnacle of his own identity as Satan comes to the precipice of a previous failure. Both the falling and the motionless standing are emblems of this central confrontation and the brevity of the scene itself catches something of the quintessential moment. Moreover if we go back to the passages which define Christ's and Satan's awareness of each other we can find a further reason for Satan's 'amazement' in a crucial and self-preserving lack of knowledge. I, 355–56 and 493–96 can be misinterpreted. These passages mean first that the protagonists know each other in that they know themselves appointed as antagonists. They also know each other as the Son of God and Satan. This is as it were, the shape of their understanding; the content must be filled in by the process of temptation and refusal. But there is also something which Satan does not see and cannot endure seeing:

His first-begot we know, and sore have felt,
When his fierce thunder drove us to the deep;
Who this is we must learn, for man he seems
In all his lineaments, though in his face
The glimpses of his Fathers glory shine   I, 89–93

The climax comes when Satan discovers that this distinction cannot be made and that when the crisis comes he must always face the same enemy. History will repeat itself and he himself has created the chain of events that makes it impossible to escape from the repetition.

Milton's presentation of the crisis on the pinnacle is striking in itself. It becomes more striking when we examine the tradition with which he had to work. As Elizabeth Pope has noted,[37] the consensus of opinion among commentators was that Christ was in no serious danger on the pinnacle. The pinnacle itself was usually thought of as the cornice surrounding a flat roof, 'the exterior circuit of the top of the house'.[38] Even those who like Henry Blackwood, were aware that a pinnacle meant something else in normal English usage, nevertheless believed that the point of the pinnacle 'hath some breath upon it wherein a man may stand'.[39] Occasionally it was suggested that the cornice itself might be an array of spires[40] on one of which Christ was placed but even for those holding this extreme view, all that was necessary was for Christ to step back on to the flat roof and to descend sedately by the staircase.[41] Something more than an architectural quibble was involved. If Christ was in no danger, the character of his temptation altered. It was usually interpreted as a temptation to vainglory, overconfidence and the performance of superfluous miracles, when ordinary means of deliverance were available.[42] Satan's partial quotation of *Psalm 91*, noted in the Geneva bible[43] and dutifully underlined by every subsequent commentator, was a reminder that God protected only those who persevered in his ways. His ways did not include uncalled-for leaps into space. Considered in this manner the temptation on the pinnacle complements the first temptation, thus implicitly justifying the sequence in *Matthew*, IV. Thus to Thomas Fuller, the first temptation is to despair and the second to presumption[44] and Richard Ward similarly observes that

Satan first tempts Christ to '*Diffidencie* and distrust' and then to 'confidence and assurance'.[45] In such circumstances 'Tempt not the Lord thy God' was read as Christ's justification for his refusal to cast himself down, rather than as a warning addressed to Satan.[46] The second view, held by what Milton might have termed 'several Ancient Fathers'[47] does not seem prominent in seventeenth-century comment.

The differences in Milton's presentation leap to the mind. The preparatory violence of the storm scene, the climactic intimidation of Satan 'swoll'n with rage', the taunt of IV, 551–52, define a crisis of isolation and peril;[48] the oracular menace of Christ's rejoinder becomes possible only because of the context; and the dramatic contrast between Christ standing and Satan falling,[49] neither in the Bible nor in New Testament commentary, is Milton's own brilliantly silhouetted image of the recurrent end of an encounter which dominates history.

The moment on the pinnacle is thus both a re-enactment and an anticipation, pulling into its blaze of understanding the beginning as well as the end of time. Its character is suggested to us not only in what Satan is compelled to see, but in the language used to describe his downfall. Epic similes are rare in *Paradise Regained* and Mrs. Lewalski counts no more than six of them.[50] Two are used in describing Christ's victory and this comparative lavishness is, as might be expected, carefully planned. Hercules was regarded as a prefiguring of Christ and Milton himself associated him with Christ in *The Nativity Ode* and in *The Passion*. His conquest of Antaeus is an example of valour. But the example is designed to point out that while Antaeus was defeated by being removed from the earth which gave him strength, Satan is vanquished in his assigned element, the air.[51] The Oedipus simile on the other hand, presents us with a victory of the mind. But if the answer to the riddle is man, that should suggest to us that there are more dangerous afflictions than that which ravaged Thebes, to which the only answer is man perfected in Christ. The balance of contemplation and valour is carefully established so that what it achieves can be carefully surpassed.[52] If we now look back to *Paradise Lost* it will be apparent that the Hercules simile can be connected to Christ's victory in heaven while the Oedipus simile connects to that later victory, not to be dreamt of as a duel, which Michael reveals on another hill to Adam. Between them, the two similes suggests something of the nature of total victory; and the sweep of one epic is potently summarized in the climax of insight that illuminates another. It is the victory in the mind that is decisive and Milton is putting it to us that the 'divine excellence' of Christ's spiritual kingdom is 'able without wordly force to subdue all the powers and kingdoms of this world'.[53] This is the central part of the story; but we neglect completeness if we insist that it is all of it.

9 *Samson Agonistes*

The unsearchable dispose

This book began by quoting the 'digression' in *The Reason of Church Government*. If it ends by doing so the result should be more than to draw the circle tight or to stress the thoroughness of Milton's achievement. In 1642 Milton proposed to himself an ancient question – whether the epic was the highest of literary forms or 'whether those Dramatic constitutions wherein *Sophocles* and *Euripides* raigne shall be found more doctrinal and exemplary to a Nation'.[1] Aristotle had answered the question in favour of tragedy. The Renaissance answered it in favour of the epic. Milton was the most competitive of poets, particularly when that competitiveness was sublimated as zeal in the service of literary Christendom. As a professional 'overgoer', he had to be accustomed to take risks; but the one risk he could not take was the risk of incompleteness. It was necessary that he should write a tragedy and it was also necessary, given the culture he was committed to surpass, that the tragedy should be on the Athenian model, with Aeschylus joining the tellingly brief list of those dramatists 'unequall'd yet by any'.[2]

Thoroughness explains much but justifies little. We condemn a man when we describe him as diligent. It is not enough to say that Milton wrote his tragedy to fulfil a literary programme or that the frustrated dramatist, compelled to throw away four drafts of *Adam Unparadiz'd*, turned in compensation to his two jottings on the theme of Samson.[3] It was aesthetically right that the epic of man should supersede the epic of England. It was also right that the blind hero should walk upon that narrow stage from which the perceptions of tragedy stab outward. Christ, Adam and the Lady surround the human condition. Samson speaks to us out of its anguished centre. The blindness is both a dramatic fact and a symbolic presence, a reminder to all of us of what we cannot see. If we permit ourselves to ask how much of tragedy is fought out in blindness we will recognize the potency of the symbol in putting to us man's relationship with reality and with the divine will which is reality in movement.

Samson has its place in the pattern in many ways. It helps to complete the envelopment of forms through which Milton's poetry moves into its core of insight. It gives us a new protagonist in a new situation at the lowest point on the wheel of man's undoing. Because constancy in recognition is best achieved through diversity in approaches we are presented with a poem of the minimum theatre, contrasted with the maximum theatre of *Paradise Lost* where cosmic time and ontological space press in inescapably on the moment of decision. In *Samson* all is stripped bare to the leanness of the Greek dramatic economy, sophistications such as the third actor are discarded and the unities are adhered to with a rigour that in lesser circumstances might be petrifying. Yet the result is not athletic grace or the achievement of that barren ideal, verisimilitude.[4] It is rather the destitution of the prison-house, with the sparseness of resources silhouetting the isolation of the hero. If the contrast with the opulence of *Paradise Lost* is striking, the affinities with *Paradise Regained* are also meant to impress themselves upon us. The brief epic as a form, is intermediate between classical epic and Athenian tragedy, sharing with the latter the starkness that is sometimes supposed to be a gift of old age. It is a starkness which underlines the similarities in the situations of the two protagonists, the need for both Christ and Samson to stand still in order to find themselves. Both protagonists also pass through the same number of confrontations, though the 'triple equation' only has its rewards if it is applied with much tact and a sense of the rights of each poem.[5] It is part of the complexities of relationships within the *oeuvre* that these resemblances should sharpen our sense of basic divergences. There is a difference between the desert and Gaza, between clarity and blindness, between Hercules surpassed and Hercules brought low in the divorce of valour from wisdom. Yet the nature of relatedness is such that these resemblances must lead us back to another and deep bond of similarity. Divine omens attend the birth of the hero.[6] One stands fast in God's image. The other, grievously imperfect, is nevertheless accepted as God's champion. The difference measures the length of the way back. The denouement tells us that the way will not be closed.[7]

Thus both the form and the embodiment pull *Samson* into an

order of accomplishment which it helps to sustain and complete and by which it is in turn contained. The pattern would be significant even if it were no more than a pattern of exploration; but it has to be remembered that the movement from innocence, through engagement, to withdrawal is almost the typical trajectory of life. In commenting on this trajectory there ought to be a place for a work of art which begins in alienation and ends in heroic involvement. Behind the individual life there stands the life of the times; and the movement from reformist hope to the disillusionment of the revolution betrayed is not peculiar to the seventeenth century. *Samson* joins the other works in embodying this movement and in giving us some sense of what it feels like to stand at various points along the curve of vision. It is the whole curve which comes closest to the whole truth. To say this is not necessarily to assign to *Samson* a certain place in the sequence of Milton's works. The probabilities still are that it is the last of five acts; but even if irrefutable evidence were produced that it is really the third act its aesthetic positioning should not be seriously affected.[8] Our concern is with what the totality means rather than with how it was put together in time. The effect of the latter on the former is less crucial than is sometimes supposed.

In that profound cry which finds two of its many echoes in a poem by Eliot and a novel by Koestler, the words 'dark, dark, dark' ring like blows of entombment sealing Samson into the dungeon of himself. The flaring out into 'blaze' of the same vowel that the repetitions lock in, makes us all the more keenly aware of the constriction. Light is felt as a conflagration in the darkness and the conflagration is the fire of life. The references to *Genesis* which follow are not simply an extension of the thought. The total eclipse into irrecoverable darkness sharpens the sense of utter alienation from the prime decree of being. It is as if man striving to remain himself, is being steadily forced down the ladder into nothingness. It is this knowledge which makes lines such as 'Scarce half I seem to live, dead more than half' much more than the rhetorical marking of time. At that central position on the scale of nature, the battle is fought and lost and the corner turned into ultimate defeat. As the symbol of blindness stirs in the reader's mind its connections proliferate and vivify. It is the physical wound and the cosmic deprivation. It is the will to creation reversing itself into chaos. It lives with inward sight as outward sight can live with inner blindness. It is humility confessing man's limits. It is the gift of the gods to those whom they wish to destroy.

The observations we make are true in themselves and together, yet as critical observations must, they fall short of the poem. The poem does more than move a symbol through a series of inter-animating contexts. Its deployment is so deeply ironic that dramatic irony seems to become a paradigm of providential irony. Because we insistently see more than any of the agents we are asked to reflect on ourselves as agents in a drama which means more than it can mean to us. Our more inclusive vision helps us to comprehend why we cannot quite comprehend the nature of a vision that includes all. The ways of God may be just and justifiable but only in so far as they are made known to us by a power of design that lies beyond us.

Riddling exchanges are part of the stuff of Greek drama but there is more than the usual amount of misunderstanding between the messenger, breathless with tragic tidings and Manoa, blindly eager to jump to conclusions. The eight successive stages of disclosure are considerably less than the closing up of truth to truth. Rather they show us the extent to which any combination of half truths must fall short of full knowledge.[9] Manoa is not the most far sighted of men and 'I cannot praise thy Marriage choises, Son' may well be regarded as the greatest understatement in the history of drama.[10] But it is an observation which is wide of the mark rather than absurdly short of it. Manoa's return to the theme in what is otherwise an oration of stately ferocity on how God protects his servants and punishes his enemies, is a reminder of how irrelevance can flourish even in the noonday of illumination. His combination of talkative insensitivity with bustling paternal solicitude evokes more serious failures than the generation gap but he has a talent for rubbing salt into Samson's wounds even if Samson is in the mood to call for more salt. The point is that Manoa is not alone in his short-comings. The chorus in its fluctuations between lyric commentary and Gaza gossip, has its fair share of half-understandings. It finds God's ways to be just and justifiable. A little later it finds them various and contrarious. Weighing the alternatives of 'invincible might' and saintly patience, it concludes that the latter is more probably in Samson's lot. Yet when it calls on the 'Holy One of Israel' to guide Samson to his destiny it is Samson's strength which is uppermost in its mind. His death in the temple is 'glorious' and

'Dearly-bought revenge' and Manoa confirms that there is no cause for lamentation since Samson 'Fully reveng'd', has heroically concluded a heroic life.[11] All may be best but it is perhaps not best in this way. If Samson is truly a Christian hero, the reaction to his death could be slightly less primitive. But this is how a humiliated people and a father troubled about the family name would react. Decorum is maintained,[12] certain things are not seen and it is we who have to ask ourselves about the full meaning of the play's 'true experience'.[13]

Less needs to be said at this stage, of the drama's two other main characters. Delilah in offering the temptation which Belial suggests for Christ and Satan dismisses, combines a laywer's intelligence with the kind of rhetoric that has to be called serpentine. She ends by seeing her tomb as a place of pilgrimage. It is Samson's tomb which is destined for this end.[14] Harapha measures God's champion by the etiquette of combat and finds him lamentably wanting.[15] He believes that Samson's strength is hung in his hair an error that is entirely understandable considering that Samson had believed in it himself. 58–59, 394–95, 401 and 497–98 reveal Samson's progress from the physical to the symbolic recognition,[16] while his exchange with the chorus in 541–61 reinforces the moral by pointing out how the lower teetotalism is meaningful only in conjunction with the higher abstemiousness. The bearing of these movements on inner and outer sight need not be laboured. Then as Samson comes to his resounding cry of renewal, his declaration of trust in the living God, he realizes that his strength is diffused through all of his being, hung on the single thread of his dedication to God's service. The diffused strength moves back to and satisfies an earlier, agonized question–why was seeing confined to the eye and not spread through every part of the body? As the movements of the language interlock we realize that they are much more than neatly fitted together; the play to the extent that it is a model of reality, invites us to contemplate the nature of wisdom and strength.

Pinned to his situation like Prometheus to his rock, Samson's function is to stand and find himself, while the play's other characters collide against his nature. It would be tidy to say that the misunderstandings of others define Samson to himself with increasing clarity. But Samson does not emerge like Christ, from each encounter with a deeper, more tranquil knowledge of what he is. There is blindness at the heart of him because blindness is part of the human condition. A guiding hand is needed to lead him on-ward and what he sees is what he is allowed to see.

A catalogue of Samson's 'blindnesses' could begin with his mis-understanding of where his strength really is and therefore of what it really is. It could then be pointed out that just as Christ enters history by refusing to enter it, Samson by closing various doors, opens the one door which he has to open.[17] The difference is that Samson, unlike Christ, does not know where his responses are lead-ing him. Indeed his first rejection virtually drives him to the brink of despair. We could look at the phrases which define Samson's sense of abandonment, noting how 460–62 and 631–32 are re-versed in the encounter with Harapha and how 521–22 is re-deemed in 1169–73. The play fits much into the turnings of its ironies. When Samson says that his race of glory and his race of shame are run (597–98) it is the second race that has been run and not the first. He will 'shortly be with them that rest' but it will be the rest of self-realization, not extinction. When he says 'This day will remarkable in my life / By some great act, or of my days the last' the day will in fact be remembered on both counts.[18]

The difficulty with such catalogues is that they do not come close enough to Samson the man, to the depths of his aloneness, to that 'prison within prison' that points the play's events to an inner stage, while not divesting them of their outer reality. Self-scrutiny has its part to play in Samson's renewal but that renewal is felt psycho-logically, as a movement into dejection and out of it rather than intellectually, as an advance into self-knowledge. Samson remains much less than perfect man 'Proudly secure, yet liable to fall' (the modulation of *PL* III, 99 is exactly judged), vulnerable to that self-contempt which is the other side of wounded self-esteem, liable to tear Delilah limb from limb with what must be judged a scarcely Christian ferocity, and, in his exchanges with the officer, conscious of the insult to his dignity, as much as of the abusing of his 'con-secrated gift'. It is because we can touch his stubborn imperfec-tions that we rejoice in his recovery, knowing that his restoration can also be ours.

To say that much of the drama of *Samson* is directed to an interior stage is to deal in one way with Johnson's objection that the play lacks a middle.[19] Johnson might have remembered an observation by Dryden: 'every alteration or crossing of a design, every new-sprung passion, and turn of it, is a part of the action, and much the noblest, except we conceive nothing to be action till they come to blows; as if the painting of the hero's mind were not more properly the poet's work than the strength of his body'.[20] Milton in his preface to *Samson* holds that the tragic effect arises from 'a kind of delight, stirr'd up by reading or seeing those passions [pity and fear] well imitated.' Aristotle on the other hand, sees catharsis as the consequence of the imitation of an *action* possessing certain characteristics.[21] Given the difference of emphasis it is well to examine that 'solid and treatable smoothnesse' which according to Milton should set out and describe 'the wily suttleties and refluxes of man's thought from within'.[22]

'Smoothness' is a word more applicable than it seems to be, for *Samson* has about it a sculptured quality in which great stresses are both contained and composed. Even the flow of the poem has a monumental deliberation with the carved cadences and the spirals of its ironies controlling it so that the forward movement seems both to be finding itself and filling out a mould. As often with Milton, the achievement is more than itself; what we see both in the unfolding of the work and in its typical contours, is self-realization as the means of the great design.

It is right that so much in *Samson* should grow out of the first soliloquy. The poem reaches out of the cage that is the man. There is before all and within all, the symbol of blindness that controls not only the poem's movement but its sense of the nature of meaning itself. There is also the wounded self-respect which is the mark of Samson's humanity, the anger of the hero turned inward against the hero's betrayal of his trust. The wheel of fortune image which the Chorus uses is anticipated in the fierce reversal of the liberator become prisoner, 'Eyeless in Gaza at the mill with slaves'. The momentum of involvement is designed to pull the reader closer to the vortex but significantly, it is twice held back. 'Let me not rashly call in doubt / Divine Prediction' and 'peace, I must not quarell with the will / Of highest dispensation' look forward in obvious ways, but the phrases also put a brake on the emotion, holding it adequately short of self-destruction. The note of responsibility is also struck with a resonance which those who read Milton should have long since learned to recognize. 'Whom have I to complain of but myself?' opens the way to Samson's more contrite admission before Manoa ('Sole Author I, sole cause') which reproduces the very accent of Adam's and Eve's repentances.

When the Chorus enters, invoking the wheel of fortune (it is later to argue that Samson's punishment goes beyond what the wheel allows)[23] we are not really meant to ruminate on the fickle state of man and the downfall of kings and princes. If the mighty are brought low by their blindness the low can also be raised; the play turns upon this double movement, applied to both Samson and the Philistines. Samson replies to the Chorus's ceremonial cadences with 'Am I not sung and proverbed for a Fool'? Once again, the subject of self-contempt is the disproportion between body and mind but the accents are those of declamation, of failure castigated before the community rather than in the solitude of the self.

The Chorus warns Samson not to tax 'divine disposal' when he has not done so and then proceeds to tax that disposal itself. The inward promptings which led Samson to his marriages have come to nothing and '*Israel* still serves with all his sons'. Samson's reply makes it clear that his sense of responsibility does not mean that he is casting himself as scapegoat in numb acceptance of the failings of others. Nations must assess themselves as sternly as individuals; to nations brought low by their vices, the cost of freedom will appear excessive and the leader will be spurned because of the demands he makes on his people.

The Chorus which has already sidestepped Samson's reproach, picks up his words on 'God's propos'd deliverance' to affirm that the ways of God are just and justifiable even though they conflict with law and seem to stand above reason. That these observations should be made in relation to Samson's marriages, is evidence that the vision of the Chorus is less than inclusive. The torment of the man before it is a far deeper basis for the doubting of God's justice, as the Chorus itself will later come to recognize. Meanwhile a tension has been set up between inscrutable omniscience and the perpetual passion of finite man to scrutinize. Those who seek to 'explain' God are like the fallen angels on Hell's hill of philosophy, but though we can say 'Down Reason then at least vain reasoning down' the naked, unmastered movement of experience will drive us to the questions which we seek to avoid.

When Manoa enters, Samson must face his first radical testing. It is tempting to arrange the three confrontations in an increasing order of difficulty, to see them as steps in a movement of regeneration, to correlate them with Christ's temptations in *Paradise Regained,* or to study them as a series of therapeutic shocks nicely adjusted to the state of the patient.[24] Perhaps the movement out of darkness into dimness is more uncertain and groping than these diagrams suggest. When Christ's inner voices draw him into the desert he says

And now by some strong motion I am led
Into this Wilderness, to what intent
I learn not yet, perhaps I need not know;
For what concerns my knowledge God reveals.   *PR* I, 290–93

Samson cannot see as clearly as Christ. He remains unfaltering in his faith but his faith is primarily the warrior's faith that the god of his people will triumph and triumph all the more decisively without that broken reed into which Samson has converted himself. His patience is his capacity to accept the onslaught of justice, without questioning that justice in the intensity of the onslaught. It is the Chorus not Samson, which comes to doubt God's ways. Samson merely petitions for extinction as the logical end of treason to the true God.

In Samson's responses to Manoa these accents are clear and dignified. Manoa begins by contrasting Samson's glorious past with his ignoble present. It is the third time this subject has been dwelt on but the third voice is significantly different from the others. The questioning of God's ways which follows and on which the Chorus is later to elaborate, is dismissed by Samson's measured acceptance of responsibility and by his passionate restatement of a familiar Miltonic theme–his external slavery is but an inadequate expression of the internal servitude into which he delivered himself. Manoa's response is typically unadjusted to the event. Samson had pleaded 'Divine impulsion' for those marriages and the matter is one which Manoa will not discuss. Having questioned God's ways and the reliability of Samson's inner voices Manoa goes on to insist that Samson's worst achievement is to have exposed God to sacrilege.

So *Dagon* shall be magnifi'd, and God,
Besides whom is no God, compar'd with Idols,
Disglorifi'd, blasphem'd, and had in scorn
By th' Idolatrous rout admidst thir wine;   440–43

It is a cruel thrust and Samson replies quietly, admitting the truth of the accusation, taking the blame unflinchingly on himself and pointing out that the way lies open for God to assert his power now that his errant champion is part of the scrap heap. The dignity of the response is such that Manoa sees for the first time before him the chained prophet rather than the wayward son.

Manoa with his talent for changing the subject, now reveals that he is negotiating with the Philistines for Samson's ransom. Samson prefers to stand and suffer. It is psychologically just that he should want to do so, now that the extent of his offence has been laid open by the cutting edge of Manoa's inconsequentiality. Remembering 'Am I not sung and proverbed for a Fool' Samson recognizes that a fool's garrulity is a social offence provoking no more than social ostracism. To desecrate God's covenant by loquacity is to invite utter alienation from God. Manoa meets his son's resolution with skill, pointing out that contrition is one thing and self-flagellation another, and that Samson may well be 'For self-offence, more than for God offended'. It is a subtle contention, particularly to an audience interested in the theological issue of Samson's 'suicide' and Samson is unable to meet the contention head on. Instead he enacts once again amid the torments of the mind's maladies, his desecration of his sacred trust. Passion rises in the language and 'Fearless of danger, like a petty God' is the kind of phrase that gives substance to Manoa's warning.[25] The point is that Samson is not quite a saint. He is a tragic hero who will accept the just accusation even if the force of the accusation breaks him. It is close to breaking him now.

We must ask ourselves more insistently why the ransom is refused. On the periphery of the language it can be argued that only Christ can negotiate Samson's ransom. In the immediate facts of the situation there is the hero's bleak, fierce knowledge that death in chains is better than death by the fireside. But there is also a blind rightness in Samson's fortitude. Manoa is not Satan, but deliverance if it comes must come in some other way. Samson has broken a covenant but he remains ineradicably loyal to its author. It is in the nature of that loyalty to sweep aside alternatives, to cry out to God for condemnation or release.

The play has now come to the depths of its own abyss. Samson's 'sense of heaven's desertion' is embodied in a tormented petition for death the lacerative quality of which writhes its way through the friction of the language. The Chorus stands behind Samson, challenging the justice which he himself accepts. Reason can be assigned its place but the voice of anguish will continue to ask 'why'? The turning point–and the extremity of the situation means that there must be a turning point–is marked by the singularly ornate simile that heralds Delilah's entrance. As a relieving simile where relief is needed, it is entitled to its digressiveness but to defend its propriety we can do more than point out that since Dagon is a sea idol, Delilah can legitimately be likened to a ship. What is actually involved is an ironic culmination of Samson's earlier comparison of himself to a vessel 'gloriously rigg'd' and the Chorus in 1044–45 continues to keep the image in mind.

Delilah's encounter with Samson is the longest of the three, thereby allowing the academic wit to suggest that *Samson Agonistes* has too much of a middle. Respect for symmetry is one reason for the length of the episode. In seeking to discover Samson's secret, Delilah prevailed only with the fourth attempt. There must be four efforts and four failures to make it evident that history will not be repeated. Delilah takes her time over these matters and so does the poem. In addition the blandishments of Belial strike at the root of Samson's weakness just as the long temptation of the kingdoms seek to strike at the pivot of Christ's destiny. If Samson is to qualify for his future he must demonstrate his freedom from his past. He does not do so with complete security 'My Wife, my Traytress, let her not come near me' is indicative of an animal tension lacking in the discussions with Manoa and the Chorus. If Samson can forgive Delilah it is only because of the detachment that distance (and the additional distance of blindness) gives him.

In between, Delilah strikes many poses. She is weakness calling for recognition by Samson's weakness, the amorous mistress coveting Samson as love's prisoner, the distraught wife torn between personal loyalty and civic duty and finally the patriot verging upon the martyr. Blindness is not without its advantages she argues, in offering Samson peace in the cradle rather than peace by the fireside. Samson to use Delilah's words, is 'implacable' and 'deaf', a raging tempest to Delilah's sumptuous ship. When she is gone the Chorus, presumably all male, indulges itself in anti-feminist comments of elephantine levity. The hierarchic principle may stand behind the sallies but the best we can say of the wit is that it is not out of character.

Milton's preface declares that Tragedy like Samson, has fallen from great heights to the 'lowest pitch of abject fortune'. In accounting for the 'small esteem, or rather infamy' with which the form was regarded, Milton blames primarily 'the Poet's error of intermixing Comic stuff with Tragic sadness and gravity; or introducing brutal and vulgar persons . . . brought in without discretion, corruptly to gratifie the people'. If Harapha is indeed the Plautine braggart, Milton's own practice is scarcely in harmony with this ringing reproof.[26] But a man's discomfiture can cause laughter without his necessarily being made of comic stuff; the laughter can arise from relief that a threat has been dispelled and that righteousness though shackled, can prevail over raw force. To see Harapha as a 'trivial and vulgar' person is to divest this episode of much of its significance and to broaden into crude comedy the witticisms that adorn Delilah's exit.

Samson's responses to Manoa brought him to the precipice. He has moved away from the dangerous edge drawn by his own torment and the deep doubtings of the Chorus. In repudiating Delilah he purged away part of himself, the stubborn snare of his sensuality. In Harapha, he faces himself once more. He does not prove himself the stronger of two contestants. Rather he proves the incompleteness of strength, 'Proudly secure, yet liable to fall'.

Recurring recognitions bind Milton's work into its characteristic and engrossing unity. Samson, facing Harapha, has links with Christ on the pinnacle. Both are in situations of peril. Both act through trust in the living God and by affirming their identities under assault. Both dissipate the force of a hostile environment by inviolably being and maintaining themselves. Preceding Christ and Samson is the Lady, 'Surpriz'd by unjust force', retaliating not with 'Spells' and 'Forbidden Arts', but by that simple righteousness which forces Comus to realize that her words are 'Set off by some superior power'.

In the depths of the play's descent into darkness Samson felt himself cast aside by God and had to console himself with the bitter knowledge that the contest was wholly between God and Dagon. He implored God's pardon but saw no reason to seek the prolonging of a useless life. He petitioned for a death which was no more than extinction. In challenging Harapha, Samson speaks ringingly as 'the power of *Israel's* God'. It is Harapha, speaking in more than one way as Samson's past, who puts it to Samson that God has cast him aside; and it is Samson who rejects the view he once held, moving away from a darkness he had to live through

Samson Agonistes

admitting that God's punishment is just, but knowing that pardon may lie beyond the punishment. Death still looms on the horizon and he who brings it is Samson's 'speediest friend'. But death now means more than the snuffing out of the man.

> Yet so it may fall out, because thir end
> Is hate, not help to me, it may with mine
> Draw thir own ruin who attempt the deed.   1265–67

These carefully positioned reversals measure the play's upward movement and sustain it so that we are aware of it not simply as a design but as a dramatic experience reviewing and reshaping itself. As the Chorus confirms the movement with 'How comely it is and how reviving' we are meant to subscribe to the reigning sense of elation. But we must also remember that Christ who defined similar objectives to himself in strikingly similar language, decided instead

> By winning words to conquer willing hearts,
> And make perswasion do the work of fear;   PR I, 222–23

Samson is not Christ, but we put it too simply by saying that he should be measured and found wanting by Christ's example.[27] He is meant to speak to us out of his flawed nature and mixed destiny. He is never completely emancipated from passion. His patience remains close to heroic endurance. His faith is primarily that men and nations bring ruin on themselves and that God will triumph despite the fallibility of his agents. He is not perfect man but he is Miltonic man, a creature of error, dignity and blindness, descended from the hill of Christ's detachment. His reinstatement as God's champion conveys more than an individual act of forgiveness.

Giants are not notable for their interest in personal hygiene but Harapha in refusing to do combat with Samson, points out that he needs 'much washing to be touch'd'. The exterior grime is of course meant to remind us that matters are otherwise with the inner man. The officer carries on this contrast, offering Samson a new set of clothes before his soul is sullied. Samson's answer is brief, precise and at this stage no more than doctrinal:

> Our Law forbids at thir Religious Rites
> My presence; for that cause I cannot come.   1320–21

As the officer persists and Samson responds to the insult to himself the 'cannot' hardens to 'will not' and the wave of poetry rises with the anger. When the officer leaves and Samson defends his attitude against the cautions of the Chorus the energy of resentment flows out and surrounds the insult to God rather than the humiliation of the hero. The dramatic process is tactful but clear and what it points to is all the more significant now that the catastrophe is approaching.

Ordinary men live longer by learning when to yield and the chorus knows that Leviathan is more difficult to deal with than Goliath. It points out to Samson that if he grinds bread for the Philistines he might as well perform at their circuses to which Samson replies with a nice observation on the limits of civil power. He had previously told Delilah of the law of nature and nations. Despite the fairly strict observance of *Decorum Personae*, it is apparent that this particular Samson has done some of his thinking in the sixteen forties.

The Chorus, agreeing implicitly that this is a matter of conscience which lies beyond the civil power, suggests that a man is not responsible for acts contrary to conscience, which are done under duress. Samson replies that he is not yet under duress but adds that God if it suits his purpose, can permit the faithful to be present at 'Idolatrous Rites'. The possibility is thrown in against the tide but a little later Samson is to feel those 'rouzing motions' which make it evident that the tide has suddenly turned.

Some reflection on what is happening is called for here. Samson in encountering Delilah, has divested himself of his weakness and in encountering Harapha, has discovered the true meaning of his strength. In refusing Manoa's peace and Delilah's peace he has qualified himself, without fully knowing it, to wage war as God's champion. He has lived through his past and by reproportioning it has repossessed it, setting his affections 'in right tune'. The inward promptings which came to him once, now come to him again as part of that deed of possession. This time they come to him creatively. The earlier promptings had set aside the law. The new 'rouzing motions' set aside the law, the urgings of conscience and the passion of the warrior for his cause. Everything is shortly to be reduced to order; but before the parts find their position in the whole we are being advised that the ways of God are inscrutable and that we walk them in blindness.

When the officer returns, Samson's capitulation is ostentatiously abject. The dramatic change of attitude puts it to us that cringing realism and lion-like defiance are both equally distant from the truth. Nevertheless, the reversal is sufficiently disturbing to have evoked further explanatory comment – including a sophisticated discussion of the meaning of the word *Agonistes*.[28] It is evident that Samson is playing a part; but to understand what his performance means we must listen attentively to the phrasing of his surrender.

Masters commands come with a power resistless
To such as owe them absolute subjection;
And for a life who will not change his purpose?   1404–6

If we take the master as God, the resistless power as the force of providence taking possession of its instrument, the absolute subjection as man's acknowledgement of his dependence on the divine, the life as life after death and the change of purpose as the acceptance of destiny, every detail of the 'capitulation' locks itself into an inner meaning. If this reading is correct this is the solitary point in the play at which Milton speaks of an after-life and that he should do so only indirectly is evidence of the strict limits within which he confines his demonstration.[29] The play because of the way in which it is shaped, reaches out beyond itself; the reaching out is all the more persuasive because the work seems to have been formed independently of what it annexes. At the same time the exterior relationship is not one which every reader is obliged to adopt and some flexibility can be permitted in making the link.

When the higher power invades Samson he only knows what the next step has to be. He does not know what it means or where it is to lead him. To trust is to surrender in blindness even to the point of denying the apparent self, the natural instinct of the hero for combat. Both in lines 1388–89 and in 1426 Samson sees only part of the whole in terms of alternatives which the final resolution is to synthesize. In between, the tenor of his parting speech suggests that he anticipates a death in which an angry mob will tear him to pieces. If he is to be crushed at the circus rather than worn down at the mill, he will accept his destiny. The obedience in darkness, the truth only half-glimpsed, is surely significantly different from the six exultant lines of *double entendre* with which Samson prefaces the last deed of his life.[30]

In speaking of tragedy Milton's reference is not merely to the two emotions made famous by Aristotle but to 'pity and fear, or terror

. . . and such like passions.'[31] Tragedy seeks not to eliminate or to purify these emotions, but 'to temper and reduce them to just measure'. This is a view of catharsis which is still respectable[32] but it is also of a piece with Milton's firm conviction that all things in the created order are good to the extent that they serve that order and its ends. The end should not be suppression but re-proportioning and reorientation. If poetry is 'of power beside the office of a pulpit' it is partly because of its capacity to 'allay the passions and perturbations of the mind and set the affections in right tune' so that they join again in the solemn music of things.[33]

The passions are reduced to 'just measure' by what Milton describes as a 'kind of delight stirr'd up' by reading or seeing them 'well imitated'. Presumably what is imitated is the passions not only in their agitation but also in their subsidence. We can go further and say that the quietening effect arises from depicting the passage through agitation to subsidence and by involving the spectator's or reader's mind in that movement. Subsidence can come about from the knowledge that ripeness is all, from the fierce consolation of the 'heroic cry in the midst of despair',[34] from the sheer force of poetry enabling us to live with the blind energy of things. It can also come from the recognition that there is an order to which all things are responsible even if we do not and cannot see all of that order. This is Milton's way though it is not the typical way of tragedy.

The Chorus in *Samson* is neither spectator nor actor, standing somewhere between them in detachment, so that the reader interprets an interpretation that is continually reformulating itself. Nevertheless, the Chorus in its own way marks out the play's milestones. It begins with the affirmation of order in the presence of suffering ('Just are the ways of God'), is driven by the impact of that suffering to a radical questioning of the ways of providence ('God of our Fathers what is man') and ends with a renewal of belief in design ('All is best though we oft doubt'). Like *Lycidas*, the play is a controlled turbulence in which an equilibrium is deliberately imperilled so that a richer, more inclusive equilibrium can be achieved through the process of disorientation.[35] 'Peace', 'consolation' and 'calm of mind' are brought about by the cohesive strength of a 'great event' that illuminates the darkness, displaying in the movement of the drama, a microcosm of the force of design in reality. This is not the precarious calm of emotion silenced by its own intensity. It is the calm of understanding, the 'peace of thought' which Adam knows on the hill.[36] It is emotion stilled within the circumference of reason and reason knowing the just bounds of its circumference. In the nature of Milton's accomplishment, catharsis must imply not simply an emotional harmonization but the restoration of understanding to its proper place in the soul's government and the rediscovery of the image of God in man. *Samson* is a work of art complete and compelling in its own right but it also takes its place in a view of life which like the poem itself, was created and held against the assault of adversity.

Milton never accepted a form without seeking to recreate it. His typical method of recreation was to stretch taut the decorum of the form against the tension of its animating forces so that its Christian potentialities were illuminated and realized. *Samson Agonistes* is in many ways his most daring experiment. More royalist than the king in its insistence on the unities, it is strikingly revolutionary in nearly everything else. It deals not with the downfall, but with the restoration of the hero. If pity is the emotion it initially arouses, it refines that pity into awe. Reversal and recognition are involved in its catastrophe but the passage from ignorance to knowledge and the difference between intention and actuality expose not fate, but the powerful presence of reason in design. The turning point comes not through *hybris*, but through self-assessment. And the catastrophe is creative not destructive, recasting experience in the proportions of truth. We are invited to contemplate *Samson* as tragedy and as more than tragedy. The question which hangs over it is whether it is tragedy at all. Can tragedy be present where there is nothing for tears, where all that happens is shown to be for the best? Can it exist where there is not merely poetic but providential justice? There will be more than one answer to these questions and perhaps the best answer is that we should look at the work instead of struggling to catch it in a definition. However Milton did say that his work was a tragedy 'according to ancient rule and best example'. If *Samson* stands at the boundary of tragedy rather than beyond it it is because awe and even dread before the infinite are aroused by the play's compelling movement towards a situation in which the providence of God requires the death of the hero.

'The hidden ways of his providence we adore and search not' is a remark of Milton which has already been quoted. *Samson Agonistes* takes up the thought.

All is best though we oft doubt,
What th' unsearchable dispose
Of highest wisdom brings about,
And ever best found in the close.　　　　1745–48

The progress of the English language has not dealt happily with the Chorus's description of God as 'uncontroulable' and 'interminable'. If we accept usages that were becoming old-fashioned even in the seventeenth century it will be apparent that one purpose of these epithets is to place the divine beyond the reach of the human. If man understands God or is able to enter into a relationship with him it is only to the extent that God has made available certain ways of understanding or certain forms of relationship. The Law is such a form but even the Law can be set aside by inner promptings, God's interior covenant with the chosen individual. *Samson Agonistes* powerfully argues this thesis with its intricate use of the symbol of blindness and with its confined, stark setting beyond which gathers the force of the unknowable. Within that unknowable lies not chaos, but the infinite design, illuminated occasionally by the 'great event'. Man confronts that design, preparing himself to see it by the exercise of responsibility and intelligence, but never able to comprehend it fully. As he qualifies himself and as the lightning flashes he knows something of the part he has to play.

Notes

CHAPTER 1

1 'Tradition and the Individual Talent', *Selected Essays* (London, 1934), p21.
2 'John Ford', *Selected Essays*, p203. In *For Lancelot Andrewes* (London, 1928) pp29–30, the earlier view seems dominant: 'Andrewes's emotion is purely contemplative; it is not personal, it is wholly evoked by the object of contemplation, to which it is adequate; his emotion is wholly contained in and explained by its object ... Donne is a "personality" in a sense in which Andrewes is not: his sermons, one feels, are a "means of self-expression".'
3 *The Spectator*, CXLVIII (1932), pp360–1.
4 'W. B. Yeats', *On Poetry and Poets* (London, 1957), pp252–62.
5 'What is Minor Poetry?', *On Poetry and Poets*, pp49–50
6 'George Herbert' in *British Writers and Their Work No 4*,

ed. J. W. Robinson (Lincoln, 1964), p63.
7 See *W. B. Yeats: A Critical Introduction* (London, 1965), pp188–92.
8 'Little Gidding', *Collected Poems 1909–62* (New York, 1965), p208.
9 For a fuller statement see 'The Overwhelming Question' in *T. S. Eliot The Man and His Work*, ed. Allen Tate (London, 1967), pp363–81.
10 Complete Prose Works of John Milton (New Haven, 1952), Vol. 1, pp807–23. Hereafter cited as *Complete Prose Works*.
11 *Ibid.*, pp813–14.
12 *Ibid.*, pp814–15.
13 *Ibid.*, pp815–16.
14 See Tillyard, *The Miltonic Setting* (Cambridge, 1938), pp168–204; Grierson *Milton and Wordsworth* (Cambridge, 1937), p72; M. M. Ross *Milton's Royalism* (Ithaca, 1943), pp98–9; and L. A. Sasek, 'Milton's Patriotic

Epic', HLQ, **XX** (1959), pp1–14. The basis is the peroration of 'The Second Defence' (*Complete Prose Works* IV, p685).

15 *The Passion*, 13–14. It may be noted in passing that the Hercules-Christ association is crucial in Sonnet **XXIII** where the rescue by force prefigures Christ's rescue by love, also prefigured in the Mosaic ceremony.

16 By including the poem, Milton like Fletcher, could claim to have written four poems on Christ's victories.

17 Hanford, 'The Temptation Motive in Milton', *SP*, XV (1918), pp176–94; Watkins, *An Anatomy of Milton's Verse* (Baton Rouge, 1955), pp87–146.

18 *Yet Once More* (New York, 1954).

19 The contrast exemplifies with considerable local force the following observation by Thomas Greene: 'The first quality of the epic imagination is extensiveness, the impulse to extend its own luminosity in ever widening circles . . . Tragic space, on the other hand, closes in to hedge and confine. It permits at best fragments of knowledge, clearings of light, islands of felicity. The space beyond the clearings remains shadowy and unknowable.' (*The Descent from Heaven*, New Haven, 1962, pp9–10).

20 *Comus*, 194–9, 330–9, 348. Quotations from Milton's poetry throughout this book are from the Columbia text.

21 See *PL* XI, 307–14. The link does not seem accidental.

22 *Comus* 662–4; *Lycidas* 64–76; *PR* I, 142–3; *PL* II, 358–62.

23 *Fourth Century*, Meditation 76; *On the Dignity of Man*, 3.

24 *The Renaissance Philosophy of Man*, edited by Ernst Cassirer, Paul Oskar Kristeller, and John Herman Randall Jr. (Chicago, 1948), p219.

25 *Complete Prose Works* II, 527; *PL* III, 108. For the classical Christian view see e.g. *Comus* 68–9, 525–30.

CHAPTER 2

1 See e.g. David Daiches, *Milton* (London, 1957), p48.

2 In 1645 the words 'Compos'd 1629.' follow the title. These words are omitted in 1673. The only other English poems

dated, are *Psalms* 114 and 136 described as 'don by the Author at fifteen years old.'

3 In 1645, the Ode is followed by *Psalms* 114 and 136 which affirm the power and providence of God. Then follows a poem of suffering (*The Passion*) succeeded by one celebrating the restoration of order (*On Time*). A second poem of suffering (*Upon the Circumcision*) is then followed by a second poem of restoration (*At a Solemn Musick*). This attractively neat scheme is not decisive since it is not preserved in 1673. *On the Death of a Fair Infant* is inserted into the sequence and it is clear from the *errata* that the *Vacation Exercise* was intended to be inserted.

4 *Comus*, 720–1.

5 The stanza is Milton's creation, though Fletcher (*The Intellectual Development of John Milton*, Vol. II, Urbana, 1961, pp496–7) cites a partial Italian precedent. Louis L. Martz notes that the use of three and five stressed lines in combination is found in many Elizabethan songs. By allowing the last line to swell out into a Spenserian Alexandrine 'Milton draws his poem out of the realm of popular song into the larger area of the poet's predestined goals'. *The Lyric and Dramatic Milton*, ed. Joseph H. Summers (New York, 1965), pp25–7. No English poet after Milton appears to have used the form. A stanza form that is created for and dies with the poetic occasion is of course, characteristic of much metaphysical writing.

6 For further comments on the appropriateness of the form to the poem see the *Poems of Dr. John Milton*, ed. Cleanth Brooks and John Hardy (New York, 1951), p104.

7 See *Metaphysical Lyrics and Poems of the Seventeenth Century*, ed. H. J. C. Grierson (London, 1931), *Intro.* p xlviii; Rosemond Tuve *Images and Themes in Five Poems by Milton* (Camb., Mass., 1962), p39; Greene, *The Descent from Heaven*, pp153, 157.

8 Broadbent's objections to Tuve (*The Living Milton*, London, 1960, pp12 ff.) are not misdirected.

9 See Austin Warren, *Richard Crashaw* (Ann Arbor, 1957), p144.

10 Crashaw, *Nativity Hymn*; Beaumont, *Psyche*, VII, 156.

11 See D. C. Allen, *The Harmonious Vision* (Baltimore, 1954), p29.

12 The difference is noted by
Louis L. Martz, *The Poetry
of Meditation* (New Haven,
1962), pp166–7.

13 Douglas Bush, *John Milton*
(New York, 1964), p36;
Mahood, *Poetry and
Humanism* (New Haven,
1950), p174 and Tuve's
words of caution, *Images and
Themes*, p42. It might be
added by way of further
caution that the account of
the poem's structure which
follows in this chapter goes
well with the view of
mannerism suggested by Roy
Daniells (*Milton Mannerism
and Baroque*, Toronto, 1963,
pp6–18).

14 *Complete Prose Works* 1,
pp751–2. Perhaps this
should have been the lady's
answer to Comus.

15 See Roy Daniells, *Milton
Mannerism and Baroque*,
pp87–99.

16 See Stapleton 'Milton and
the New Music' *UTQ*,
XXIII (1953–54) reprinted
in *Milton: Modern Essays in
Criticism*, ed. A. E. Barker
(New York, 1965), p39.

17 Lowry Nelson Jr. in *Baroque
Lyric Poetry* (New Haven,
1961), pp51–62 perceptively
examines Milton's
manipulation of tenses. Less
alert critics should beware of
regarding the historic present

as a sign of the Baroque lest
Damon Runyon emerge as a
master of Baroque style.

18 A. E. Barker, 'The Pattern of
Milton's Nativity Ode' *UTQ*,
X (1940–41), p177.

19 The phrase is of course, in
immediate contrast to the
death on the Cross. But in a
larger context it suggests that
the consequences of the divine
intervention in history have
only begun and will not
grow to completion until the
last judgement. 165–7 is in
accord with such a reading.

20 Christ is described as the
'Prince of Light' eclipsing the
sun's 'inferior flame' (a
popular conceit which the
pun makes almost
unavoidable). In
Animadversions Christ is
described as 'the ever-
begotten light, and perfect
Image of the Father'
(*Complete Prose Works* 1,
p705). This is in keeping with
Donne's description of Christ
as 'essential light' as distinct
from the natural light of
reason and the supernatural
light of faith and grace
(*Sermon preached on Christmas
day 1621*). For discussion of
the traditions behind Milton's
light symbolism see in
particular, Merritt Y.
Hughes, *Ten Perspectives on
Milton* (New Haven, 1965),

pp63–103. The false gods, in contrast, are uniformly described in terms of darkness. 'Twilight Shade', 'midnight plaint', 'Temples dim', 'shadows dred', 'profoundest Hell', 'Anthems dark' and 'dusky eyn' (an affectation indulged in because rhyme to 'twine' was needed) are typically evocative.

21 *Complete Prose Works* 1, p817.

22 See Chapter 7 below.

23 Tuve, p56.

24 See the editions by Hanford, Bush, Hughes and Broadbent in *The Living Milton*, p24.

25 Browne in describing nature as the art of God, is playing with the idea. For Tasso's statement of it see *Literary Criticism: Plato to Dryden*, ed. A. H. Gilbert (New York, 1940), pp292, 300. Further discussion can be found in Robert M. Durling, *The Figure of the Poet in Renaissance Epic* (Camb, Mass., 1965), pp124–6.

26 *Job* 26. 7 is the primary source. Hughes also cites Ovid, *Met* I, 12 and Gilbert's citation of Galileo's *Dialogue*. That the idea is not uncommon is apparent from its appearance in as unlikely a place as Castiglione's Courtier: 'Behold the constitution of this great

fabric of the world . . . the round heaven, adorned with so many divine lamps, and the earth in the center, surrounded by the elements and sustained by its own weight.' Trans. Charles S. Singleton (New York, 1959), p343.

27 *PL* III, 99.

28 *PL* XII, 539.

29 See in particular McColley, 'The Epic Catalogue of *Paradise Lost*', *ELH*, IV, pp180–9, and in refutation, Whiting, *Milton's Literary Milieu* (Chapel Hill, 1939), pp177–217.

30 *PL* I, 356–75; Lactantius, *Divine Institutes*, ii, 1, 3, 15–19; iv. 27; Tuve, pp66–7 cites Augustine, Tertullian and Minucius Felix. See also McColley *Paradise Lost* (Chicago, 1940) p104. Hooker, *Ecclesiastical Polity* 1, IV, 3 is a widely known statement of the idea.

31 *Complete Prose Works* 1, p817.

32 Such images find their climax in the 'infernal jail' in which the powers of darkness are imprisoned. Again, it is noteworthy, that they 'troop' to the jail instead of being driven there.

33 The catalogue in *PL* dwells at length on the territorial jurisdiction of each deity.

This is part of the epic ritual but it also gives the 'general relapses' a certain specificity by rooting them in time, place and corruption.

34 A similar view is taken by C. A. Patrides, *The Phoenix and the Ladder* (Berkeley, 1964), pp59–61.

35 *Divine Institutes*, VII, 24.

36 *Institutes*, VII, 15.

37 For a fuller discussion see Ernest Lee Tuveson, *Millennium and Utopia* (New York, 1964), pp1–70; Norman Cohn, *The Pursuit of the Millennium* (New York, 1961), pp1–21; William Haller, *Foxe's Book of Martyrs*

and the Elect Nation (London, 1963), pp130–7.

38 Haller, *passim*; Fixler, *Milton and the Kingdoms of God* (London, 1964), pp13–45, 98–101.

39 Tuve, p68.

40 Daiches (*Milton*, p67) and Bush note that the lines suggest the infant Hercules strangling the serpents. The association of Christ with Hercules is made both in *The Passion* and in *Paradise Regained*. Satan is linked to Typhon in *PL* I, 197–200, a link which Hughes notes, is traced back by Conti to Theodorus.

CHAPTER 3

1 Charles Williams, Intro. to *The English Poems of John Milton* (London, 1946), p x.

2 Milton: *Poems and Selected Prose*, ed. M. Nicolson (New York, 1962), p6.

3 *Ikon: John Milton and the Modern Critics* (Ithaca, 1955), pp1–34.

4 References to Milton's poetry follow the text and lineation of the Columbia edition. 166–9 in the text generally adopted, appear as 166–8 in the Columbia edition and the lineations cease to coincide at this point.

5 See e.g. Douglas Bush's edition of the poetry (New York, 1965).

6 *Milton's Poetical Works. Facsimile Edition*, edited by H. F. Fletcher, Vol. 1 (Urbana, 1943), p633.

7 W. B. Yeats, *Collected Poems* (London, 1950), p57.

8 W. B. Yeats, *Collected Plays* (London, 1952), p693.

9 *Ibid.*, pp693–4.

10 Helen H. Vendler, *Yeats's Vision and the Later Plays* (Camb., Mass., 1963), p238.

11 Tuve, *Images and Themes in Five Poems by Milton*, p116.

12 G. M. Trevelyan, *English Social History* (London, 1942), p238; John Arthos *A Masque Presented at Ludlow Castle* (Ann Arbor, 1954), p15.
13 Sonnet XXII; *PL* I, 497.
14 Ben Jonson, *Works*, ed. C. H. Herford and Percy Simpson, Vol. II (Oxford, 1925), p250.
15 Welsford, *The Court Masque* (Cambridge, 1927), p320.
16 Herford and Simpson, pp304–9; Welsford, pp316–18; Allen, *The Harmonious Vision*, p31 and in rejoinder Adams, pp2–3. Gretchen Finney in '*Comus*, Drama per Musica,' *SP* XXXVII (1940), pp482–500 suggests a different *genre*.
17 This is often regarded as a characteristic of the Baroque writer. See e.g. Austin Warren, *Richard Crashaw* (Ann Arbor, 1957), p65; Molly M. Mahood, *Poetry and Humanism* (New Haven, 1950), pp135–8; Frank J. Warnke [Ed.], *European Metaphysical Poetry* (New Haven, 1961), pp1–2 and Roy Daniells, *Milton Mannerism and Baroque*, p54.
18 Herford and Simpson, Vol. II, p250.
19 Emile Haun, 'An Inquiry into the Genre of *Comus*', *Studies in Honour of Walter Clyde Curry* (Nashville, 1954), pp221–39.
20 Herford and Simpson, Vol. II, p309.
21 Rosemond Tuve (pp111–21, 153–6) is particularly sensitive in perceiving how Milton uses these propensities.
22 Tillyard, *Studies in Milton* (London, 1954); Woodhouse, 'The Argument of Milton's *Comus*', *UTQ* XI (1941), pp47–71 and '*Comus* Once More', *UTQ*, XIX (1950), pp218–23.
23 See however *Milton*, ed. Maynard Mack (Englewood Cliffs, 1961), *Intro.*, p8 and Northrop Frye, *The Return of Eden* (Toronto, 1965), p43.
24 For Comus's long history from Philostratus to Ben Jonson, see Madsen, 'The Idea of Nature in Milton's Poetry', *Yale Studies in English* Vol. CXXXVIII (New Haven, 1958), pp185–8. Madsen finds some basis for Comus's descent from Bacchus but none for the full parentage. See also Arthos, pp53–8n.
25 Augustine (*Confessions*, X, 36) speaks of corporeal light in contrast to heavenly light, as 'a tempting and dangerous sweetness, like a sauce spread over the life of this world for its blind lovers.' Quotations from the *Confessions* are in Rex Warner's translation (New York, 1963).

There are other significant contrasts, beside the two that have been mentioned. Comus assumes a disguise for purposes of deception while the Attendant Spirit does so for a beneficent end. Several other differentiations are cited by Madsen (p197). Such contrasts are in keeping with Frye's view (p23) that parody is a mode of the demonic and look forward to the far more comprehensive structure of parody in *PL*.

26 In *Mythology and the Renaissance Tradition* (1963 edn.), p274, Bush notes that 'incomplete metamorphosis' and 'unconsciousness of degradation' are found in *Orlando Furioso*, VI, 60–6. Hughes in 'Spenser's Acrasia and the Circe of the Renaissance', *JHI* IV (1943), pp383–6, notes more than one argument in favour of life on the animal level with suggestions that beasts share in the rational nature of man. Milton is of course, putting the idea to more advanced use and the reference to perfect misery is deeply evocative of what is to come in his work.

27 *The Complete Poetry of Henry Vaughan*, ed. French Fogle (New York, 1964), p184.

28 *Enneads* I, 6, 8; See also *Enneads* V, 9, 1. Quotations from the *Enneads* are in the translation by Elmer O'Brien (New York, 1964). Sandys's commentary on the *Metamorphoses* (London 1632, pp480–1) is a statement which would have been familiar to many of Milton's readers.

29 Comus who presides over a fully developed world of error, offers a semblance of reason for the true reason he destroys (757–9).

30 *SA* 151–61. Augustine, *Confessions*, X, 5, is not without relevance.

31 The anticipation is noted by Hughes in his edition of Milton's complete poetry and selected prose (New York, 1957), p104n.

32 Dante is inevitably quoted For an older example see Augustine, *Confessions*, X, 35; 'In this enormous forest, so full of snares and dangers, many are the temptation which I have cut off and thrust away from my heart, as you, God of my salvation have granted me the power.' In Indian Literature the forest is normally a place of enlightenment as it is indeed in *Purgatorio* XXVIII.

33 Woodhouse as is well-known, equates temperance, chastity, and virginity to the state of

nature, a state intermediate between nature and grace and the state of grace ('The Argument of Milton's Comus', *UTQ*, pp49–50). It may be possible to reconcile these distinctions to the text; but the text does not enforce them or urge the reader to attend to them. Indeed the Elder Brother as Woodhouse himself recognizes (p56), makes no clear differentiation between chastity and virginity. Comus who derides temperance (and is the first to mention it), speaks of virginity but not of chastity; The Lady up to the temptation scene, speaks only of chastity; in replying to Comus she speaks of temperance, chastity and virginity but not in terms which suggest the different 'realms' to which the three qualities belong. Finally, in the crucial passage of the *Apology (Complete Prose Works* 1, pp889–93; see Woodhouse, *op. cit.*, pp50–1), virginity is not even mentioned and it is chastity (compatible with marriage) which enables one to apprehend those 'high mysteries' of which the Lady also speaks in *Comus* (784). The essence of Woodhouse's interpretation is that *Comus* affirms a certain continuity between the realms of Nature and of Grace. By positing an intermediate realm, the sense of continuity is strengthened; but the third realm is not essential to Woodhouse's argument and does result in demanding from the text a stratification to which it is perhaps not fully committed.

34 This observation is not meant to belittle the value of a reading such as Sears Jayne's 'The Subject of Milton's Ludlow Masque', *PMLA*, LXXIV (1959) pp533–43. Much in Professor Jayne's interpretation is illuminating and there should be no quarrel with his view that Milton read Plato as Ficino read him. But there is more in *Comus* than Professor Jayne's reading can extract.

35 Madsen, *op. cit.*

36 Tillyard, *op. cit.*

37 This I take it, is the view of Brooks and Hardy.

38 Simple botching, of which Milton is sometimes accused is hardly worth discussing. Watkins, pp90–100 provides an intelligent statement of the view that the poem suffers from a divided *imaginative* allegiance.

39 F. R. Leavis, *Revaluation* (London, 1936), pp47–52.

40 Madsen, pp187–92.
41 Bush, *English Literature in the Earlier Seventeenth Century* (Oxford, 1962), p385; *John Milton* (New York, 1904), pp54–5.
42 735, 781. The point is noted by Brooks and Hardy, p217–8.
43 Fletcher, *ed. cit.*, 1 p331.
44 *Ibid.*, 72–3, 209, 289–90, 422–3.
45 *Comus* 671; *Complete Prose Works*, Vol. I, p892.
46 Fredella Bruser, 'Comus and the Rose Song', *SP* XLIV (1947), pp625–44. *FQ* II, XII, 70–6 with its reproduction of *Gerusalemme Liberata* XVI, XV is in particular, not absent from Milton's mind.
47 Fletcher, *ed. cit.*, Vol. I, pp72–4, 208–10, 288–92, 330–2, 421–5.
48 *Ibid.*, pp78–9, 214–15, 298–9, 339, 344, 431–3.
49 *Complete Prose Works*, II, p516.
50 Barker's remarks (*Milton and the Puritan Dilemma*, Toronto, 1941, pp9–13) on the inadequacy of the Lady's rejoinder are particularly instructive since Barker certainly cannot be accused of failing to understand the Puritan mind.
51 Robson, *The Living Milton*, p127 and Watkins, pp90, 92 are among those who see poetic merit in the Lady's 'flame of sacred vehemence'.
52 John Arthos, 'Milton, Ficino and the *Charmides*', *Studies in the Renaissance*, VI (1959), pp261–74.
53 e.g. Malcom Mackenzie Ross, *Poetry and Dogma* (New Brunswick, 1954), p196.
54 *Enneads* I, 6, 6; 1, 2, 3.
55 *Complete Prose Works* I, pp892–3.
56 W. Haller, 'Hail Wedded Love' *ELH* XIII (1946), pp79–97. The link with Spenser is strengthened by the Lady's reference to the sage and serious doctrine of virginity and the use of the same words in Milton's commendation of Spenser in *Areopagitica* (*Complete Prose Works* II, p516).
57 Woodhouse, *Comus Once More* pp219–23; Brooks and Hardy pp212–15, 224–7. A small bibliography could be compiled on 'haemony'; the basic article is by Le Comte in *PQ* XXI (1942), pp283–98.
58 Sandys, pp480–1.
59 Daniells (*op. cit.*, pp32–3) argues that a designed lack of balance characterizes *Comus* as mannerist and contributes to its appeal. This reasoning seems more applicable to the asymmetry of the *Nativity Ode* (which

Daniells does not discuss) than to *Comus*. In *Comus* the argumentative content is so considerable that the lack of a resolution cannot but be dissatisfying to many of its readers.

60 *Works*, Columbia Edition. Vol. XV, p25.

61 *Complete Prose Works* I, pp751–2; see *PL* V, 618–27.

62 *Comus* 393–7, 980–3; *PL* IV, 249–51.

63 *FQ* III, VI, 30. The interpretation of the Epilogue which follows draws upon, adds to and differs from Woodhouse (pp65–71), Tillyard (pp84–7), Brooks and Hardy (pp228–34) and Arthos, 'The Realms of Being in the Epilogue of *Comus*' *MLN* LXXVII (1962) pp821–4.

64 *FQ* III, VI, 37.

65 *Ibid.*, 39–42.

66 *Ibid.*, 47.

67 *Ibid.*, 34–6, 43–4.

68 *Ibid.*, 35.

69 *Ibid.*, 49–50.

70 Madsen, p218.

71 *Complete Prose Works* I, p892.

72 As in *FQ* III, VI, 50.

73 E.g. The Variorum Spenser III, p261.

74 *Enneads*, VI, 9, 9.

75 *Vide* Bush's note.

76 *Enneads*, VI, 9, 11.

77 Part of the effectiveness of the epic catalogue in Book I of *PL* turns on the suggestion that the inglorious likeness is not only revelled in but actually worshipped.

78 *Conf.* XII, 11. See also the reference in XII, 16 to 'that chaste city of yours, our mother which is above, and is free and eternal in the heavens.'

79 *Comus*, 216.

80 The ladder of self-realization is referred to again in *The Reason of Church Government*: 'How shall a man know to do himselfe this right, how to performe this honourable duty of estimation and respect towards his own soul and body? Which way will lead him best to this hill top of sanctity and goodnesse above which there is no higher ascent but to the love of God which from this self-pious regard cannot be assunder?' (*Complete Prose Works* I, p842). Milton returns to Virtue's hill (an image possibly behind *Hamlet* III, IV, 52–61) in his ninth sonnet and in *PR* II, 216–19.

CHAPTER 4

1 See *Milton's Lycidas. The Tradition and the Poem*, ed. C. A. Patrides (New York, 1961), and in particular, 'Five Types of Lycidas' by M. H. Abrams, pp212–31. Wherever possible, quotations are made from this volume, hereafter cited as *Patrides*. For Baroque and Mannerist interpretation, see Sypher *Four Stages of Renaissance Style* (New York, 1955); Roy Daniells, *Milton Mannerism and Baroque*, pp37–50; Lowry Nelson, Jnr., *Baroque Lyric Poetry* pp64–76, 138–52 and Rosemond Tuve's cautions in 'Baroque and Mannerist Milton', *Milton Studies in Honour of Harris Francis Fletcher* (Urbana, 1961), pp209–25.

2 The image is offered in response to the fears expressed by R. M. Adams: *Ikon: John Milton and the Modern Critics*, pp160–2.

3 For the view that *Lycidas* is transcribed, see. e.g. *The Poems of John Milton*, ed. H. J. C. Grierson (London, 1925), Vol. 1, pp XIV–XVII and Ants Oras, 'Milton's Early Rhyme Schemes and the Structure of "Lycidas" ', *MP* LII (1954) p17n.

4 Quotations from the Trinity Manuscript are from H. F. Fletcher's facsimile in *John Milton's Complete Poetical Works*, Vol. 1 (Urbana, 1943).

5 These changes occur in the 'trial-sheet' of the MS, which follows 'Comus'. It is assumed that Milton having recast the first lines, then wrote out the main text which incorporates these changes and subsequently returned to the trial-sheet to further revise the 'Orpheus' and 'flower' passages. Darbishire's view, in her edition of Milton's poetry (Vol. II, London, 1955, p336n) that 'this famous "flower-passage" was an afterthought' is too easily reached. The deletion in the main text may mean that Milton was dissatisfied with his language and not that he had jettisoned his idea.

6 *John Milton: a Reader's Guide to his Poetry* (New York, 1963), p xv.

7 *Ibid.*, pp107ff.

8 'The Pattern of Milton's Nativity Ode' pp171–2.

9 See e.g. J. Milton French, 'The Digressions in Milton's *Lycidas*', *SP* L (1953) pp486, 489; Abrams, pp227ff; and A. S. P. Woodhouse, 'Milton's Pastoral Monodies'

in *Essays in Honour of Gilbert Norwood* (Toronto, 1952), p273. Woodhouse observes that the first two parts of *Lycidas* culminate in passages that 'shatter the pastoral tone, while the third does not shatter but rather transcends it.'

10 *John Milton* (New York, 1964), p62.

11 For the history of the image see Mayerson, 'The Orpheus Image in Lycidas'. *PMLA* LXIV (1949), pp189–207 and D. C. Allen, 'Milton and the Descent to Light', *Milton Studies in Honour of Harris Francis Fletcher*, pp10–13.

12 Nicolson reminds us (p95) that it is the Fates not the Furies who cut the thread of life and that the Furies are not notable for their blindness. Milton's alteration is as always, significant. Death is removed from the realm of order however inscrutable, to that of arbitrary punishment; the Furies calculating in their victimization, are blind in the choice of their victim.

13 Daiches in *Patrides*, pp111–12.

14 Daniells, p45. Christ's equally quietist dismissal ('For what is glory but the blaze of fame') echoes *Lycidas* but is made from the far side of a sea which the earlier poem is only beginning to enter.

15 *The Harmonious Vision*, p57.

16 The revisions to lines 153 and 154 are in the Trinity manuscript, that to line 157 in the 1645 text. However both the Cambridge University copy of 1638 and one British Museum copy have 'humming' replaced by 'whelming' in what is regarded as Milton's hand.

17 'Milton 1', *On Poetry and Poets* (New York, 1961), pp163–4.

18 Allen (*The Harmonious Vision* pp68ff), however locates the turning point in the flower passage.

19 Abrams, pp226ff; Nicolson, p96n; J. Milton French, p489.

20 The line is usually taken as alluding to Arion. Mabbott in *Explicator* v (1947), no. 26 follows Richardson and Newton in reading it as alluding to Palaemon. Michael Lloyd in 'The Two Worlds of "Lycidas" ' (*Essays in Criticism* xi, 1961, pp397–8) notes that in 'Servius's version of the myth, Phoebus Apollo himself in the guise of a dolphin rescued his drowning son Icadius and carried him to Mount Parnassus'. This

interpretation of the myth would fit best into the pattern here suggested.

21 The omission of this line in the 1638 edition is presumably accidental. It appears in the MS and in the 1645 and 1673 texts and is restored in two copies of 1638 [See above note 16].

22 See Ransom 'A Poem Nearly Anonymous' in *Patrides*, pp69ff. Precedents for Milton's rhyme and stanzaic structure are found by Prince in the canzone (*Patrides*, pp153–6), by Oras (p20), in the madrigal and by Finney in the *dramma per musica* ('A Musical Background for "Lycidas" ', *HLQ* XV, 1951–52, pp325–50).

23 Oras (p17) notes that the design of the paragraphs of *Lycidas* 'closely mirrors the broader architectonics of the poem as a whole, beginning regularly and clearly, then becoming more and more intricate and involved and eventually reverting to transparent regularity.' A study of repetitions of phrase in the poem bears out this conclusion. Such repetition, particularly when it occurs with the first or second syllable of succeeding or closely-linked lines (as in 8, 9; 15, 17; 162, 63; 167, 68; and 190, 91), strengthens the impression of pastoral performance. Phrase repetition is most frequent in the first forty-nine lines of the poem (when the pastoral convention has not yet been undermined) and in the last twenty-nine (when the convention is re-established).

24 *Patrides*, p167.

CHAPTER 5

1 Walter Raleigh, *Milton* (London, 1915), pp81–2.

2 E. M. W. Tillyard, *Studies in Milton* (London, 1951), p43.

3 See in particular, Millicent Bell, 'The Fallacy of the Fall in *Paradise Lost*', *PMLA*, LXVIII (1953), pp863–83 and H. V. S. Ogden 'The Crisis of *Paradise Lost* Reconsidered' *PQ*, XXXVI (1957), pp1–19.

4 Tillyard, *Studies in Milton*, pp13–14.

5 G. A. Wilkes *The Thesis of 'Paradise Lost'* (Melbourne, 1961). Wilkes observes (p42) that 'The weight of Milton's conception is not poised on one episode analysed by

Professor Waldock or on another singled out by Dr. Tillyard: its weight is distributed through the whole structure and all twelve books of the poem help to support it.'

6 Marvell's phrase has been used as the title of a recent book on Yeats.

7 See Kester Svendsen '*Paradise Lost* as Alternative', *The Humanities Association Bulletin* XVIII (1967), pp35–42. Professor Svendsen's article appeared after this chapter was written.

8 Watson Kirkconnell, *The Celestial Cycle* (Toronto, 1952), Intro. p xxii.

9 '*Paradise Lost*' *and the Seventeenth Century Reader*, pp35 and 145n.

10 *Works*, Columbia Edn., Vol. XV. pp33–5.

11 Allan H. Gilbert 'The Outside Shell of Milton's World', *SP* XX (1923), pp444–7; Harry F. Robins 'The Unnecessary Shell of Milton's World', *Studies in Honour of T. W. Baldwin*, edited by D. C. Allen (Urbana, 1958), pp211–19.

12 A. S. P. Woodhouse, 'Notes on Milton's Views on the Creation: the Initial Phase', *PQ* XXVIII (1949) pp211–36 and esp. p229, n30.

13 Walter C. Curry, *Milton's Ontology, Cosmogony, and Physics* (Lexington, 1957), pp48–91; A. B. Chambers, 'Chaos in *Paradise Lost*' *JHI*, XXIV (1963), pp55–84.

14 *PL* III, 380; VII, 233; I, 63. See also V, 599.

15 The *De Doctrina* (*Works*, Columbia edn., XV, pp373–5) restricts its claim of support to Luther, Chrysostom, and 'some later divines'.

16 *PL* I, 73–4.

17 *PL* I, 593–4; I, 247. See also I, 97; IV, 835–51. The reverse of this process can be found in the *Paradiso* where Beatrice becomes more and more beautiful as she rises to the ultimate light.

18 Milton had an important precedent for his presentation of Heaven in Tasso but even if he had not read Davenant's *Preface to Gondibert* he could not have been oblivious to the kind of objection that Davenant urges against Tasso's presentation. See *Critical Essays of the Seventeenth Century*, edited J. D. Spingarn (Oxford 1908), Vol. ii, p5.

19 Merritt Y. Hughes, *Ten Perspectives on Milton*, pp108–11. Hughes is responsible for drawing attention to the relevance of

Hope Travers's *The Four Daughters of God* (Bryn Mawr College Monographs, VI, 1907). See also Patrides, *Milton and the Christian Tradition* (Oxford, 1966) p24. T. M. Greene in *The Descent from Heaven* (New Haven, 1963, p175) observes in another connection that the first person addresses the second in Folengo's *L'Umanita dei Figliuol di Dio* (1533).

20 *Works*, Columbia edn., XV, p105; Grant McColley, 'Milton's Battle in Heaven and Rupert of St. Heribert', *Speculum*, XVI (1941), pp230–5; '*Paradise Lost*' *and the Seventeenth Century Reader*, pp146–7, n. 20.

21 Elnathan Parr observes that 'Creation is a Worke proper onely to God, undividedly common to the Father, the Sonne, and to the Holy Ghost'. *The Ground of Divinitie* (London; date defaced), p73. To the same effect see James Ussher, *A Body of Divinitie* (8th edn., London, 1702), pp82–3. William Ames goes so far as to say that 'By the *Creation*, God is known, but not God the Father, Sonne and Holy Spirit, because that effecting power whereby the world was created, pertains to the

essence of God and not to his personal subsistence.' *The Marrow of Sacred Divinitie* (London, 1642), p35.

22 D. Taylor Jr., 'Milton's Treatment of the Judgement and the Expulsion in *Paradise Lost*', *Tulane Studies in English*, X (1960), p71.

23 Arnold Stein. *Answerable Style* (Minneapolis, 1953), p116.

24 *PL* V, 506–12; V, 477–9; IV, 181. III, 80–4 acquires new meaning against this background.

25 *PL* VII, 230–1, 166–7.

26 *Poetics* 5; Lane Cooper, *Aristotle on the Art of Poetry* (Revised ed., Ithaca, 1947), p15; *Literary Criticism: Plato to Dryden*, ed. W. H. Gilbert (New York, 1940) p275; Grant McColley, *Paradise Lost* (The newest estimate is 33 days) pp16–17.

27 The best available account of Milton's use of space is in Roy Daniells's *Milton, Mannerism and Baroque*, pp87–99. See also Jackson I. Cope *The Metaphoric Structure of Paradise Lost* (Baltimore, 1962).

28 *Poetics*, 24.

29 *Poetics*, 7.

30 See in this connection John C. Demaray, 'The Thrones of Satan and God: Backgrounds to Divine Opposition in

Paradise Lost', *HLQ* XXXI (1967) pp21–33 and esp. p27. Dr. Demaray's essay appeared after this chapter was written.

31 *Comus* 243–63; *PL* IX, 465.
32 *PL* IX, 348–9.
33 *PL* III, 99.
34 James H. Sims, *The Bible in Milton's Epics* (Gainesville, 1962), pp261–2.
35 Sims, pp271–3, 10–11.
36 Sims, p262.
37 *Complete Prose Works*, Vol. II, p292. The text in the background is *Rom* II, 33. Luther, in commenting on it says 'It is not for us to inquire into these mysteries, but to adore them'. His subsequent answer to the question 'Why did God let Adam fall?', is on the same lines and is in sharp contrast to *PL* ('The Bondage of the Will', in *Martin Luther, Selections from his Writings*, ed. John Dillenberger, New York, 1961, p195). We should remember however that Milton's position on free-will was closer to Luther's at the time he wrote the divorce tracts than it was when he wrote *Paradise Lost*.
38 On Milton's relative use of perfection see Ogden, p6 and Ruth Mohl, *Studies in Spenser Milton and the Theory of*

Monarchy (New York, 1949), pp125–6.
39 See Chapter I, p8.
40 *PL* IX, 351–2; VI, 181.
41 The view that the disclosure of the Incarnation occasioned the rebellion in Heaven (Williams, *The Common Expositor*, p118; McColley, *Paradise Lost*, pp32–3) may have provided Milton with the basis for his 'invention' but is not the same thing as the invention itself.
42 Daniells who regards will as the axis of Milton's universe (*Milton Mannerism and Baroque*, pp64–86) finds this fact indicative of Baroque achievement rather than artistic failure. Perhaps it can be argued that a universe built round the primacy of the divine will is Augustinian as much as it is baroque. Herschel Baker notes for instance that 'Augustine's radical departure from the humanistic tradition is apparent in his substituting of will for reason in his hierarchy of values' *The Image of Man* (1961 ed.),p172.
43 A fuller discussion of the concept than is possible here will be found in R. A. Hoopes *Right Reason in the English Renaissance* (Camb., Mass., 1962).
44 Christ in *PR* exemplifies the

whole of this description and
not simply its first line.

45 *PL* VIII, 589–92; IV,
750–7; V, 483–8; XII, 98.

46 The nature of the image of
God in man is discussed by
Williams in *The Common
Expositor*, pp72–5. The
image is both inward and
outward. Outwardly, the
image is expressed in Adam's
dominion over the creatures
(as in *PL* VIII, 540–6) and
according to some
commentators, in Adam's
dominion over Eve. The
inward image is found to
quote Ussher's typical
wording, in 'the perfection of
his [Adam's] Nature, indued
with Reason and Will,
rightly disposed in Holiness
and Righteousness, Wisdom
and Truth; and accordingly
framing all Motions and
Actions, both inward and
outward.' *A Body of Divinitie*,
p92. See also Elnathan Parr,
The Grounds of Divinitie, p122
and William Ames, '*The
Marrow of Sacred Divinitie*'
(London, 1642), p38. Milton
describes the image as
consisting of 'Wisdom,
Purity, Justice, and rule over
all creatures'. (*Complete Prose
Works* II, p587). In *PL*, he is
not only providing a
description of the inward
image, but suggesting in

line 295 that the outer image
depends upon the inner.

47 *Comus* 528–9.

48 *The Letters of W. B. Yeats*,
edited Allan Wade (New
York, 1955), p824.

49 *Gen.* II, 21–2 does not
mention the side from which
Eve was created. Davis P.
Harding in pointing out how
the birth of Sin diabolically
distorts the birth of Pallas
Athene, notes that 'on the
theory that the rib from which
Eve was fashioned must have
been extracted from a region
near Adam's heart, most
commentators had concluded
that the rib was taken from
the left side. Milton
apparently subscribed to this
view. But, so far as I have
been able to discover, no
mythographer had ever
designated the side of the
head from which Pallas
Athene was born. Milton,
very likely, therefore, invented
this detail.' *The Club of
Hercules* (Urbana, 1962), p75.

50 *PL* V, 65. Note the echo at
IX, 890.

51 *PL* VIII, 571–3. In the
Reason of Church Government
Milton describes 'this pious
and just honouring of
ourselves' as 'the radical
moisture and fountain head,
whence every laudable and
worthy enterprize issues

forth.' *Complete Prose Works* I, p841.

52 Eve's Areopagitican argument is not employed inconsistently or absentmindedly. See Arnold Williams, 'Eve, the Devil and *Areopagitica*' *MLQ* V (1944), pp429–34.

53 *PL* IX, 355–6.

54 *PL* VIII, 530–7.

55 *PL* VIII, 560.

56 *PL* IX, 900–7.

57 *PL* III, 150–64. A double connection is at work, for IX, 901 recalls III, 208.

58 *PL* IX, 913–14; 955–6. Death's remarks in X, 243–51 with their specific echo of X, 1010 are a grim commentary on the real nature of the link.

59 *PL* VIII, 511; IX, 1036; I, 193–4; see also II, 386–8; IX, 1036 it will be observed, develops the destructive implications of VIII, 532–3. Williams (*The Common Expositor*, p84) says that Milton in speaking of wedded love before the fall 'is going farther than most of the commentators warrant.' McColley (*Paradise Lost*, p178) describes as distinctly uncommon, the idea that there was lustful intercourse in Paradise after the fall. Once again Milton breaks with tradition to achieve an important contrast.

60 *PL* IV, 241–3; V, 294–7; IX, 792–3.

61 Analyses of this scene are not lacking. For one particularly relevant to the view expressed here see Dennis H. Burden, *The Logical Epic* (London, 1967), pp80–93.

62 Milton's originality in this detail was pointed out to me by Professor Svendsen.

63 Godfrey Goodman, *The Fall of Man* (London, 1616), p429.

64 This view is similar to that put forward in detail and with subtlety by Stanley E. Fish in *Surprised by Sin* (London, 1967). See also pp xxvi–xxviii of the introduction to the present author's edition of the first two books of *PL* (Bombay, 1964).

65 *Johnson's Life of Milton*, ed. C. H. Firth (Oxford, 1888), p76.

66 *PL* X; 1092, 1104.

67 Ussher, *A Body of Divinitie*, p123.

68 Luther, *De servo arbitrio* tr. J. I. Packer and O. R. Johnson (1957) pp103f.

69 See above, n. 15.

70 The agreement is noted by A. S. P. Woodhouse, *The Poet and His Faith* (Chicago, 1965), p107. See in particular, Luther's Commentary on *Galatians*.

71 *Complete Prose Works*, I, pp613–14; II, p293; II, pp519–20.

72 Peter Du Moulin, *The Anatomy of Arminianism* (London, 1626), p85.

73 Elnathan Parr, *The Grounds of Divinitie*, p30.

74 See *PL* X, 1–8 where prevenient grace is mentioned for the only time in the epic. Ephraim Pagitt in discussing the concept observes: 'The Papists say that man's will worketh with God's grace in the first conversion of a sinner by itself: we say that man's will worketh with God's grace in the first conversion, yet not of itself but by grace.' *Heresiography* (London, 1654), pp129–30. For contrasted views on the relation of grace to fallen nature see Dick Taylor Jr., 'Grace as a Means of Poetry: Milton's Pattern for Salvation', *Tulane Studies in English* IV (1954), pp57, 73 and Jackson C. Boswell 'Milton and Prevenient Grace'. *SEL* VII (1967), pp84–94.

75 Thomas Edwards *Gangraena* (London, 1646), pp63, 74–6.

76 For the association of Arminianism with the religious right see Godfrey Davies, 'Arminian versus Puritan in England, *c.* 1620–50', *Huntington Library Bulletin* V (1934), pp157–79. The background of Anglo-Dutch Arminianism is succinctly discussed by Rosalie Colie in *Light and Enlightenment* (Cambridge, 1957), pp1–21.

77 *The Arminian Nunnery* (London, 1641). The author goes on (p10) to describe Arminianism as a bridge to Popery and 'a great part of the Clergie of this Land' as 'downright Arminians'.

78 See e.g. 'The five articles of the Remonstrants' *Documents of the Christian Church*, ed. Henry Bettenson (London, 1943), pp374–6; Peter Du Moulin, *The Anatomy of Arminianism*; Ephraim Pagitt, *Heresiography*, pp105–12; Alexander Ross, *A View of All Religions of the World* (London, 1673), pp367–9; Daniel Featley, *Pelagius Redivivus* (London, 1626). A synthesized account, based on the above, might read as follows:

Christ died for all mankind and not for the elect alone. No man is doomed only for original sin. Eternal life is given to all that believe and all men are given grace and sufficient power to believe.

Salvation depends on free-will applying itself to grace universally offered. But grace is not irresistible. A man may hinder his own regeneration or not make use of the strength given him. Election depends on the free assent of man's will, which even with the help of saving grace may choose otherwise. [*PL* III, 173–202 is relevant here. Maurice Kelley in *PMLA*, 1937, pp75–9 has shown the agreement of this passage with the *De Doctrina* and its differences from the Westminster confession]. Election may further be incomplete and the incompletely elected may become reprobate. Consequently the number of the elect is not fixed. [The Remonstrants fifth article has misgivings at this point].

Man after the fall is not dead in sin. He is able to thirst after righteousness. If the darkness is cleared from his understanding and his unruly affections tamed, his will is not incapable of choosing good. There is a common grace left to man after the fall which is basically the light of nature; by good use of this common grace man can attain to evangelical or saving grace. [The bearing of these propositions on the events in Book X will be apparent.]

In addition to a general and conditional election, there is another election of particular men whom God foresees from eternity would believe in Christ and persevere in the faith. 'God hath precisely and absolutely decreed to save some certaine men, for their faith fore-seen' [Du Moulin, p114. The proposition illuminates *PL* III, 183–4.]

Milton's position on the universality of grace has affinities with that taken by Melanchthon. See *Melanchthon on Christian Doctrine*, ed. Clyde L. Manschreck (New York, 1965), pp60, 187–91.

79 C. A. Patrides *Milton and the Christian Tradition* (Oxford, 1966), p195; John Hales *Golden Remains* (London, 1673), Introductory letter.

CHAPTER 6

1 E. N. S. Thompson, 'For *Paradise Lost*, XI–XII,' *PQ*, XII (1943), pp376–82.
2 *A Preface to Paradise Lost* (London, 1942), p125.
3 See in particular, *'Paradise Lost' and the Seventeenth Century Reader* (London, 1947), pp78–92; F. T. Prince, 'On the Last Two Books of *Paradise Lost*' E. & S, XI (1958), pp38–52; William G. Madsen, 'The Idea of Nature in Milton's Poetry, in *Three Studies in the Renaissance* (New Haven, 1958), pp256ff; G. W. Whiting, *Milton and this Pendant World* (Austin, 1958), pp129–200; John E. Parish, 'Milton and God's Curse on the Serpent,' *JEGP*, LVIII (1959), pp241–7; John M. Steadman, 'Adam and the Prophesied Redeemer (*Paradise Lost*, XII, 359–623)', *SP*, LVI (1959), pp214–25; Joseph Summers, *The Muse's Method* (London, 1960), pp186–224; D. Taylor Jr., 'Milton's Treatment of the Judgement and the Expulsion in *Paradise Lost*', *Tulane Studies in English*, X (1960), pp51–82; Lawrence A. Sasek, 'The Drama of *Paradise Lost* Books XI and XII in *Louisiana State University Studies, Humanities Series* XII (1962), pp181–96, (references to this article are to the reprint in *Milton: Modern Essays in Criticism*, edited A. E. Barker, New York, 1965, pp342–56); Bernard Wright, *Milton's 'Paradise Lost'* (London, 1962), pp190–206; Barbara K. Lewalski, 'Structure and the Symbolism of Vision in Michael's Prophecy, *Paradise Lost*, Books XI–XII', *PQ*, XLII (1963), pp25–35; C. A. Patrides, 'The "Protevangelium" in Renaissance Theory and in *Paradise Lost*' *SEL* III (1963), pp19–30; *The Phoenix and the Ladder* (Berkeley, 1964), pp58–68; Louis L. Martz *The Paradise Within* (New Haven, 1964), pp141–67; H. R. MacCallum 'Milton and Sacred History' in *Essays in English Literature from the Renaissance to the Victorian Age, Presented to A. S. P. Woodhouse*, ed. Millar MacLure and F. W. Watt (Toronto, 1964), pp149–68; Michael Fixler, *Milton and the Kingdoms of God* (London, 1964), pp226–34. Robert A. Bryan, 'Adam's Tragic Vision in *Paradise Lost*', *SP*, LXII (1965), pp197–214;

Mother Mary Pecheux, 'Abraham, Adam and the Theme of Exile in *Paradise Lost*', *PMLA*, LXXX (1965), pp365–71; Arnold Stein, 'The Paradise Within and the Paradise Without', *MLQ*, XXVI (1965), pp597–600; Larry S. Champion, 'The Conclusion of *Paradise Lost* – A Reconsideration', *CE*, XXVII (1966), pp384–94; Virginia R. Mollenkott, 'The Cycle of Sins in *Paradise Lost* Book XI', *MLQ*, XXVII (1966), pp33–40.

4 *PL*, I, 100.

5 *PL*, XI, 809; XII, 372–3, 468. Bentley noted these passages and made them part of his reasons for amending the final lines of the poem.

6 In the most literal sense the reader is shown the kingdoms of the world. It is no accident that nearly all of them are tyrannies. Adam apparently is only shown the location in space of what is to happen in time, but the roll-call is evocative of what is to come and there is mordant irony in the remark that Adam's eyes were opened to 'nobler sights'. The film spread over his vision by the 'false fruit' is removed so that he can see what fruits the fruit has brought forth and three drops from the well of life equip him

to see the progress of death in the universe.

7 Whiting, pp169–92; MacCallum pp150–68.

8 Taylor, p71.

9 *Ibid.*

10 *PL* XI, 117.

11 *PL* XI, 286, 334, 421.

12 *PL* XI, 453.

13 Merritt Y. Hughes shows how Milton's early illustrators falling back on the traditional 'woeful' treatment, fail to convey the mood of the quiet close. 'Some Illustrators of Milton' reprinted in *Milton: Modern Essays in Criticism* ed. A. E. Barker pp363–5.

14 *Works* (Columbia edn.) Vol. XVIII, p232.

15 *Vide* Summers, p197.

16 *PL* XI, 475–7; 515–19; 477–88 of which 485–7 were added in 1674; 634–5.

17 *PL* XI, 632–3.

18 *PL* XI, 681. In XI 874–88 Adam develops his recognition further. In grasping the relationship between the one just man (Noah) and the world restored he prepares his mind (and that of the reader) for the Atonement.

19 Summers, p198; Lewalski, pp28–9.

20 Hughes, note on *PL* XI, 700. Arnold Williams in *The Common Expositor* pp149–50

provides a basis in commentaries on *Genesis*. Ainsworth notes that 'by this translation of *Enoch* God assured all the faithfull of their resurrection and eternall life.' *Annotations Upon the Five Books of Moses* (London, 1639), p28. According to Ames, Adoption was declared by 'the translation of *Enoch* into the heavenly inheritance' and Glorification was 'publickly sealed both by the example of *Enoch* and the conservation of *Noah* with his family from the flood.' *The Marrow of Sacred Divinitie*, pp172–3. Milton, as Williams observes, may be singular not in emphasizing the virtue of Enoch, but in presenting him as the one just man in a wicked world.

21 Ainsworth's comment on *Gen.* VIII, 22 which lies behind this passage is as follows: 'It is a promise to conserve the orderly course and state of the world through all ages, unto the end; under which also the promise of stability of grace in Christ is spiritually covenanted unto the faithfull'. *Annotations Upon the Five Books of Moses* p38.

22 This passage is not studied by Albert L. Cirillo in his article, 'Noon-midnight and the Temporal Structure of *Paradise Lost*', *ELH* XXIX (1962), pp372–95.

23 See e.g. Sasek pp352–3.

24 *PL* III, 56–9.

25 Summers, pp207–8; Lewalski, pp27–8, supports this suggestion and adds others.

26 A conspicuous exception is Adam's response to the deliverance of Noah (XI, (871–83) which opens the way to his responses in the last book.

27 *Lex Rex*, quoted Woodhouse, *Puritanism and Liberty* (London, 1938), p204. Hughes, in his edition of the 'Tenure', *Complete Prose Works*, Vol. III p226 notes that Milton's arguments resemble Rutherford's while not mentioning the latter.

28 *PL* V, 788–97. *Vide* Martz, p158.

29 '*Paradise Lost*' and the *Seventeenth Century Reader*', pp86–8, 158–9n, Arnold Williams, *The Common Expositor* pp222–3.

30 *PL* XI, 829–38. The importance of these lines is stressed by Northrop Frye in *The Return of Eden*, pp41, 54, 110. In *The Common Expositor* p99 Williams states that it was commonly believed that 'Paradise had been destroyed or greatly altered by the

deluge.' Ussher states that though the place remains, the 'Beauty and Commodities' of Paradise have been almost abolished by the flood and by man's sin. However 'it is a very fruitful Place still'. *A Body of Divinitie* (8th edn., London, 1702), p112. The physical uprooting of the site which Milton describes is, according to Don Cameron Allen 'a geographical matter that the commentators had discussed at length.' 'The Legend of Noah', *Illinois Studies in Language and Literature* Vol. XXIII, nos. 3 and 4 (1949), pp153–4. Helen Gardner (*A Reading of 'Paradise Lost'*, London, 1965, pp80–1), however considers it one of Milton's 'grand inventions.'

31 *The Collected Poetry of W. H. Auden* (New York, 1945), p111.

32 'Eikonoklastes', *Complete Prose Works* Vol. III, p598. The Bible does not mention Nimrod, either as the founder of monarchy or the builder of Babel but there are ample precedents for Milton's treatment. See e.g., *'Paradise Lost' and the Seventeenth Century Reader*, p158, n. 19; *The Common Expositor* pp160–1, 222–3; Ainsworth, *Annotations*, p44

and possibly *Paradiso*, XXVI, 124–6. The obvious connection between Babel and Pandemonium is made by the English language subsequent to Milton, but Milton does make the connection in I, 692–9.

33 The relevant paradoxes are deployed with care in X, 58–62. In X, 183 Milton is even willing to borrow from Catholic thought to bring out his symmetries.

34 *PL* X, 173, XII, 543. The account which follows draws upon Steadman and C. A. Patrides, *Milton and the Christian Tradition*, pp121–8.

35 *PL* X, 1030–2; XI, 153–61.

36 *PL* XI, 22–30; IX, 194–6; X, 267–9.

37 *PL* XI, 113–16.

38 *PL* XII, 105–6. Compare the darkening of the thought in XII, 537–8.

39 *Complete Prose Works* I, pp614–16; I, pp703–7; II, pp552–3.

40 *Works* (Columbia edn.), XIV, 97–9.

41 *PL* XII, 124–6; XII, 147–8; XII, 449–50. Adam uses the phrase at XII, 276–7.

42 MacCallum, p167 argues that this acceleration takes place because 'Events are seen through the eyes of Adam and this involves a

reversal of perspective.' The suggestion does not quite take the sting out of his earlier rhetorical suggestion that Milton is 'like an inexperienced student at a history examination, simply running out of time.' A further possibility is that Adam has learned the pattern of the contention. It is therefore possible to pass over events more rapidly without repeatedly showing how history repeats itself.

43 For the tradition see Steadman.
44 *PL* V, 477–9.
45 *Comus* 68–72, 525–30.
46 *PL* XII, 294; III, 210–15.
47 *PL* V, 574–6.
48 *PL* V, 573.
49 Notably Maurice Kelley in *N & Q* CLXXXI (1941), p273.
50 The interpretation developed here is similar to the one offered by Madsen in 'Earth the Shadow of Heaven: Typological Symbolism in *Paradise Lost*', *PMLA*, LXXV (1960), p525.
51 *PL* VI, 852.
52 *PL* VI, 781–4.
53 *PR* IV, 561–2.
54 Martz (p124) notes how in this sense, the battle in heaven prefigures 'the later defeat of Satan by the crucified Christ'.

55 An interesting discussion of the relationship between the paradise within and reformation in history can be found in John P. Dolan's *History of the Reformation* (New York, 1967), pp66–71.
56 *PL* XI, 829–39; I, 17–18; *PR* IV, 288–90, 321–6.
57 *PL* XII, 307–15.
58 *PL* XII, 621–3; XI, 167–9; XII, 469–78. Kermode in *The Living Milton*, p120 considers Eve's recognition as 'much more central to the mood of the poem than the famous *felix culpa*.' Since both paradoxes are rooted in traditional ideas and images it seems more satisfying to regard both as complementary affirmations of what might be called the style of Providence.
59 Argument, Book XII.
60 Malcolm M. Ross, *Poetry and Dogma* (New Brunswick, 1954), pp103–7.
61 Martz, p165.
62 Ernest L. Tuveson, *Millennium and Utopia*, pp7–70.
63 See above n. 39.
64 *Comus.* 664.
65 Paul Tillich reported in *Time*, Feb. 26, 1965, p38.
66 *PL* XII, 553–60; IX, 1121–6.
67 *PL* XII, 507ff; *Lycidas* 113–31.

68 *Complete Prose Works*, II,
pp549, 564–5.

69 'Seventh Prolusion',
Complete Prose Works I, p296.
In fairness to the continuity
of Milton's thought it should
be added that immediately
afterwards (p297), Milton
observes that those who
possess learning enjoy 'a
kingdom in themselves far
more glorious than any
earthly dominion.'

70 2 *Pet.* 1, 5 and 6 on which the
latter half of this passage is
based, is interpreted as
enumerating the four cardinal
virtues with virtue equalling
justice, knowledge equalling
prudence, temperance
equalling continence and
patience equalling fortitude.
See Ames, *The Marrow of*

Sacred Divinitie, p205. See
also the reference in the
Reason of Church Government to
those 'wise and artful
recitations' which lead to 'the
love and practice of justice,
temperance and fortitude'.
(*Complete Prose Works*, I,
p819). In *Eikonoklastes*
Milton relates the 'happiness
of a Nation' to the four virtues
and adds that those in whom
these virtues dwell 'need not
kings to make them happy,
but are the architects of their
own happiness; and whether
to themselves or others are
not less than kings.'
(*Complete Prose Works*, III,
p542).

71 They also look forward to
Christ's dismissal of the
temptation of learning in *PR*.

CHAPTER 7

1 Pope was among the first to
recognize that *Paradise Lost*
had more than one style. See
Milton Criticism, edited James
Thorpe (London, 1951),
p349. See also John M.
Steadman 'Demetrius, Tasso
and Stylistic Variation in
Paradise Lost' *ES*, XLVII
(1966), pp329–41. Note 1 of
this article contains references
to those who have discussed
the variety of styles in *PL*.

2 Tasso's convictions on unity
in variety (*Literary Criticism:
Plato to Dryden* ed. Allan H.
Gilbert, New York 1940,
pp498–501) are based on
the proposition that the
microcosmic work of art
should reflect the
characteristics of macrocosmic
reality; but it follows that the
language of the work should
bring the qualities of the
work into life. It is doubtful

if any poem exemplifies
Tasso's views on this matter
more fully than *Paradise Lost*.

3 Christopher Ricks, *Milton's
Grand Style* (Oxford ,1963)
p10. The present author's
attempt to look at the style
in terms of the Milton
controversy is contained in
Milton's Epic Poetry, ed. C. A.
Patrides (London, 1967)
pp276–97.

4 F. T. Prince's, *The Italian
Element in Milton's Verse*
(Oxford, 1954), is the most
important effort in this
direction.

5 *Complete Prose Works*, II,
p405; Thomas Kranidas, *The
Fierce Equation* (The Hague,
1965), p96.

6 *Complete Prose Works*, I, p813.
Other interpretations have
been put forward e.g., by
C. S. Lewis in *A Preface to
'Paradise Lost'* (London,
1942), pp5–6.

7 Yeats tells us in 1916 that
'All imaginative art remains
at a distance and this
distance, once chosen, must
be held firmly against a
pushing world.' 'Certain
Noble Plays of Japan', *Essays
and Introductions* (London,
1961), p224.

8 Joseph Hone, *W. B. Yeats*
(London, 1942), p459.

9 Yeats is the twentieth century
master of this strategy.

Coleridge in the penultimate
paragraph of *Biographia
Literaria* Ch. XIV, provides
the theoretical basis.

10 *PL* III, 142.

11 Donald Davie 'Syntax and
Music in *Paradise Lost*', *The
Living Milton*, ed. Frank
Kermode (London, 1960),
p78.

12 *PL* II, 426–9 and II,
138–42 provide the crucial,
though not the only contrast.
The discriminations implied
will be apparent but attention
may be invited to the sardonic
sense of judgement which
describes Satan as
'transcendent' (the word is
used only three time in *PL*)
and the contrast between
Satan 'Conscious of highest
worth, unmov'd' and Christ
visibly moved by divine
compassion.

13 *PL* II, 557–61; IV,
236–40; V, 620–4; IX,
494–500; X 829–33. *See
Answerable Style*, pp66–7 and
A. Bartlett Giamatti; *The
Enchanted Garden* (Princeton,
1966), pp303–6. The
references to the fifth and
tenth books are necessary to
complete the picture. Milton
in speaking of 'mazie error'
is playing upon two meanings
of 'error' to suggest one of
the shapes of possibility; but
the other contexts keep us

aware that there is another road which can be taken.

14 *PL* IV, 241–3; V, 294–7; IX, 792–4; IX, 1013–15. The word 'boon' is used only twice in *PL*.

15 The use of three tenses in describing the fall of man is meant to heighten our awareness of this 'simultaneous present'.

16 The first book has an equally striking unity of imagery. Beginning with the Vallombrosa Simile, a series of regenerative and inflationary similes come to their climax in the building of Pandemonium. Then follows a deflationary series so that the angels who made the assembled armies of history look like pygmies are themselves compared to bees, elves and pygmies. There is more of the Alice in Wonderland strategy in the

seating arrangements for Pandemonium. Infinitely large numbers must contract themselves into infinitely small dimensions to enter a structure that surpasses man's mightiest works. But the decision-making élite remain 'in thir own dimensions like themselves'. The manipulation of 'size' is considerably more than artful. See, in this connection, Kingsley Widmer, 'The Iconography of Renunciation: The Miltonic Simile' *Milton's Epic Poetry*, ed. Patrides, pp127–30.

17 James Whaler, 'The Miltonic Simile': *PMLA*, XLVI (1931), p1034.

18 Arnold Stein, *Answerable Style*, pp93–4, 101–2.

19 For a kindred discussion see Rosalie Colie, *Paradoxia Epidemica* (Princeton, 1966), pp169–89.

CHAPTER 8

1 Donne also maintains that 'David is a better poet than Virgil' (*The Sermons of John Donne* ed. Simpson and Potter, Berkeley 1953–62, Vol. IV, p167).

2 In the *Defence of Poesy* Sidney observes: 'Nay truly learned men have learnedly thought,

that where once reason has so much overmastered passion as that the mind has a free desire to do well, the inward light each mind has in itself is as good as a philosopher's book'. The similarity to Christ's argument in *PR* need not be laboured. Ferrar in *Ferrar Papers*, p63, is more emphatic: 'In as much as all the Comedyes, Tragedyes, Pastoralls etc: and all those they call Heroicall Poems, none excepted; and like wise all the Bookes of Tales, wch they call Novells, and all feigned Historyes written in Prose, all love Hymns, and all the like Bookes are full of Idolatry, and especially tend to the Overthrow of Christian Religion, undermining the very Foundations thereof, and corrupt and pollute the minds of the Readers, with filthy lusts, as, woe is me, I have proved in my self. In this regard, therefore, to show my detestation of them to the World, and that others may take warning, I have burned all of them, and most humbly have, and do beseech God, to forgive me all my mispent time in them, and all the Sinns that they have caused in me, wch surely, but for his infinite Grace, had carryed my soule down into Hell long ere this.' See Louis L. Martz, *The Paradise Within*, pp158–9.

3 *Enneads* 1, 6, 6.

4 In *Institutes* 2.2.16 Calvin observes: 'If the Lord has willed that we be helped in physics, dialectic, mathematics, and other like disciplines, by the work and ministry of the ungodly let us use this assistance.' Luther declares that those who consider a knowledge of scripture alone apart from the classics as sufficient 'must always remain irrational brutes'. *Luther on Education* (St. Louis, n.d.) p183. The thing said changes according to the polemical context and Luther can be quoted differently as in Barbara Lewalski, *Milton's Brief Epic* (London, 1666), pp295–6. Augustine in *De Doctrina Christiana* (bk. 11, Chapter 40) tells us that 'the beliefs of the Gentiles contain not only fables and invented superstitions and useless requirements of labour, which each of us must despise and shun as we follow Christ out of the pagan world, but also the liberal arts, which are more proper for the use of truth, and certain precepts useful in governing our lives, even verities which reveal the one God.'

5 *The Renaissance and English Humanism* (Toronto, 1939), p125. For kindred observations by others see Lewalski, p282.

6 The argument is advanced more emphatically in Bush's

John Milton (London, 1965), pp189ff and in his edition of Milton's poetry (New York, 1965), p461. See also Irene Samuel, 'Milton on Learning and Wisdom', *PMLA*, LXIV (1949), pp708–23.

7 *Complete Prose Works*, 1, pp808–23. The view (p816) that 'those frequent songs throughout the law and prophets . . . not in their divine argument alone, but in the very critical art of composition may be easily made appear over all the kinds of Lyrick poesy to be incomparable' is specifically remembered in *PR* IV, 334–49.

8 *Paradise Regained: the Tradition and the Poem* (reissued New York, 1962).

9 *Milton's Brief Epic*, pp281–302. Mention must also be made of Arnold Stein's thoughtful comments in *Heroic Knowledge* (Minneapolis, 1957) pp94–111.

10 Lewalski, op. cit., p66. The six pages on the vanity of learning contained in John Downame's *Christian Warfare* (London, 1634), a volume of over a thousand pages, are significant in more than one way.

11 *Ibid.*, p120.

12 *Ibid.*, p128.

13 *Ibid.*, p127.

14 Louis L. Martz, 'Paradise Regained: the Meditative Combat', *ELH*, XXVII (1960), pp223–47.

15 *Paradise Regained*, pp13–29.

16 The relative length and elaborateness of this temptation seem to be without precedent.

17 This technique has been studied in an earlier chapter on the *Nativity Ode*.

18 *PL* VI, 472.

19 *Dan.* II, 35 and *Dan.* IV, 11 are customarily cited but *Matt.* 20, 44 is not without its relevance and Donne's typical exposition of this double-edged text (Simpson and Potter, *ed. cit.*, Vol. IV, 180–96) is instructive in putting before us the relationship between what the audience does know and what Satan cannot know.

20 The repudiation of Athens is distressing to many because if Christ is perfect man undergoing the temptations in his human aspect, his 'rejections' become examples which we are inexorably called on to follow. One way out is to suggest that what Christ says is relative to the context of argument: thus Socrates can be commended in one place and the limits of his knowledge severely

exposed in another. The basic difficulty can also be bypassed by suggesting that we are not inescapably called on to follow Christ's example at all points. This is the effect of Howard Schultz's view that Christ as head of the church puts forward counsels of perfection meant 'not primarily for the Christian layman but for the Church and its ministers'. (*Milton and Forbidden Knowledge*, New York, 1955, p233). The view suggested in the present chapter is that while Christ may be perfect man, he is also the historic Christ, exhibiting in his responses an emerging awareness of his destiny. Such a way of reading is not implausible and by adopting it we would enrich substantially the poems natural ironies.

21 *PR* IV, 235.
22 *Comus*, 707. *PL* II, 564.
23 *PR* IV, 352.
24 That Christ's rejections are not ultimately rejections is suggested by III, 433–40 and by the saving 'yet' in IV, 131. Once again the play is between the reader's knowledge of Christ's transforming mission, Christ's emerging knowledge of it, and Satan's ignorance.
25 *PL* IV, 297.
26 *PR* IV, 143.
27 *Complete Prose Works* II, pp366–7.
28 *Ibid.*, pp377–9.
29 *SA* 51–4; 173–4; 206–9. Samson in his regeneration, is seen as combining 'plain heroic magnitude of mind' with 'celestial vigour' (1279–80).
30 See in particular Stein, *Heroic Knowledge*, pp126–34; Lewalski, *Milton's Brief Epic* pp313–19; Fixler, *Milton and the Kingdoms of God*, pp267–9.
31 The Geneva Bible describes *Psalm* 91 as telling us 'in what assurance he liveth that putteth his whole trust in God, and commiteth himselfe wholly to his protection in all tentations.' Though both the quotation and the counter-quotation (the third occasion on which Christ has used *Deuteronomy*) are prescribed by the Bible, the poetic context invites a connection to Christ's praise of 'Sion's songs' in IV, 331–49.
32 *PL* I, 43.
33 *PR* IV, 594, 618, 630; *PL* VI, 855–8.
34 *Milton's Brief Epic*, pp313–19.
35 Frye (*The Return of Eden*, p141) notes the ironic relevance of *Psalm* 91, 13: 'Thou shalt tread upon the lion and adder; the young

lion and the dragon shalt thou trample under foot.' 618–20 echoes this text as well as *Luke* X, 18.

36 III, 215–20 is also relevant.

37 Pope, pp84–7.

38 Henry Hammond, *A Paraphrase and Annotations upon All the Books of the New Testament* (London, 1659), p21.

39 Christopher Blackwood, *Expositions and Sermons Upon the Ten First Chapters of the Gospel of Jesus Christ according to St. Matthew* (London, 1659), p97.

40 Pope, p85.

41 Pope, p87. Blackwood (p102) similarly observes that Christ's temptation was 'to cast himself down when there were steps to go down'.

42 See e.g. Daniel Dyke *Two Treatises: the One of Repentance the Other of Christ's Temptation* (London, 1619), pp283ff.

43 Geneva Bible on *Matt.* IV, 6.

44 See Thomas Fuller's chapter headings in *A Comment on the Eleven first Verses of the Fourth Chapter of St. Matthew's Gospel* (London, 1652).

45 Richard Ward on *Matt.* 4, 6 in *Theological Questions, Dogmatical Observations and Evangelical Essays upon the Gospel of Jesus Christ according* to *Saint Matthew* (London, 1646). Also Blackwood, p103.

46 Geneva Bible on *Matt.* IV, 7; John Diodati on *Matt.* IV, 7 in *Pious and Learned Annotations Upon the Holy Bible* (London, 1651); Fuller on *Matt.* IV, 7; David Dickson, *A Brief Exposition of the Evangel of Jesus Christ according to Matthew* (London, 1647), p38.

47 Pope, pp83, 103.

48 Don Cameron Allen's phrase 'poorly concealed murder' (*The Harmonious Vision* p115) hardly fits the commentary but is a not unreasonable response to Milton's text.

49 Much is also said by a situation in which the Second Adam stands while the victor over the first Adam falls. See Thomas Langford 'The Temptations in *Paradise Regained*' *Texas Studies in Language and Literature*, IX (1967), p43.

50 *Milton's Brief Epic*, p335.

51 *PR* I, 39–46; II, 115–18; IV, 618–20.

52 Mrs. Lewalski notes (p319) 'that Hercules's conquest of Antaeus was usually interpreted as an allegory of reason's conquest over all sensual or earthbound passions and desires.' However, the coupling with the Oedipus simile suggests

that the 'valorous' side of the victory should not be forgotten.

53 'A Treatise on Civil Power', *Works* (Columbia edn.), VI, p22.

CHAPTER 9

1 *Complete Prose Works*, I, p814.
2 Preface to *SA*.
3 Namely 'Samson pursophorus or Hybristes, or Samson marrying or in Ramath Lechi. Jud. 15' and 'Dagonalia. Jud. 16.' *Works*, Columbia edn., XVIII, p236.
4 It is realized that Milton in the preface to *SA* does pay service to the ideal of verisimilitude.
5 Pope *Paradise Regained*, pp51–69. Krouse, *Milton's Samson and the Christian Tradition* (Princeton, 1949), pp124ff. Parallels between Samson and Christ abound. Krouse in the illustrations to pp68–9 provides an insistent example.
6 There is an extraordinary insistence on the divine portents surrounding the birth of the hero. See 23–31, 361–4, 524–5, 1430–5.
7 While the date of *Samson* can be disputed it cannot be disputed that both *Samson* and *PR* were published in one volume. It is possible to argue that Milton's publisher found his brief epic too brief

and that Milton decided to pad the book with his refurbished tragedy from the forties as Eliot padded *The Waste Land* with his notes. It can also be argued that the two books are in the same volume because they have something to do with each other. See e.g. Stein, *Heroic Knowledge*, pp207ff.
8 As Hughes indicates (*Complete Poems and Major Prose*, 1957, p531), *Samson* has been variously assigned to 1666–70, 1660–61, 1647–53 and to an even earlier time.
9 Stein (*Heroic Knowledge*, p194) is not entirely just to this passage in referring to its 'set ironies'.
10 *'Paradise Lost' and Other Poems* ed. E. S. Le Comte (New York, 1961), p420n.
11 *SA* 293–4; 667–70; 1269–96; 1627–40; 1660; 1708–12. Other examples of Manoa's failure to see completely are found in his warning to Samson to leave the 'execution' to 'high disposal' when in fact Samson's actions are to bring

about precisely that result (506–8 and 1745–8 the former passage being matched by Samson's parallel rebuke at 373–5); in the contrast between 346–8 and Samson's treatment of Harapha; in the use of the fountain image at 581–5 to suggest outward rather than inward sight, a limited view of regeneration which is reiterated in 1502–3; in the adoption in 1500–1 of Samson's words at 566–70; and in the 'higher' reading of 517–18 to which the movement of the play directs us.

The chorus is of course both wrong and right in numbering Samson among those whom patience 'finally must crown'. It also declares more than it knows in citing patience as the 'truest fortitude'. The alternatives which human understanding poses (as in 1268–96) are brought together in the completed truth. For further discussion of 1268–96 see William O. Harris, 'Despair and "Patience as the Truest Fortitude" in *Samson Agonistes*' *ELH*, XXX (1963), pp107–20.

12 Here as in *Comus*, the poem is kept within strict bounds so that it can be seen as opening out into a fuller

meaning rather than as having that meaning stamped upon it. It is possible to characterize this 'opening out' typologically but this is not the only possible characterization and caution is called for in defining the relationship between the type and the truth. Milton's adherence to the properties of a pre-Christian event is apparent even in such matters as the uniform use of 'disposal' for 'providence' (60–2, 210, 373, 506, 1746).

13 *SA* 1756. The 'true experience' is more than retributive justice but should not bypass or sublimate that justice. It is worth remembering that the Geneva Bible on *Judges* XVI, 28 describes Samson's 'vocation' as the executing of 'Gods judgements upon the wicked'. The relationship between *SA* and the Geneva Bible is explored by Whiting in *Milton and This Pendant World*, pp201–22.

14 Roger B. Wilkinfeld, 'Act and Emblem: the Conclusion of *Samson Agonistes*' *ELH*, XXXII (1965), p168.

15 Hughes (p535) cites Edith Buchanan's doctoral thesis on the Italian Neo-Senecan Background of *SA*. See also Ralph Nash, 'Chivalric

Themes in *Samson Agonistes'*,
*Studies in Honour of John
Wilcox* (Detroit, 1958),
pp23–38.

16 In commenting on *Judges*
XVI, 19 the Geneva Bible
states that Samson's strength
left him 'Not for the losse of
his haire but for the contempt
of the ordinance of God'.
Samson's strength returns
(comment on XVI, 22) when
he has 'called upon God and
reconciled himselfe'. Daniel
Dyke observes that 'in this
faith apprehending Gods
strength lies our strength as
Sampsons in his lockes, and
therefore the Divell knowing
this, labours to do to us,
which Delilah did to *Sampson*,
even to cut off our lockes'.
Two Treatises, pp241–2.
Milton himself (*Complete
Prose Works* I, p859) refers
to Samson's hair as 'the
golden beames of Law and
Right'.

17 E. M. W. Tillyard, *Milton*
(London, 1930), pp343–4.

18 '*Samson Agonistes*' and the
Shorter Poems of Milton, ed.
Isabel G. MacCaffrey (New
York, 1966), *Intro.* p xxxv.

19 *Rambler* 139 (1751). In the
Life of Milton (ed. C. H.
Firth, Oxford, 1888, p79) the
charge is that 'the
intermediate parts have
neither cause nor consequence,

neither hasten nor retard the
catastrophe'.

20 *Of Dramatic Poesy and Other
Critical Essays*, ed. G. Watson
(London, 1962), I, p52.
Lisideius is speaking of the
French Drama. This makes
all the more interesting
Francis Fergusson's
conclusion that the word
'action' as used in
Corneille's *Trois Discours* and
in Racine's prefaces 'does not
suggest the notion which I
have attributed to Aristotle
... it does not mean action
so much as its results: not the
movement or focus of the soul
which actualizes its essence
moment by moment but the
overt deeds, chains of events
reportable as facts, which
action produces.' *The Idea of
a Theater* (Anchor Books
edition), p61.

21 The point is made by John
Arthos, *Milton and the Italian
Cities* (London, 1968),
pp130–2 and 187–90n.

22 *Complete Prose Works*, I, 817.

23 167–9; 682–90.

24 The last possibility is
suggested by Una Ellis
Fermor (*The Frontiers of
Drama*, London, 1945, p27).
For a further possibility see
Arthur E. Barker, *Essays ...
Presented to A. S. P. Woodhouse*,
pp177–9. The triple equation

has already been mentioned as a structural hypothesis.

25 It is a phrase duly undercut by 532 but the tone suggests identification with the past as well as awareness of its folly.

26 W. R. Parker (*Milton's Debt to Greek Tragedy in Samson Agonistes*, Baltimore, 1939, pp122–4) sees Harapha as a blusterer descended ultimately from Euripides. For Boughner ('Milton's Harapha and Renaissance Comedy', *ELH*, XI, 1944, pp297–306), the source is the continental forerunner of Beaumont and Fletcher. Boughner treats the play as inconsistent with the preface. In dissent see D. C. Allen, *The Harmonious Vision* pp91–3. To Steadman (*JEGP*, LX, 1961, p789), 1 *Samuel*, 17 remains the primary source. According to G. R. Waggoner ('The Challenge to Single Combat in *Samson Agonistes*', *PQ*, XXXIX, pp82–92) Milton is drawing on 'contemporary interest in single combat, especially judicial combat on the part of both legal writers and the public.'

27 See William Madsen, *From Shadowy Types to Truth* (New Haven, 1968), pp181–202. It is not disputed that

Christ's remarks in *PR* II, 222–23, with their roots in Plato (*Laws*, IV, 718), the early prose (*Complete Prose Works* I, 746) and the Sonnet to Cromwell (10–11), are an imporant current in Milton's thought.

28 P. Sellin, 'Milton's Epithet *Agonistes*', *SEL*, LV (1964), pp137–62. For an exercise in Christian semantics not directly bearing on this passage, see Krouse, *Milton's Samson*, pp108–18.

29 Douglas Bush the most resolute dissenter from the Christianizing of Samson, notes (*Milton*, p200) that in *Samson* 'no specifically Christian doctrines are admitted, no clear statement of the working of grace, not even faith in Samson's immortality.' William R. Parker, in *Milton. A Biography* (Oxford, 1968, Vol. 1, p294) finds Samson 'starkly devoid of theology'.

30 The end is in contrast to the interpretation offered by the Geneva Bible in commenting on *Judges* XVI, 30. 'He speaketh not this of despaire, but humbling himselfe for neglecting his office and the offence thereby given.'

31 Preface to *SA*. Butcher limits the tragic effect to the

catharsis of pity and fear. Bywater's less restrictive translation ('arousing pity and fear wherewith to accomplish its catharsis of such emotions') is followed by several critics.

32 See in particular Humphry House, *Aristotle's Poetics* (London, 1961), pp100–11. The affinities between Milton's and Minturno's view of catharsis were pointed to by Spingarn in 1899 (*Literary Criticism in the Renaissance*, 1930 edn., pp79–81). Gilbert in his collection *Literary Criticism: Plato to Dryden* (New York, 1940, p517), has suggested Guarini as a source. P. Sellin ('Sources of Milton's Catharsis: A Reconsideration', *JEGP*, LX, 1961, pp712–30) makes a claim for Heinsius. In offering an interpretation here which while similar to House's, is set in a much more inclusive context, I am bearing in mind the highly-charged nature of phrases such as 'just measure' and 'in right tune' for those familiar with Milton's thought.

33 *Complete Prose Works*, I, pp816–17.

34 W. B. Yeats, *Letters*, p837.

35 I. A. Richard's views on poetry are suggested.

36 Stein (*Heroic Knowledge*, pp210–11) sees the catharsis of *SA* as both Socratic and Aristotelian.

Index

Abrams, M. H., 53, 158n., 159n.
Adam, completion of, in Eve, 69; divine image, in 28–30, 63-4, 90, 164n.; education of, 85-6, 89, 94; hierarchical function of, 71–2; Paradise, departure of, from, 9, 83; repentance of, 75; *see also* Christ.
Adams, Robert M., 23, 24, 152n., 153n., 158n.
Aeschylus, 128
Ainsworth, Henry, 170n., 171n.
Allen, Don Cameron, 51, 149n., 159n., 171n., 179n., 183n.
Ames, William, 162n., 164n., 170n., 173n.
Andrewes, Lancelot, 13
Ariosto, 24
Aristotle, 62, 63, 101, 102, 128, 162n.
Arminius, Jacobus, 77, 166–7n.
Arthos, John, 153n., 156n., 157n., 182n.
Auden, W. H., 86, 171n.
Augustine, 43, 151n., 153n., 154n., 157n., 163n., 176n.

Barker, Arthur E., 14, 48, 150n., 156n., 158n., 182n.
Beaumont, Joseph, 12, 149n.
Bell, Millicent, 160n.
Bentley, Richard, 169n.
Bible, citations of, 65–6; Geneva version of, 125, 178n., 179n., 181n., 182n., 183n.; *Daniel*, 177n.; *Deuteronomy*, 124, 178n.; *Galatians*, 165n.; *Genesis*, 60–1, 73, 130, 170n.; *Hebrews*, 84; *Job*, 4-5; *Luke* 118, 179n., *Matthew* 125, 177n., 179n.; *Peter*, 173n.; *Psalms*, 15, 123–4, 125, 178n.; *Romans*, 17, 162n.; *Revelations*, 5, 60
Blackwood, Henry, 125, 179n.
Boswell, Jackson, C., 166n.
Boughner, D. C., 183n.
Broadbent, J. B., 149n., 151n.
Brooks, Cleanth, 149n., 155n., 156n., 157n.
Browne, Thomas, 151n.
Bruser, Fredella, 156n.
Bryan, Robert A., 168n.
Buchanan, Edith, 181n.
Bullinger, Henry, 21
Burden, Dennis, 165n.
Bush, Douglas, 13, 34, 49, 113, 150n., 151n., 152n., 154n., 156n., 176n., 183n.
Butcher, S. H., 183n.
Bywater, Ingram, 183n.

Callimachus, 5
Calvin, John, 113, 176n.
Castiglione, Baldassare, 151n.
Chambers, A. B., 161n.
Champion, Larry S., 169n.
Christ, 60–1; and celestial light, 150n.; and creation, 13, 18; exaltation of, 67; judgement by, 82, 86; and Hercules, 5, 126, 129, 148n.; 152n.; and Oedipus, 126; and Orpheus, 50; and Samson, 129, 132-3, 135-6, 139, 140; and Satan, 82, 91, 93, 113-27; as Second Adam, 8, 37, 81, 91

Chrysostom, John, 161n.
Cirrillo, Albert L., 170n.
Cohn, Norman, 152n.
Coleridge, S. T., 79, 102, 174n.
Colie, Rosalie L., 166n., 175n.
Comes, Natalis, 152n.
Cooper, Lane, 162n.
Cope, Jackson I., 162n.
Corneille, Pierre, 182n.
Crashaw, Richard, 12, 149n.
Curry, Walter C., 161n.
Cyprian, 22, 93

Daiches, David, 50, 148n., 152n., 159n.
Daniells, Roy, 50–1, 150n., 153n., 156–7n., 158n., 159n., 162n., 163n.
Dante, Alighieri, 3, 17, 43, 59–60, 154n., 161n.
Darbishire, Helen, 106, 158n., 175n.
Davenant, William, 161n.
Davie, Donald, 105, 174n.
Davies, Godfrey, 166n.
Demaray, John C., 162–3n.
Dickson, John, 179n.
Diodati, John, 179n.
Dolan, John P., 172n.
Donne, John, 113, 150n., 177n.
Downame, John, 177n.
Dryden, John, 133–34, 182n.
Du Moulin, Peter, 76, 166n.
Durling, Robert M., 151n.
Dyke, Daniel, 179n., 182n.

Edwards, Thomas, 77, 166n.
Eliot, T. S., 1–4, 52, 130, 147n., 180n.
Ellis Fermor, Una, 182n.
Ellwood, Thomas, 81
Euripides, 128, 183n.
Eve, and the Lady, 37; as preserver, 93, 172n; and Satan, 36; self-sufficiency of, 70–1; and Sin, 69, 149n.; *see also* Adam.

Featley, Daniel, 166n.
Fergusson, Francis, 182n.
Ferrar, Nicholas, 113, 175–6n.

Ficino, Marsilio, 37, 155n., 156n.
Finney, Gretchen, 153n., 160n.
Fish, Stanley, E., 165n.
Fixler, Michael, 152n., 168n., 178n.
Fletcher, Giles, 5, 148n.
Fletcher, Harris, F., 149n., 152n., 156n.
Ford, John, 2, 147n.
Freedom, and departure from Paradise, 96; in fallen man, 75–6; and foreknowledge, 65, 69–70, 110–11; as nucleus of man's nature, 74; and perfection, 66; and responsibility, 6–9, 74, 77; in repentant man, 76–7.
French, J. Milton, 158n., 159n.
Frye, Northrop, 16, 153n., 170n., 178n.
Fuller, Thomas, 125, 179n.

Galileo, 151n.
Giamatti, A. Bartlett, 174n.
Gilbert, A. H., 151n., 161n., 184n.
Goodman, Godfrey, 22, 73
Greene, Thomas, 148n., 162n.
Grierson, H. J. C., 149n., 158n.
Guarini, Giambattista, 185n.

Hakewill, George, 22
Hales, John, 167n.
Haller, William, 152n., 156n.
Hammond, Henry, 179n.
Hanford, J. H., 6, 148n., 151n.
Harding, Davis P., 164n.
Hardy, John, 149n., 155n., 156n.
Harris, William O., 181n.
Haun, Emile, 153n.
Heinsius, Daniel, 185n.
Herbert, George, 2
Herford, C. H., 153n.
Homer, 4, 62
Hone, Joseph, 174n.
Hooker, Richard, 151n.
Hoopes, R. A., 163n.
House, Humphrey, 183n.
Hughes, Merritt Y., 17, 150n., 151n., 152n., 154n., 161n., 169n., 180n., 181n.

Jayne, Sears, 155n.
Johnson, Samuel, 7, 12, 45, 75, 133, 182n.
Joyce, James, 25

Kelley, Maurice, 167n., 172n.
Kermode, Frank, 172n.
King, Edward, 45
Kirkconnell, Watson, 161n.
Koestler, Arthur, 130
Kranidas, Thomas, 175n.
Kristeller, Oskar, 8, 148n.
Krouse, F. Michael, 180n., 183n.

Lactantius, 20–1, 151n.
Langford, Thomas, 179n.
Lawes, Henry, 35
Leavis, F. R., 30, 101, 155n.
LeComte, E. S., 6, 147n., 156n., 180n.
Lewalski, Barbara, 26, 114, 124, 126, 168n., 169n., 170n., 176n., 178n.
Lewis, C. S., 79, 101, 174n.
Lloyd, Michael, 159–60n.
Lucretius, 58
Luther, Martin, 21, 76, 93, 162n., 165n., 176n.

MacCaffrey, I. G., 182n.
MacCallum, Hugh, 82, 168n., 169n. 171n.
Mack, Maynard, 153n.
Madsen, William, 41, 153n., 154n., 155n., 156n., 157n., 168n., 172n., 183n.
Mahood, Molly M., 153n.
Mantuan, 12
Marlowe, Christopher, 113
Martz, Louis, 94, 115, 149n., 150n., 168n., 170n., 172n., 176n., 177n.
Marvell, Andrew, 44, 161n.
Mayerson, Caroline W., 159n.
McColley, Grant, 151n., 162n., 163n.
Melanchthon, 167n.
Mercator, 53
Milton, John, poetry of: Baroque in, 13, 17–18, 150n., 153n., 158n., 163n.; Chain of being in, 27, 61–2, 90; Christian heroism in, 122—3; Christian humanism in, 68; Christian liberty in, 37, 89; Christian warfare, in, 7, 25, 31, 88; continuity in, 4–10, 16–19, 63–4, 81, 91, 95–6, 116, 123–4, 126–7, 129–30, 139; contraries in, 27–32, 47, 59–60, 61, 88, 93, 103, 108–9; decorum in, 18–19, 46, 101–2, 111–12, 132, 141; discipline and energy in, 25, 40; irregularity in, 14, 15, 46, 48–9, 115–16; mannerism in, 50–1, 150n.; Mosaic Law in, 76, 82, 89–91, 145; pattern and process in, 49, 108–9, 110–11; spatial treatment in, 6, 13, 14, 16, 22, 62–3, 80
Writings of:
Adam Unparadized, 62, 83, 128
Apology for Smectymnuus, An, 43, 155n.
Areopagitica, 8, 32, 37, 66, 79, 95, 98, 156n.
At a Solemn Music, 95, 149n.
Bridgewater Manuscript, The, 34, 35
At a Vacation Exercise, 149n.
Comus, 2, 5, 7, 8, 11, *23–44*, 48, 63–4, 67, 69, 95, 97, 113, 119, 122, 148n., 150n., *152–7n.*, 172n., 178n., 181n.; chastity in, 37–38; Christian-classical synthesis in, 43; Epilogue of, 40–4; light imagery in, 28; masque form of, 25–7; textual changes in, 34–5
De Doctrina Christiana, 39, 42, 57, 58, 60, 67, 87, 161n.
Defensio Secunda, 79, 86
Doctrine and Discipline of Divorce, The, 65–6
Eikonoklastes, 171n., 173n.
Elegia Sexta, 11
Il Penseroso, 24
Lycidas, 5, 12, 15, *44–55*, 97, 143, *158–60n.* 172; digres-

Index

Milton, John—*Continued*
sions in, 47; textual changes
in, 46, 47, 52; three-part
structure of, 48, 53; un-
rhymed lines in, 54
Of Education, 123
On the Death of a Fair Infant, 16,
17, 149n.
*On the Morning of Christ's
Nativity*, 5, *11–22*, 26, 63–4,
95, 127, *148–52n.*, 156–7n.;
alexandrine in, 16–17; antecedents of, 12; catalogue of
Gods in, 20–1; historical
process in, 21–2; *Paradise
Lost*, affinities with, 17–19,
20–2; stanza of, 11; three-
part structure of, 14–16.
Paradise Lost, 2, 5, 8, 10, 17, 18,
19, 26, 29, 31, 35, 36, 38, 51,
56–112, 113, 116, 117, 119,
120, 122, 124, 126–7, 129,
135, 144, 151–2n., 157n.,
160–75n., 178n.; anticipatory devices in, 109–11;
celestial cycle in, 57, 93;
cosmography of, 58–9; crisis
of, 56; dramatic oppositions
in, 59–60; fortunate fall in,
93–4; historical process in,
79–99; perfection in, 66–74;
pessimism of, 94–6; redemption in, 57, 67, 72, 86, 89–90;
six ages of history in, 82;
syntax of, 104–5; verse paragraph of, 103–4
Paradise Regained, 6, 7, 81, 86, 91,
113–27, 129, 136, 140, 157n.,
159n., 173n., *175–82n.*,
Christ's victory in, 126–7;
irony in, 121; pinnacle in,
125; precedents for, 114–15;
renunciation in, 114; Stoicism in, 119–20
The Passion, 17, 127, 149n.
Prolusion VII, 98–9
Psalm 144, 13, 149n.
Psalm 136, 13, 149n.

Reason of Church Government, The,
4, 13, 14, 39–40, 113–14, 128,
157n., 164n., 173n., 177n.
Samson Agonistes, 2, 6, 7–8, 13,
26, 31, 85, 98, 123, *128–45*,
178n., *180–4n.*, blindness in,
31, 130–1; Chorus in, 135,
141, 143; Christianity in,
137, 142; Comedy in, 139;
Delilah's part in, 132, 138;
Harapha's part in, 132, 139;
interior drama in, 133–4;
Manoa's part in, 131, 136–7;
tragic effect in, 142–4; triple
equation in, 129; typological
reading of, 181n. *see also* Christ
Sonnet IX, 157n.
Sonnet XXIII, 148n.
*Tenure of Kings and Magistrates,
The*, 85–6
Trinity Manuscript, 24, 35, 45–7,
128, 158n., 159n., 180n.
Minturno, Antonio, 62, 185n.
Minucius Felix, Marcus, 151n.
Mollenhott, Virginia R., 169n.

Nash, Ralph, 181–2n.
Nelson, Lowry, Jr., 150n., 158n.
Newton, Thomas, 159n.
Nicolson, Marjorie, 23, 47, 53, 152n.,
158n., 159n.

O'Brien, Elmer, 154n.
Ogden, H. V. S., 160n.
Oras, Ants, 158n., 160n.
Ovid, 17,39

Pagitt, Ephraim, 166n.
Paradise, first and final, 21; location
after deluge, 170–1n.; interior
reality of, 79, 86, 93, 107, 114
Parish, John E., 168n.
Parker, William R., 183n.
Parr, Elnathan, 76–7, 162n., 164n.,
166n.
Patrides, C. A., 152n., 162n., 167n.,
168n., 171n.

Pecheux, Mother Mary, 169n.
Pico della Mirandola, 8, 66
Pindar, 5
Plato, 37, 38, 90, 155n.
Plautus, 139
Plotinus, 28, 38, 42, 113, 154n. 156n., 157n.
Pound, Ezra, 25
Prince, F. T., 160n., 168n., 174n.

Quarles, Francis, 115

Racine, Jean, 182n.
Raleigh, Walter, 56, 160n.
Ransom, John Crowe, 160n.
Richards, I. A., 185n.
Richardson, Jonathan, 159n.
Ricks, Christopher, 101, 174n.
Robins, Harry F., 161n.
Robson, W. W., 156n.
Ross, Alexander, 20, 162n., 166n.
Ross, Malcolm Mackenzie, 172n.
Runyon, Damon, 151n.
Rutherford, Samuel, 85, 170n.

Samuel, Irene, 177n.
Sandys, George, 20, 39, 154n., 156n.
Sannazaro, Jacopo, 12
Sartre, Jean-Paul, 8
Sasek, L. A., 147–8n., 168n.
Satan and Comus, 63; and interior paradise, 93; language of, 106–7; *see also* Christ.
Schultz, Howard, 178n.
Selden, John, 20
Sellin, P., 183n., 185n.
Shakespeare, William, 1, 2, 62, 157n.
Sidney, Philip, 113, 175n.
Sims, James H., 65, 162n.
Sin, 74; and celestial and infernal trinity, 60; and Death, 61; and degree, 61; *see also* Eve.
Sophocles, 5, 128
Spenser, Edmund, 24, 37, 38, 40–1, 58, 156n., 157n.
Spingarn, J. E., 184n.

Stapleton, Laurence, 150n.
Steadman, John M., 168n., 171n., 172n., 173n., 183n.
Stein, Arnold, 100, 111, 162n., 169n., 175n., 177n., 180n., 185n.
Summers, Joseph, 168n., 169n., 170n.
Svendsen, Kester, 161n., 165n.
Sypher, Wylie, 158n.

Tasso, Torquato, 4, 12, 101, 151n., 161n., 173n.
Taylor, Dick, Jr., 162., 166n., 168n., 169n.
Tertullian, 151n.
Theodorus, 152n.
Thompson, E. N. S., 79, 168n.
Tillich, Paul, 96, 172n.
Tillyard, E. M. W., 27, 56, 147n., 153n., 155n., 157n.
Traherne, Thomas, 8, 11
Travers, Hope, 162n.
Trevelyan, Sir G. M., 25, 153n.
Tuve, Rosemond, 2, 12, 22, 25, 55, 149n., 150n., 151n., 152n., 153n., 158n.
Tuveson, Ernest, 95, 152n., 172n.

Ussher, James, 75, 162n., 164n., 165n., 171n.

Vaughan, Henry, 28, 154n.
Vendler, Helen H., 152n.
Virgil, 4, 15, 21, 43, 48, 58, 62.

Waggoner, G. R., 183n.
Ward, Richard, 125–6, 179n.
Warner, Rex, 153n.
Warnke, Frank J., 153n.
Warren, Austin, 149n. 153n.
Watkins, W. B. C., 6, 148n., 155n., 156n.
Welsford, Enid, 153n.
Whaler, James, 175n.
Whiting, G. W., 82, 151n., 168n., 169n.

Widmer, Kingsley, 175n.
Wilkes, G. A., 56, 160n.
Wilkinfeld, Roger, B., 181n.
Williams, Arnold, 163n., 164n., 165n., 169n., 170n.
Williams, Charles, 23, 152n.,
Woodhouse, A. S. P., 27, 153n.,

154–5n., 156n., 157n., 158–9n., 161n., 165n., 170n.
Wright, Bernard, 106, 168n.

Yeats, W. B., 2, 3–4, 18, 24–5, 69, 103, 147n., 152n., 161n., 164n., 174n., 185n.